LAW & SOCIETY *Redefined*

LAW & SOCIETY *Redefined*

GEORGE PAVLICH

OXFORD
UNIVERSITY PRESS

OXFORD
UNIVERSITY PRESS

8 Sampson Mews, Suite 204, Don Mills, Ontario M3C 0H5
www.oupcanada.com

Oxford University Press is a department of the University of Oxford.
It furthers the University's objective of excellence in research, scholarship,
and education by publishing worldwide in

Oxford   New York

Auckland   Cape Town   Dar es Salaam   Hong Kong   Karachi
Kuala Lumpur   Madrid   Melbourne   Mexico City   Nairobi
New Delhi   Shanghai   Taipei   Toronto

With offices in

Argentina   Austria   Brazil   Chile   Czech Republic   France   Greece
Guatemala   Hungary   Italy   Japan   Poland   Portugal   Singapore
South Korea   Switzerland   Thailand   Turkey   Ukraine   Vietnam

Oxford is a trade mark of Oxford University Press
in the UK and in certain other countries

Published in Canada by Oxford University Press

Copyright © 2011 Oxford University Press Canada

The moral rights of the author have been asserted

Database right Oxford University Press (maker)

First Published 2011

Library and Archives Canada Cataloguing in Publication

Pavlich, George Clifford

Law and society redefined / George Pavlich.

Includes bibliographical references and index.

ISBN 978-0-19-542980-0

1. Sociological jurisprudence. I. Title.

K370.P39 2010   340'.115   C2010-900344-6

Cover image: iStockphoto.com/MBPHOTO, INC.

Oxford University Press is committed to our environment. This book is printed on Forest
Stewardship Council certified paper, harvested from a responsibly managed forest.

Mixed Sources
Product group from well-managed
forests and other controlled sources
www.fsc.org Cert no. SW-COC-000952
© 1996 Forest Stewardship Council

Printed and bound in Canada.

1 2 3 4 — 14 13 12 11

Contents

Acknowledgements

Many are those who have contributed—advertently or not—to the pages that follow: Peter Fitzpatrick generously read and, with his customary insight, commented on several chapters; Lois Harder offered encouraging words on a rough first draft; Patrick McLane provided valued research assistance throughout; several colleagues in the Faculty of Law formed an attentive and thought-provoking reading group that helped immeasurably with readings of Fuller and post-colonial thought; Colin Perrin discussed ideas of mutual interest with an infectious enthusiasm, bringing valuable references to my attention (including Latour); many students over the years have helped shape my views about the value of socio-legal studies; three anonymous referees for Oxford University Press imparted constructive comments on an earlier draft; Maria Jelinek's copy-editing was most helpful; my siblings (Dennis, Colleen, Posh) offered support in their inimitable ways, as did my mother Tally; and the University of Alberta graciously provided me with an opportunity to devote a chunk of time to the project at a crucial moment. I gratefully acknowledge all of their various contributions to the book, fully accepting that all flaws are entirely of my own doing. Two long-standing friends, Paul Hollingworth and Harold Salant, knew me when I first encountered some of the authors here discussed, and their thoughtful reactions to muses for this book made a long-awaited reunion even more captivating. I especially want, however, to thank two exceptional people in my life, who give so much and ask so little: Carla Spinola and Seth Pavlich; this book is dedicated to Seth.

For Seth

Introduction

For most of us, it is difficult, if not impossible, to imagine a society without law. In our everyday lives, we encounter the law in many different ways—here is a courthouse with architecture designed around symbols of legal authority, there a police car's siren reveals law enforcement in action, and across the street suited lawyers bustle about the business of practising law, just as newspaper headline banners announce a heinous criminal act and a lawsuit between two famous singers. Yet, many of us would have a hard time defining law exactly. Suppose you are pushed to do so by a circle of friends over a meal. You end up saying something like: 'laws are orders that tell us what to do and what not to do in given circumstances', adding triumphantly, ' . . . with the threat of force if we choose to ignore what is required'. A friend deflates your obvious sense of achievement by pointing out that this definition would mean an armed thug is practising law when he demands your wallet and threatens to hurt you if you don't comply! To quiet the guffaws, this friend pointedly asks whether anyone else has something better to offer. Breaking the awkward silence, another friend acknowledges the problems with the earlier definition, adding that authentic laws differ from the commands of a mugger because they are based on reason, passed by parliamentary processes, written as statutes, enforced through official institutions, adjudicated by trained lawyers and judges, and, moreover, can be justified morally, i.e., shown to be just. Someone else notes that as a **constitutional monarchy**[1] and a **representative democracy** (which separates powers between the executive, legislative, and judicial branches of government), Canada's laws are legitimate in ways that the mugger's decrees are not.

Budding lawyers in the group elaborate further, arguing that law needs to be understood as a complex rule-bound system—to discover what it is requires training and the ability to scrutinize the principles, rules, and rationales judges use to reach a given decision. 'No mugger's "law" can do this', they gloat, adding that wider philosophical arguments could also be used to show whether a given law is moral, legitimate, or valid. This is precisely why lawyers, judges, and legal philosophers receive special training at law schools. More sociologically inclined friends counter immediately with a blunt rebuttal: law is nothing more than a **social control** to make sure that people conform to an established order. In other words, for them, law is simply a device to compel people to act in ways that conform to, rather than oppose, a given society. Law's ultimate purpose is to safeguard and serve established interests or, less frequently, to change a particular society. Leaving that congenial discussion here, let us consider some of the ideas raised as an invitation to the pages that follow.

Objectives of the Book

At the outset, it is important to declare that this book does not try to defend one definition of law. Rather, it describes numerous ideas within a well-established law and society field, focusing on various attempts to understand law in relation to social contexts.[2] It does not claim to be a comprehensive review of all theories in the field, but, like any books of this kind, selectively appraises the contributions of key figures and their impact on shaping its current contours. It has three main objectives:

First, it examines selected theories that have at different times assembled the boundaries of a field of study variously called **law and society** and **socio-legal studies**.[3] Influenced by **jurisprudence** (broadly, the philosophy of law) and **legal theory** (a field of study dedicated to theoretical formulations of law), the socio-legal arena may be distinguished by a basic assumption: 'Law can be said to have a distinctly *social basis*; it both shapes—and is shaped by—the society in which it operates' (Comack and Brickey 1991: 15). In other words, the field assumes ' . . . that law is a social phenomenon and that legal doctrine and actors are integral parts of the social landscape' (Lipson and Wheeler 1986: 2). As such, the law and society field 'is identified broadly with the study of law and its social context' (Munger 1998: 25). The field orbits around concepts of 'law' and 'society' as well as the relations between them (Milovanovic 2003; Hunt 1993). The first two sections of the book describe how the field has emerged through formative texts that either understand law as a basic element with social consequences, or, by contrast, more sociologically inspired approaches that view society as the architect of law.

The book's second objective is to review several endogenous critiques that have transformed the field in a rather unusual way. These critiques have contested the field's early anchor in discrete concepts of 'law' and 'society' as independent categories of being, with essential and timeless characteristics. As I will argue, the various critical approaches may de-emphasize and even oppose specific formulations of law and society, but they do not entirely jettison the concepts (even if some may aspire eventually to so doing). Instead, they radically reframe these as historically specific ideas and processes of currently accepted visions of law and society.

But without distinctive images of 'law' or 'society', what is to become of the law and society field and its well-developed socio-legal analysis? This question announces the third of the book's objectives—namely, to consider how such critiques might redefine the field. This aim signals a deliberate attempt to renew the vitality with which the law and society field once breathed new life into old jurisprudential debates, to welcome anew the critiques that opened the field to its current limitations, and that increasingly appear fatigued by the effort. If my assessment is correct, several theoretical renewals are well underway, appearing in attempts to frame the field not through versions of *being*, but through images of *becoming*. As noted, their focus has shifted from a logic that tries to discover the essence of a supposed **being** (say, law or society) to a logic that emphasizes how changing images of 'law' and 'society' emerge in specific historical contexts. Now local images of law and society are considered to be unfolding contextual achievements, emphasizing how their becoming is propelled by various promises of enhanced futures (justice, fairness, equality, etc.). The full implications for the field are very much in development, but the contours of a stimulating reinvigoration are evident in several possible directions discussed at the end of this text.

The Book's Parts

Each of the three parts describes debates that have significantly contoured the law and society field. The first part focuses on debates guided by the view that law is an absolute entity, and that it has social effects. This part is entitled 'Law *Sui Generis*' (meaning 'of its own kind; peculiar, unique'[4]) to signal that theorists discussed here—different though their approaches may be—consider law to have an essential being, distinct from other sorts of being. The analysis focuses particularly on the contributions from jurisprudence and legal theory. It explores scholars' different ways of describing law on its own terms and then examining its purported effects on society.

The second part—'Society *Sui Generis*'—describes various reversals of this law-society approach. Specifically, it focuses on contributions from the sociology of law, socio-legal studies, and critical theories that frame society as a being 'of its own kind', conceptualizing law as a more or less derivative predicate thereof.

The final part, 'Promising Justice: The *Becoming* of Law and Society' changes tack by discussing several theories that still address law and society but no longer accept either of these concepts as *beings* of their own kinds. I have here avoided the glib tendency to lump such theories under banners like **postmodernism**[5] or **post-structuralism**[6], preferring instead to deal with specific themes through which these approaches conceive of legal and social relations as historical creations that emerge out of power and knowledge relations. The theorists discussed focus variously on processes that shape law and society in the making—power, violence, sovereignty, governance, post-colonial regulation, and justice. The point is not to explore the essential *being* of either law or society but to highlight how these are always historical accomplishments framed by wider socio-political and cultural matters.

In that sense, as suggested, the focus of this section of the book is not on the *being* of law and society, but on the logic of how they *become*, how they are calculated, and the effects of such calculations, in specific contexts. The theories here offer various ways to conceptualize such becoming, and in the process are relieved of paying allegiance to fixed, essential images of law and society. The implications of these gestures for the future of law and society research are profound, raising this question: what will likely happen to the law and society field when its previously targeted objects of analysis (law and society) are radically transformed into dynamic processes without a fixed, or universal, essence? The concluding chapter, entitled 'After Law and Society', examines the prospects of that very turn. Let us examine each part of the book in more detail.

Part I: Law *Sui Generis*

To be sure, the term 'law' pops up in many conversations, and not only with reference to legal arenas. For example, we speak of laws governing language (grammar), culture, and musical form, and in science we refer to the laws of, say, chemistry, physics, politics, biology, and even nature. So what is the difference between these various sorts of laws and the 'law' of courthouses? Turning to responses from jurisprudence and legal theory that have influenced law and society research in consequential ways, the book outlines several attempts to define courtroom law. In general, scholars of these disciplines tend to understand their object— the *law*—as referring to the practices, processes, procedures, and texts that surround police, prosecutors, court administrators, lawyers, judges, legislators, etc., who operate in the name of 'law' (see Davies 2008: 4; Raz 2005). As Davies suggests, 'A minimal, and reasonably non-controversial, definition of the law is that it is something devised by humans to create order within our society. Law regulates human behaviour, and the relationships between members of the society. Beyond this, of course, it may attempt to enshrine certain ideals, such as equality, freedom, and justice (2008: 6).'

What about law in Canada? We might add to what has already been said, that in Canada, law is often located in the statutes created by parliament, but equally adjudicated by judges' decisions. They decide what the law is in a given situation. But the courts where they make decisions are hierarchically ordered, from provincial administrative tribunals (e.g., human rights tribunals, labour relations boards, liquor licensing commissions), provincial inferior courts (e.g., courts of justice, provincial courts, small claims courts, territorial courts), and superior courts (e.g., Supreme Courts, Courts of Queen's Bench, Courts of Appeal), to the highest court of the land—the Supreme Court of Canada (see Horner 2007: 24). There are other courts (e.g., various federal and military courts), but decisions made in courts higher up in the hierarchy are considered binding on those below and often on future decisions of that court. To the extent that this structure adjudicates the law in context, it quite literally defines what Canadian law is at a given point in time.

However, there is a wrinkle in all this: determining the law is complicated in Canada by the historical influences of two different European legal traditions that were historically supplanted over Aboriginal law—**civil law** and **common law** systems (Horner 2007: 36–65). Civil law systems, such as the one pursued in Quebec, have ancient roots, but their basic precepts prominent in Roman law (e.g., the written codes of the Emperor Justinian) provided citizens with publicly available, written laws that were supposed to be universally applicable. The distinguishing feature of the system lies in its claim that law is to be found in these codes (e.g., the Napoleonic Code). In practice, this means that judges are supposed to apply and follow the law only as it is enshrined in relevant legislated, written, and publicly available laws that declare rules and standards of conduct. In this system, judges allegedly do no more than apply the law as articulated by a code to a given set of events.

By contrast, a common law system supposedly underlies legal practices in the rest of the country ('supposedly' because this overlooks the important foundations of Aboriginal law). Common law systems try to capture unwritten customs assumed to form the foundation of a given social group, and to be the source of law. Statutes may supplement and/or reflect customs, but true law appears through a judge's ability to find and declare custom through law in specific cases. Past decisions bind future judgments of inferior courts, or courts of similar standing facing similar cases. Law thus grows out of what has gone before. This **doctrine of precedent** signals an important common law idea that the principles and rules used in past decisions should serve as precedents for deciding future cases with equivalent facts. In common law systems, then, judges typically examine the facts of a given case in relation to the principles and rules implied by relevant statutes or past decisions by other courts (hierarchically ordered). Thereafter, judges offer reasoned argument to arrive at legally defensible decisions (i.e., the *ratio decidendi*), and such decisions form part of an amalgam that is referred to collectively as the law.

Since many jurisprudential scholars discussed in this book assume variants of the common law system in their approaches, it may be helpful at least to point to some of its early protagonists. Classical common law theories took law to be an expression of ancient custom, and jurisprudential scholars of the sixteenth to eighteenth centuries—principally Coke (see Stoner 1992), Blackstone (2001), and Hale (1971)—were instrumental in carving out an image of law as such (see Cotterrell 2003: 21–39). They conceived of law as guided in large measure by its assessment of justice and the common good, regardless of what kings (or parliaments) may say. However, their point was not that judges make law; rather judges are said to discover and publicly enunciate—declare—unwritten, timeless, and eternal customs of ancient origin.

On this basis, Blackstone portrays judges as the vehicles by which 'maxims' or customs are declared: they are the 'living oracles' who authoritatively declare the law based on knowledge acquired through 'experience and study' of established law. As soothsayers, judges must suspend personal opinions and base their decisions purely on reasons that declare known 'customs' and laws of the land.

Other classical common law theorists offered a somewhat different view of law (see Davies 2008: 39ff.). Coke, for example, insisted on the hallowed and ancient origin of law, demanding a fidelity to a relatively stable—but mystical—customary heritage as the only secure basis of law. Hale, for his part, was more inclined to accept that the law, and the custom from which it derives, changed over time within a particular social group. Recognizing that law developed continuously, he nevertheless saw it as directly connected to some stable core, comparing it to a rebuilt ship, and a man Titus:

> As the Argonauts Ship was the same when it returned home, as it was when it went out, tho' in that long Voyage it had successive Amendments, and scarce came back with any of its former Materials; and as Titus is the same man he was at 40 Years since, tho' Physicians tell us, That in a Tract of seven Years, the Body has scarce any of the same Material Substance it had before (1971: 40).

With such approaches in mind, one can perhaps better understand the jurisprudential quest to expose law's essential being *sui generis* (see Raz 2005). Chapter 1 examines the view of several **classical natural law** theorists for whom law, by definition, must comply with the doctrines of a higher, eternal, moral authority conceived in various ways (e.g., God, right reasoning). Chapter 2 focuses specifically on two recent **natural law** approaches that view law as an ordering, rule-driven, and morally defensible process. One version (**Lon Fuller**) requires that any process to govern people through rules and claiming to be law must reflect a minimal 'internal morality'. Another version (**John Finnis**) argues that law should serve a more encompassing set of basic morals that enable human beings to flourish as human beings. Chapter 3 examines **legal positivism**, which still dominates many areas of law in Canada. As we shall see, this approach defines and is concerned only with law as it is 'posited' by a given authority in a given context. It is not concerned with the morality or virtues of a given law, but only with those rules that can be scientifically observed to serve as laws in a specific context. In other words, rules or norms that can be shown scientifically to serve as laws in a given society are in fact laws. There is nothing more to the definition of law. Chapter 4 rounds out this section by describing a reform-minded movement called **legal realism** (and an allied **sociological jurisprudence**) that challenges the prevailing 'myths' of formal law. For example, it rejects the idea that judges decide 'neutrally', and that one can predict law by examining the rules used to produce reasonable decisions. Rather, for legal realists, law is a real process that, like any other, is fraught with human frailty. Judges let personal values and beliefs cloud their decisions, use reason to rationalize their previously made decisions, and are swayed by entirely extra-legal determinants—social, cultural, political, and psychological. Not surprisingly, these approaches call upon social sciences to relate to the law, and open the way to the second part of the book.

Part II: Society *Sui Generis*

If jurisprudence presupposed the 'law' as its grounding auspice, socio-legal approaches and the sociology of law privileged concepts of the 'social' as the foundation of law. An early version of such thinking is commonly attributed to a nineteenth-century analyst, Henry Sumner Maine (1822–88). He argued that in 'progressive' (modern) societies, law's stable, conservative basis is often at odds with the transformations of an advancing society. In such contexts, he tells us:

> . . . social necessities and social opinion are always more or less in advance of Law. We come indefinitely near to the closing of the gap between them, but it has a perpetual tendency to reopen. Law is stable; the societies we are speaking of progressive. The greater or less happiness of the people depends on the degree of promptitude with which the gulf is narrowed (1979: 19).

Maine famously identified in progressive societies a clear movement away from relations of 'status' that tied people to traditional kinship patterns, to those of 'contract' that allow individuals greater freedom to choose how to relate with others. One detects here a framing element of the sociology of law; namely, that law is inextricably fashioned out of, and serves, the societies in which it appears. The point was developed further by an early proponent of the sociology of law, Eugen Ehrlich (1862–1922), who dismissed 'ordinary jurisprudence' as insufficiently scientific, failing to consider law as a social phenomenon: 'Juristic science has no scientific concept of law. . . . The jurist does not mean by law that which delivers and is operative in human society as law, but . . . exclusively that which is of importance as the law in the judicial administration of justice' (2002: 9–10).

Although obscure, Ehrlich's statement emphasized the importance of understanding law as no more than a social process—he even distinguished between '**living law**' and abstracted judicial understandings of law. Living law is real law, the pulsating, changing patterns of those whose lives are lived out in legal institutions. Law's true identity, this living law, is always a social product. In other words, the social defines law: 'At the present as well as at any other time, the centre of gravity of the legal development lies not in legislation . . . nor in juristic science, nor in judicial decision, but in society itself. This sentence, perhaps, contains the substance of every attempt to state the fundamental principles of the sociology of law (2002: Foreword).'

So, for Ehrlich, the sociology of law, unlike jurisprudence, studies law scientifically as it lives in particular societies. It is not concerned with the technical details of how 'law' ought to perform its functions (e.g., resolving conflict), but merely describes and explains its social operations—an approach commonly found in socio-legal studies and the sociology of law (e.g., Deflem 2008; Banakar and Travers 2002; Black 1989; Milovanovic 1988). Here, society becomes the lens through which to analyze law at any moment in history (cf. Gurvitch 2001); as a social construct, predicated upon, and recursively helping to shape various historically specific social processes, law is studied sociologically. Jurisprudence's attempt to find the essence of law is reversed; now the primary question becomes '*what is the nature of this society?*' and, once answered, it becomes possible to offer secondary versions of law.

This particular approach to law is canvassed through three chapters, each highlighting different ways that key sociologists of the late nineteenth and early twentieth centuries conceptualized society, and their contributions to the law and society field. Chapter 5 starts with **Émile Durkheim**, a famous French sociologist, who focused his attention not on what motivates individuals to act as they do (as in psychology), but rather on the ways that broader **social facts** shape particular kinds of individuals. For him, these social facts are independent phenomena and actually shape individuals—the sum (society) of all the parts (individuals) forms a distinct being that is greater than each part. That is, society exists *sui generis*, has a specific nature, shapes its members' individuality, and forms the proper subject matter of sociology. As well, Durkheim understood law to be an indicator—a sort of measuring device—for a specific type of society; but, simultaneously, it is always a product of the society it serves.

Chapter 6 explores **Karl Marx**'s rather different sense of society as historically produced out of underlying economic forces. His analysis of capitalist society locates law as an **ideology** (a system of ideas that shape how we see the world) that for the most part helps to reproduce an alienating and exploitative society. For him, revolution is the only way to bring about significant change, to overthrow capitalist society, and to usher in a socially orientated communist (or socialist) society. Marx did not examine law in a sustained way, but several debates have emerged in the law and society field that engage directly with the legacy of his ideas.

Another prominent sociologist, **Max Weber**, who is usually considered a key proponent of the **sociology of law**, is discussed in Chapter 7. For him, individual action directed to other people is the basis of society; and specifically modern societies tend to comprise people whose relations with others are rationally framed and understood. These rationalized societies also reflect more rational approaches to law, which he distinguished from early forms of law. He offered an intriguing view of law as a legitimate order backed up by a staff of people who are specifically there to coerce others to conform to such orders. The shape of a given society will determine how orders are created and issued, how they are adjudicated, and how staff will be organized to enforce these orders. In this more complex way, Weber held onto the sense that law is ultimately a social product.

Chapter 8 discusses a late 1970s **critical legal studies** movement that largely emerged in reaction to liberal jurisprudence (explicitly radicalizing legal realism), and that drew extensively on various sociologists (especially Marx and Weber) to offer a comprehensive critique of law. They focused on how law replicates the alienating and unequal hierarchies of capitalist society through its law schools, law practices, and the judicial structures that decide cases. It mystifies and masks such hierarchies, and so helps to perpetuate capitalist inequalities. Calling for radical transformations in law, critical legal studies wanted to change lawyers' (and budding lawyers') ideas and practices fundamentally, thereby radically altering legal institutions from within. They specifically sought to eliminate law's class, gender, and race inequities, but also summoned law to help remove these inequities from wider society. The aspiration was echoed by feminist jurisprudence and critical race theory, but both saw limitations within critical legal studies, and so developed their own analyses and strategies. The admittedly diverse approaches that I have gathered around this movement have a common image of law as shaped by a wider society, but also as shaper of the society in which it operates. Law does not merely determine a society any more than *vice versa*. At this point, the mutual constitution of 'law' and 'society' as historical manifestations is rendered clear, and this effectively contests conceptions of law and society as clearly independent beings, as entities *sui generis*.

Part III: Promising Justice: The *Becoming* of Law and Society

If neither law nor society is cast as fixed objects, whose essence can be determined, the character of early forms of study in the law and society field appears ripe for significant modification. For example, some critics argue that to declare one image of law or society as the only 'correct' formulation, to universalize a given instance as it were, is to privilege dominant versions of either. This invariably propagates existing hierarchies (of, for example, class, race, gender, sexuality), as well as past socio-political oppressions (e.g., colonialism). The idea that many different types of law always coexist (**legal pluralism**) in given social contexts is accompanied by claims that have overturned once popular versions of modern, 'advanced' (or civilized) society—so much so that some even now allege the 'death of the social' (Rose 1999). Such fundamental critiques within the field generate an important conundrum: what is to become of a field that developed around 'law' and 'society' when that field begins to question the very existence of such founding concepts? Can a 'law and society' field survive? Is there a way to reformulate the field without assuming law and society to be discrete objects of study?

Part III describes several approaches that have expanded the field in new ways, and implicitly responded to questions of this kind. The work of **Michel Foucault** has proved deeply influential to subsequent socio-legal analysis, even though he did not emphasize law in his work. Thus, in Chapter 9 we examine his focus on shifting power relations and how specific images of law and society come into being at given historical junctures. In particular, Foucault's work: highlights historical events that enable entities to emerge as fixed *beings* in everyday life; focuses on power relations and their accompanying forms of knowledge; and is attentive to the critical possibilities of changing historical ways of being. His influential analyses of modern political formations provide a novel way to understand legal and social relations as effects of underlying power relations. This chapter also describes how other scholars have developed Foucault's rather fragmentary comments on law. It shows how his analyses of power have enabled socio-legal analysis of local knowledge and practices that claim to be operating in the name of law, society, or justice.

Foucault's focus on the *becoming* of such entities as law and society is implicitly or explicitly allied with the critical socio-legal work that is the subject of Chapter 10. Here the becoming of specific images and practices of law and society in our times is diagnosed and its effects evaluated. Many of these approaches recognize that 'Law seeks to work in the world. It seeks to order, change, and give meaning to the society of which it is a part . . . but what gives law its special character is the fact that when all is said and done, it can, and does, deploy violence' (Sarat 2004b:1).

The chapter selectively reviews four themes: how contemporary law emphasizes violence and the need to protect existing social orders over any allegiance to justice (e.g., the theories of **Robert Cover** and **Walter Benjamin**); **Giorgio Agamben**'s idea that our supposedly democratic states and laws operate through a harmful politics where sovereigns except themselves from law and create depraved 'bare' lives for subjects; the arguments of **Judith Butler** that we are currently being governed by new ways of using law—a politics that relies on unfettered sovereign power, much like the monarchs of old; and, finally, the various post-colonial discussions that describe the plural, contested, and historical processes that have deposited law amongst the deaths of so many in the post-colonial settings. Such discussions open the way to the penultimate Chapter 11 that explores **Jacques Derrida**'s influential essay on law and justice. Amongst other things, it theorizes the *becoming* of law (and society) as local calculations of infinite promises (justice) that are never fulfilled, but remain forever on the horizon of what could be. That work has enabled new socio-legal approaches that describe the logic involved in the becoming of law (**Peter Fitzpatrick**) and society (**Jean-Luc Nancy**), and open the field in important new ways.

The overall prospect for the future of socio-legal studies, 'After Law and Society?', is the subject matter of the concluding review. That review provides glimpses of several options confronting contemporary socio-legal scholars, and suggests some exciting new avenues for scholars who no longer remain committed to 'discovering' what is assumed to be an underlying, static, and unchanging essence of either 'law' or 'society'. Encountering the flow of legality and social forms continuously on their historical paths to something else, and in the name of such laudable promises as justice, is precisely the complex task that faces a regeneration of the field that is gathered around changing images of 'law and society'.

Suggested Readings

Banakar, R., & Travers, M. (eds.) (2002). *An Introduction to Law and Social Theory*. Oxford: Hart.

Cotterrell, R. (2008). *Living Law: Studies in Legal and Social Theory*. Aldershot: Dartmouth.

Hunt, A. (1993). *Explorations in Law and Society: Toward a Constitutive Theory of Law*. London: Routledge.

PART I

Law *Sui Generis*

1 Classical Natural Law

Questions to Consider

- ⊛ Are rulers bound to a higher moral authority (e.g., God, reason)?
- ⊛ In order to be valid, must the laws created by human rulers conform to an eternal notion of justice?
- ⊛ Are subjects duty-bound to obey unjust laws?

Being ruled by neutral laws that seek justice for all is, for many people, the basic requirement of a legitimate order. This is meant to restrain arbitrary decrees by rulers, especially those with a despotic or tyrannical bent. The implication here is that rulers should follow a higher moral authority, and that their laws should conform to justice. Classical natural law approaches develop this basic starting point in various ways. This chapter offers a brief survey of selected influential classical natural law scholars—Plato, Aristotle, Cicero, St Augustine, St Thomas Aquinas, Grotius—who, over many centuries, based their work on the idea that if human laws are to be valid, they must reflect a universal and natural justice. At the heart of **classical natural law**, then, is a collection of ideas that consider 'natural justice' as a stable, Archimedean starting point for all human laws—it assumes an unbreakable link between morality and valid law. Moreover, rational human beings can discover this link because of their exclusive access to reason. Sophocles (an ancient Greek tragedian whose work has survived through the ages) exposes some of the key themes of classical natural law theory in his play *Antigone*.

An Illustrative Case: Sophocles's *Antigone*

In jurisprudence, *Antigone* is often used to illustrate natural law theories because its tragic plot involves a clash between a higher, divine law and a humanly created law (Butler 2000; Ricouer 2000; Douzinas and Warrington 1994). The drama unfolds in a strife-torn milieu, where a proud king named Kreon rules over the Greek city of Thebes. Polynices, one of his sons, mounts a war against his brother Eteocles to recover a sceptre that is supposedly Polynices's right to possess. Both brothers are killed in the ensuing battle, and Kreon proclaims that Eteocles, who defended the city, be buried with full funereal and religious rites. In flagrant contravention of what was then considered to be essential for dealing with the dead, Kreon orders that his other son, Polynices, be abandoned on the battlefield, to perish unburied as fodder for birds and wild beasts. This diktat evokes a heartrending response from the brothers' sister, Antigone. Distraught by their tragic deaths, Antigone cannot accept Polynices's fate; she calls upon her sister Ismene to help bury him, against Kreon's will. Ismene refuses and pleads with Antigone not to disobey the king, but Antigone is unyielding. She violates the edict and performs abbreviated burial rights on her brother. Antigone is reported to Kreon, who summons her to appear before him. He angrily accuses her of disregarding his will, and Antigone openly confesses her deed, acknowledging knowledge of the edict:

> **Kreon**:   And yet you dared to overstep the law?
> **Antigone**: It was not Zeus who made that proclamation
> To me; nor was it Justice, who resides
> In the same house with the gods below the earth,
> Who put in place for men such laws as yours.
> Nor did I think your proclamation so strong
> That you, a mortal, could overrule the laws
> Of the gods, that are unwritten and unfailing
> (2003: 73, lines 495–501).

In these words, we detect Antigone's appeal to an eternal and higher order of justice that can never be overruled by mere mortals. Therefore, she remains entirely unrepentant, knowing only too well that death is her likely fate. But, given the awful situation, she actually welcomes the prospect:

> By dying? So for me to happen on
> This fate is in no way painful. But if
> I let the son of my own mother lie
> Dead and unburied, that would give me pain.
> This gives me none. And now if you think my actions
> Happen to be foolish, that's close enough
> To being charged as foolish by a fool (2003: 73, lines 512–18).

In a passionate rage, Kreon commands that Antigone be buried alive as punishment for her defiance, even though she is betrothed to his son, Haemon. Kreon remains obstinate and unbending, ignoring Haemon's frantic pleas for him to recant. Haemon subsequently commits suicide in the same tomb that Antigone has already hanged herself, and Kreon's distraught wife, Eurydice, stabs herself in grief-stricken sadness.

As these tragic events unfold, Sophocles' 'chorus' notes the dire consequences for those— including kings—who dare to transgress divine justice.

It is the ultimate and eternal authority, capable of inflicting great sorrow on any transgressors. The play is rich with lessons and nuanced appreciations of life, and elegantly draws a distinction between finite laws created by human beings and a 'higher' order of divine laws; the latter ultimately govern the world, including the finite laws of human rulers. In other words, human laws ought always to follow an eternal and infinite law of nature and/or justice. This basic theme has reappeared over the centuries, and is specifically developed by Greek philosophers (e.g., Plato and Aristotle), as well as the Roman stoics whom Marcus Tullius Cicero draws upon to frame his classical natural law theory.

Greco-Roman Ideas and Natural Law

In Plato's (427–347 BCE) work, we have an ambiguous rendition of natural law theory. As Kainz warns, 'we run into semantic problems when discussing natural law in Plato' (2004: 3) because he does not consistently promote its basic precepts. For example, in Book X of *Law*, he suggests that principles of justice and changes to law 'have no basis in nature, but are of authority for the moment and at the time at which they are made' (Plato 1964, X, 889e–898a). At the same time, however, Plato's dialogues do reflect several ideas consonant with natural law; for instance, his well-known **doctrine of forms** differentiates between a rarefied realm of eternal knowledge and finite, earthly manifestations, or copies thereof.[1] As well, *The Republic* addresses the question of justice directly, expressing it as a formal virtue arising from our individual and social makeup.

In many ways, Plato's thinking represents a response to the crumbling fortunes of Athens wracked by the instabilities of protracted warfare. Several decades before his birth, Athens was a thriving imperial power that ruled many surrounding city-states through a confederation. But a few years before he was born, Athens had embarked on a fateful Peloponnesian War with Sparta that was to last for about 27 years; it ended in a crushing defeat that shook the erstwhile democracy. In the aftermath, Plato witnessed his former teacher, Socrates, being tried and condemned to death for impiety and corrupting the minds of youth—and one might speculate whether Plato's own sense of justice as an idea, distinct from law in action, was shaped by that experience. Regardless, he begins *The Republic* with basic questions such as 'why we ought to be virtuous, or just (rather than evil)', and 'why we ought to be law-abiding or ethical'. Thrasymachus, a participant in the dialogue, makes a 'might makes right' argument, which sees justice as whatever the strongest in society deem it to be. In response, Plato puts forward his idea of justice as the natural state of civilized societies and individual beings. He views justice as having an essential and purified nature that we can decipher by careful use of reason and logic.

Famously, Plato argues that human societies comprise three classes of people—craftsmen who provide the basic necessities of life, guardians who ward off external aggression, and rulers, a small elite group of philosophers trained in the Academy to rule wisely. For him, these three classes correlate with three basic elements of the individual human body—the abdomen (appetite), the chest (will), and the head (facility to reason). When in harmony, a body functions in a coordinated fashion, allowing parts to perform their respective tasks according to the way things are in nature. Justice at the level of the individual involves keeping these three dimensions in balance: 'The just man will not allow these three elements which make up his inward self to trespass on each other's functions or interfere with each other, but by keeping all three in tune, like the notes of a scale . . . will in the truest sense set his house in order, and be his own lord and master and at peace with himself' (Plato 1971: [443], p 196).

Equally, for Plato, a just society is one that respects the divisions and hierarchy noted above, seeking the wise rule of the philosopher kings, the elite, to steer that society by the dictates of reason. Respective parts of the social structure must be appropriately educated to meet their tasks for a just state to exist.

Interestingly, this comparison of society to the structure of the body foreshadows an **organic analogy** that will reappear in other (especially sociological) approaches to be discussed in this book. As we shall see, the organic analogy takes the human body as an analogy for how societies work. Just as, say, the circulatory system has complex components of its own, it also works in harmony with other systems (breathing, immune, etc.) to ensure that the whole body works; similarly, one might say that various systems of society (education, political, economic) work in harmony to produce a healthy society. In any case, according to Plato, when the natural body is actually replicated in a specific community, there may be no need for law—rulers who possess the virtue of wisdom make legal adjudication unnecessary. Although this viewpoint appears in *The Republic* (Parts 7 and 8), Plato's later work acknowledges the sheer difficulty of nurturing wise rulers, given the significant commitment that a life of reasoning requires. Consequently, law becomes necessary, but any legal institutions should always reflect an eternal, natural justice.

Aristotle (384–323 BCE) also wrestled with the foundations of classical natural law theory. Against Plato's view of justice as a formal essence, however, Aristotle opts for a 'real world' sense of both natural and human laws. A Macedonian who travelled to Athens at the age of 17, Aristotle was enthralled by the intellectual stimulation of the city, and even attended Plato's Academy. He stayed there for some 20 years before moving to Assos, a city ruled by Hermeias (a devotee of Plato). He later took on the job of tutoring Alexander, Phillip of Macedon's son, and none other than the spectacularly successful military leader now commonly referred to as Alexander the Great.

Under Alexander, Macedon became a formidable ruling empire that eventually controlled Athens. Aristotle returned to Athens in 335 BCE and set up his own school, the Lyceum, writing several of his most influential texts during a decade-long stay. Upon Alexander's death in 323 BCE, anti-Macedonian feelings encouraged him again to leave Athens, and he died shortly thereafter in the city of Chalcis.

One of Aristotle's basic philosophical assumptions is this: every being has a naturally assigned purpose, or *telos*, and this differentiates it from any other being. For Aristotle, human beings have a natural *telos*, and when they pursue that purpose, they flourish. He termed the human purpose **eudaimonia**. Usually translated as 'happiness', this state is the end to which all human pursuits naturally aspire—it is a state of being that allows human beings to flourish according to their natural dispositions, namely, 'living well' and 'doing well' (Aristotle 2004: 23). People voluntarily and consciously act in pursuit of happiness, and this shapes how they live. In other words, just as a tree requires certain basic conditions (water, good soil, sunlight, etc.) to flourish and achieve its natural purpose, so human beings require appropriate conditions to thrive.

One important condition for people to flourish is the presence of a suitable political environment that allows people to pursue happiness. Aristotle ties this condition to living a virtuous (good) life. He makes a key claim: the things that we regard as good, the 'virtues', are never fully determined by nature, but rather, 'We are furnished by nature with a capacity for receiving them, and are perfected in them through custom' (2004: 39). Thus, in order to be virtuous, human beings must *acquire* the attribute of good character. To do this, they choose dispositions that lead them to form good habits—and the latter are developed through appropriate 'training'. That training is best carried out through good government, and good government includes appropriate laws that explicitly develop 'characters' who habitually pursue virtues (like justice), and so happiness (2004: 227ff.).

For Aristotle, justice is a complex matter; it cannot be defined through neat and tidy principles that explain its essence. Instead, he sees justice as something that arises (or not) in the everyday world of action: ' . . . just acting is a mean between acting unjustly and being acted unjustly towards' (2004: 88). So, justice is a moral state reflected in how just people act—it is 'the aptitude for practising the just in the way of moral choice' (2004: 88). That is, justice is a real condition in the world of the here and now. To be just, individuals must cultivate the habit of acting justly, of being fair. Once cultivated, this habit produces a 'character' that always tends toward just acting. Moreover, just characters are nurtured and cultivated through good governance that pursues happiness.

Aristotle distinguishes between broader forms of governing justly for others, and a more local 'social' justice that involves a 'man', 'his wife', and 'slaves'

(2004: 91). It is, of course, a revealing commentary on his time that Aristotle should consider patriarchal and master-slave relations as potentially just.[2] Nevertheless, he distinguishes between two different kinds of social justice: 'natural and conventional; the former being that which has everywhere the same force and does not depend upon being received or not; . . . the latter being that which originally may be this way or that . . . all matters of special decree' (2004: 91). In this important passage, Aristotle makes a distinction between 'natural' forms of justice and those that depend on 'convention'. Having rejected Plato's eternal, universal, and abstract ideas of justice, he argued (like Heraclites) that everything is always changing and appears through real world actions or choices. As such, natural justice arises from the nature of things: ' . . . allowing that everything is subject to change, still there is that which does exist by nature and that which does not' (2004: 91). Consequently, the distinction between natural and conventional justice hinges on this: while certain acts are just *naturally*, other acts become just by virtue of 'human intervention'. The former are universally just, whereas the latter depend on specific contexts. The distinction Aristotle (2004: 92) draws between 'justice' and 'lawful' is congruent with the main drift of natural law theory, but he offers a specific claim that justice is always bound to the actions of a just character, not to some abstract idea.[3]

Furthermore, Aristotle regarded human beings as by nature political animals, who—in pursuit of happiness—form political states that strive to be just. They do so naturally because happiness (their *telos*) is only secured through proper governance. Let us recall too that he insists nature 'makes nothing in vain'; everything has a purpose. In pursuing their political purpose it becomes clear that people are also moral beings: ' . . . it is characteristic of man that he alone has any sense of good and evil, of just and unjust, and the association of living beings who have this sense makes a family and a state' (Aristotle 2004: 200).

The 'association' to which Aristotle refers is rendered secondary to a state and its laws: ' . . . the state is by nature clearly prior to the family and to the individual, since the whole is of necessity prior to the part' (2004: 201). Like Plato, he evokes an organic analogy to underscore his point: '. . . if the whole body be destroyed, there will be no foot, or hand' (2004: 201). This aligns with his view that politics is pivotal for nurturing just characters and allowing just action to express human nature in social contexts.

For Aristotle, then, law is prior, and essential, to securing a just society: 'A social instinct is implanted in all men by nature, and yet he who first founded the state was the greatest of benefactors. For man, when perfected, is the best of all animals, but when separated from law and justice, he is the worst of all' (2004: 201). In other words, a primordial instinct towards sociability can secure the ultimate moral purpose of happiness only when it is harnessed by a political state that cultivates just human characters and

actions. Law is pivotal to cultivating justice and an appropriate 'political society': 'Justice is the bond of men in states, and the administration of justice,
which is the determination of what is just, is the principle of order in political society' (2004: 201). In this sense, Aristotle emphasized law as crucial to
developing social instincts to express a natural justice, thus allowing human
beings to flourish.

Both Plato and Aristotle establish key ideas that later natural law theories
have developed. However, the precise direction of natural law theory was
shaped by stoic philosophy that informed much of Roman thinking about
laws, especially the notion that laws, which did not subscribe to reason and
the common good, could not really be considered as proper or valid law. Perhaps most influential, and drawing on the stoic philosophy of his day, was
Marcus Tullius Cicero (106–43 BCE).

Living through remarkable upheavals in Rome, Cicero became an important political critic and figure, but was caught up in the struggles between
the republican sentiments of older Senators, and the imperial visions of
Julius Caesar, Crassus, and Pompey.[4] The conflicts peaked in 49 BCE with
Caesar crossing the Rubicon, and Rome's well-known descent into civil
war. Caesar's subsequent dictatorship marginalized Cicero, who continued
intellectually to defend the defeated Roman republic and challenge the new
imperial leaders, such as Mark Antony. As someone who lived by the principles he expressed, one might have expected him to encounter opposi-
tion—but certainly not to be murdered, as was the case, and at the behest
of Antony!

In any case, Cicero developed the idea that human laws should always express an underlying natural law. Laelius, a character in one of the remaining fragments of Cicero's dialogue, *The Republic*, utters words that are worth
quoting at length:

' . . . law in the proper sense is right reason in harmony with nature. It is spread
through the whole human community, unchanging and eternal, calling people
to their duty by its commands and deterring them from wrong-doing by its
prohibitions. When it addresses a good man, its commands and prohibitions are
never in vain; but those same commands and prohibitions have no effect on the
wicked. The law cannot be countermanded, nor can it be in any way amended,
nor can it be totally rescinded. We cannot be exempted from this law by any
decree of the Senate or the people; nor do we need anyone else to expound or
explain it. There will not be one such law in Rome and another in Athens, one
now and another in the future, but all peoples at all times will be embraced by a
single and eternal and unchangeable law; and there will be, as it were, one lord
and master of us all—the God who is the author, proposer, and interpreter of
that law. Whoever refuses to obey it will be turning his back on himself. Because
he has denied his nature as a human being he will face the gravest penalties for

those alone, even if he succeeds in avoiding all the other things that are regarded as punishments . . .' (1998: Book III, 33, pp 68–9).

Embedded in this quotation are several key elements of Cicero's approach to natural law. To begin with, he believes that the universe is ordered by rational design, human beings constitute a distinct species between God and animals, and they can only ever realize their full potential in communities governed by laws. Such laws, for Cicero, are based not on opinion but on nature, i.e., an **ontology**[5] that defines what exactly it means to be a human being. If a law does not support that nature (i.e., what it is to be a human being), then it is not a law. So, any humanly created 'true law' must align with the natural order of things because 'Nature is the source of law' (1971: 186). Moreover, 'it is contrary to nature for one man to prey upon another's ignorance' (1971: 186), and any such action ' . . . strikes at the roots of human fellowship', destroying the 'link that unites every human being with every other' (1971: 166). Philosophy and law employ 'different methods' to combat crooked or 'sharp practice': the former uses reason and logic to combat deception, pretense, and so on, whereas law does so through 'forcible coercion' (1971: 184). Such coercion is valid only if based on 'nature's rational principle', because that principle 'governs gods and men alike' such that 'everyone who wants to live according to nature's laws must obey it' (1971: 167). Here, he clearly offers a view of law as an entity *sui generis*, as one that has an essence to be discovered through reason.[6]

Before proceeding to Christian revisions of these basic ideas, it may be worth pausing to note an important, and common, criticism of classical natural law theory. Although it assumes many different guises, let us here refer to this dispute as the **fact-value** debate that centres on whether or not the moral value of law (what it *ought to be*) can ever be derived from our actual existence. As Davies (2008: 116ff.) usefully outlines, critics contest natural law's basic claim to derive what human laws *ought* to be from immutable 'laws of nature' (what *is*). This point may be explained further in this way. Human beings—unlike, say, plants—are only partly determined beings. We have a unique capacity to make choices about how to exist (e.g., as a law-abiding citizen, kind person, or ambitious rogue). But when dealing with these undetermined realms of our lives, we are involved with moral and ethical choice. Critics argue that this realm is entirely different from, and so cannot be derived from, the determined world of the way things are by nature. In responding to this criticism, natural law theorists mostly refuse to accept that these domains are radically distinct, especially in the context of human law. Their overall point is that the moral (ought) and factual (is) worlds cannot be divorced from one another; facts are forever tinged with value, just as values are always deployed in worlds of fact. There may be differences, but the two worlds are inextricably related. With this claim in mind, several Christian forms of classical natural law refer to God to make the link between the two realms.

Christian Revisions of Natural Law

'What are states without justice but robber-bands enlarged?' (Augustine 1950: 112).

In the fourth century CE, St Augustine of Hippo (354–430) argued that any eternal idea of a natural state is part of a Christian God's kingdom. Born in North Africa, he was educated in Carthage, and later taught in Rome before being appointed the Bishop of Hippo in 395. Although probably most famous for his *Confessions*, it is in *The City of God* that we find several important ideas on natural law. Augustine is reputed to have read Cicero carefully, and worked with Plato's doctrine of forms. His famous statement, quoted above, insists that there is no difference between robber-bands and state rulers when the latter do not subscribe to clear notions of justice. And for him justice is inevitably a religious (Christian), moral matter.

Although not initially raised a Christian, he converted in the year 386 at a time when Christianity was the official religion of the Roman Empire. But over the course of his life, the Empire declined, and he became a critic of the rapidly changing times. Consequently, there is a decidedly pessimistic tone to St Augustine's writings, where he hankers after a world of innocence lost in the 'sinful' times before him. He continuously worried about a lost paradise, an ideal and harmonious state of nature that is only to be found in God's city, prior to Adam and Eve's fall in the Garden of Eden. For him, this catastrophic fall unleashed destructive sin into the heart of communities and destroyed their once blissful and divinely natural forms. The upshot was increasingly wicked states, and he calls on Christians to reclaim their true nature by reaching out to the 'city of God.'

So, for Augustine, there can be no justice as long as sin prevails and human laws do not mirror a Christian God's eternal laws of nature. That is why he is reputed to have said, *Lex iniusta non est lex* ('an unjust law is no law'). Apparently emphasizing a distinction between eternal law (*lex aeterna*) and human law (*lex temporalis*), Augustine takes the latter to be a way to expunge sin from everyday social life, and to express the eternal laws of God's justice. By framing the 'state of nature' in divine terms, he takes both natural justice and natural law to be God's creations. By emphasizing the 'fall of man', Augustine (1950) is gripped by the effects of the so-called original sin of society, calling for a harmonious, pastoral society, characterized by innocence, no slaves, and no sin. But the drift of his work is often negative, highlighting the sinful, fallen, and impure state of societies that pervert a natural social order by their perpetual exposure to sin. Consequently, human law must eliminate sin; it must forcefully and coercively ensure that people meet their obligations and duties to behave according to a God-given nature. And this is possible only if law reflects and ensconces a Christian God's natural order. Justice can only appear through God's embrace; as such, the force of state legislators is no different from that of robber barons, unless it is placed in the service of God's justice.

St Thomas Aquinas's (1225–74) much later version of Christian thinking is less concerned with eliminating sin through law; influenced by Aristotle, he wanted to develop a progressive state of living together within God's embrace. Born in the town of Roccasecca, Aquinas studied at the University of Naples, where he outlined an approach to natural law theory that reconciles human reason with Christian belief (see 1952: 3ff., vol. 1). Like Aristotle, he viewed human beings as 'political animals' with an ability to reason; this perspective helps us to understand how to live according to our eternal nature. However, for Aquinas, God embeds moral values in our souls and grants us the capacity to reason practically. By using these powers of reason, we grasp God's eternal moral principles. Thus, in his analysis of law, Aquinas argued that we can only reveal true law by using our God-given powers of reason. When we do so, we find that our laws exist only in 'complete communities' (*civitas*), and derive their authority from an eternal natural law.[7] More specifically, and following Aristotle, he claimed that the law should be directed to happiness and that 'every law is ordained to the common good' (1952: 90, 206, vol. 2). Aquinas also recognizes that laws must change; indeed, if based on reason and if they secure a common good, such changes are central to human progress and our final reconciliation with a Christian God (1952: 236, vol. 2).

Aquinas also differentiated between four different types of law. First, he referred to a primary, **eternal law** (*lex aeterna*), which is the 'rational governance' by God as the infinite ruler and creator of the universe, and not fully available to finite human beings. Secondly, **natural law** (*lex naturalis*) takes the form of law through which rational creatures participate in eternal law, and affirm a natural aspiration to secure their proper (Aristotelian) ends. Hence he argues, 'the natural law is nothing else than the rational creature's participation of the eternal law' (1952: 209, vol. 2). Thirdly, **divine law** (*lex divina*) is revealed through scriptures, and guides human beings to live Christian lives. Finally, **human law** (*lex humanis*) relies on reason to enact statutes for the common good in a local context. A key point one could derive from Aquinas is this: to the extent a government abuses its authority, by proffering unreasonable laws that are not in the common good, it lacks the moral authority to be obeyed; it involves a 'corruption of law'. But one should be cautious here: Aquinas was no radical, and did not see his philosophy as providing a carte blanche endorsement to disobey unjust edicts (Finnis 1998). On the contrary, he considered it important to obey laws, except in very rare cases.

In both Christian formulations discussed so far, separated though they are by many centuries, there is a common appropriation of the idea that human law ought to serve an eternal and universal 'natural justice'. But here, the concept of the 'natural' is viewed through Christian images of a primordial

God who creates a perfect world either subverted by sin and fallen beings (Augustine), or that is yet to be attained by imperfect political beings (Aquinas). In either case, for a human law to have any legitimacy, it must promote a Christian God's eternal laws.

Grotius's Secular Revisions

If these Christian approaches championed a theologically inspired natural law theory, early modern Enlightenment thinkers de-emphasized (and even rejected) religious doctrines and instead embraced secular reasoning. One of the leading jurisprudential thinkers at the time was Hugo Grotius, or Huig de Groot (1583–1645), more commonly known as Grotius. Quite remarkably, Grotius attended the University of Leiden at the age of 11 and was eventually appointed as advocate-fiscal of Holland at the ripe age of 24. He was exceptionally successful until a conservative faction executed the prime minister for whom Grotius had worked. Grotius was imprisoned for his Calvinist inclinations. As a Protestant, he had challenged the Catholic teachings of both Aquinas and Augustine, and in 1625 wrote an important text, *De Jure Belli ac Pacis* (*The Law of War and Peace*). It outlined his understanding of natural law not simply as an ideal moral state, but one that develops through a series of natural progressions.

For Grotius, modern law is both guided and limited by human nature, and its decisions are based entirely on human reason. Emphasizing human rationality and its ability to advance a common good, he considered progressive social development as only possible through reason (and not religious dogma). As law embraces reason and extends its jurisdiction over more areas of social life, so society is pushed in a progressive direction. For example, he referred to the increasing use of rational laws to deal with matters of private property, and argues that these laws spurred the development of capitalism and the progress of modern society. Such social progress may be taken as an indication of nature's grand design in action, and hence he considered the development of capitalism as a natural social progression.[8] So, for Grotius (1964), and unlike St Augustine, the movement away from a 'primitive' state of nature in a pastoral society to a modern one where private property flourishes should not be seen as a fall from grace. On the contrary, it is a natural advancement guided by the reason-based laws of 'nature'. Whilst one might rightly identify echoes of Aquinas's 'common good' idea in Grotius, we should be careful because Grotius emphasizes secular reasoning in his discussions of law, and pointedly omits any references to God as central to natural law.

More particularly, despite personally believing in divine creation, Grotius was clear that natural law is a product of the innate rationality of human nature. He argued that 'right reason' always provides the foundations of law—reason has its own force, regardless of divine sanction. He even went as far as to insist that his analysis ' . . . would have a degree of validity even if we should concede that which cannot be conceded without the utmost wickedness, that there is no God, or that the affairs of men are of no concern to him' (1964: Prolegomena, 11).

His secular conception of natural law has widely influenced modern legal theorists and humanists who in various ways emphasize human nature's ability to reason and so develop law naturally. From this vantage, all human laws ought to be based on right reason and accord with the historical 'nature of society'. Of course, such laws still appeal to a higher moral authority, but in a dawning age of Enlightenment that authority need not be understood as emanating from a God. Secular appeals to the reason-based nature of all things would now suffice.

Concluding Reflections

As will become clearer from later chapters, many legal theorists have re-worked, or responded to, central concepts articulated in classical natural law theory. To reiterate, classical natural law theorists variously singled out human law as a distinct object of analysis, as something with an essence to be discovered through careful analysis. Law appears as an independent entity in and of itself (i.e., *sui generis*), but one that always derives from higher orders of justice (morality), nature, and reason. This law is granted an internal logic appropriate to its nature. In a sense, then, one of the discursive achievements of classical natural law theory was to have isolated law as a distinct category of being, and to have framed that being as always stemming from a higher, more eternal, moral authority. In so doing, classical natural law separated justice as a moral and natural state from the laws posited by human legislators and adjudicators. The latter are then, as we have seen, variously considered as valid, and so worthy of being obeyed, only when they conform to the basic precepts of the former. Sophocles's *Antigone* approached the theme through a tragic tale of a king who did not heed the call of natural justice. Plato, Aristotle, and Cicero developed the theme, Augustine and Aquinas gave it a religious twist, and Grotius reformulated it by elevating the power of human reason. That secular revision has echoed through the ages, and one finds it revealingly embedded in Jean-Jacques Rousseau's critique of eighteenth-century laws in France in his novel *Emile*:

> One aspires in vain to liberty under the safeguard of laws. Laws! What are the laws, and where are they respected? Everywhere you have seen only individual interest and men's passions reigning under this name. But the eternal laws of nature and order do exist. For the wise man, they take the place of positive law. They are written in the depth of his heart by conscience and reason. It is to these that he ought to enslave himself in order to be free (Rousseau 1979: 473).

Reason, nature, and moral images of justice (conceived in various ways) have since then prominently featured as ways to determine the validity of human laws. All law— if it is even to count as 'law'—must be grounded in a higher moral authority, revealed through a careful use of reason. In such concepts we have the foundations of natural law theory that continue to preoccupy many contemporary debates in jurisprudence and legal theory.

Discussion Questions

1. Without notions of justice, is valid law ever possible?

2. Is justice best formulated as an abstracted moral essence (Plato) or as a way of living one's life in pursuit of happiness (Aristotle)?

3. Are the rules that govern members of a gang any different from the state's laws used to prevent gang activities?

4. Do we have a universally agreed upon sense of justice that might make it the arbiter of human laws?

Suggested Readings

Finnis, J. (1986). 'The "Natural Law Tradition"'. *Journal of Legal Education*, 36(4), 492–5.

Kainz, H. (2004). *Natural Law: An Introduction and Re-examination*. Chicago: Open Court.

Murphy, M.C. (2006). *Natural Law in Jurisprudence and Politics*. New York: Cambridge University Press.

Relevant Websites

http://classics.mit.edu/Aristotle/politics.html
www.ucmp.berkeley.edu/history/aristotle.html
www.utexas.edu/depts/classics/documents/Cic.html
http://plato.stanford.edu/entries/natural-law-ethics/
www.historyguide.org/intellect/allegory.html

2 Natural Law Theory: Morality and Law

Questions to Consider

- Does any attempt to define the nature of law necessarily involve morality?
- Does law have an 'internal morality' reflected by its internal procedures?
- What makes a human law just (moral) and so worthy of being obeyed?
- Is the nature of law necessarily tied to the nature of human beings?

Lawyers are often involved with creating, legislating, adjudicating, or enforcing laws that prescribe behaviour in given situations. That prescriptive function is what links, for the **natural law** approaches discussed in the present chapter, law and morality. They agree that legal analysis differs from philosophical discussions of morality (and ethics), but both are ultimately concerned with how subjects ought to act in given sets of circumstances when different actions are possible. Stated differently, natural law approaches contend that since law is directly or indirectly involved in specifying what ought to be done in specific situations, it cannot but involve moral matters in one way or another. So, while law and morality may well offer different visions of suitable 'codes of conduct' in given social contexts, they are necessarily related.

We have, of course, encountered a version of this idea in the classical natural law theories of the previous chapter, where a higher, moral authority was said to found all human law. While the natural law theorists of the present chapter accept the overall thrust of this argument, they nevertheless revise it in important ways. I will focus on two influential natural law scholars who distill classical natural law approaches in significant ways—Lon Fuller (1969, 1958) and John Finnis (1980). Both agree that notions of morality (justice) in law emerge out of the actual ways that we do things, rather than through abstract moral principles. To help clarify their respective revisions, let us consider an immoral apartheid law (see Thompson 1990).

Apartheid and the *Prohibition of Mixed Marriages Act,* 1949

The law as it is applied, the law as it has been developed over a long period of history, and especially the law as it is written and designed by the Nationalist Government, is a law which, in our view, is immoral, unjust, and intolerable. Our consciences dictate that we must protest against it, that we must oppose it, and that we must attempt to alter it (Nelson Mandela, quoted in Derrida and Tlili, 1987: 39).

With these words, Nelson Mandela unswervingly challenged the apartheid system of law in South Africa that was eventually to criminally convict and imprison him (and others) for life in the famous Rivonia Trial (see Joffe 2009). In declaring apartheid law as 'immoral, unjust, and intolerable', he questioned the moral authority of a legal system that divided its population along racial lines, systematically discriminated against a majority of that population, enforced unjust laws with horrendous effects, and used the rule of law to ensconce the domination of privileged white subjects (see Abel 1995). And the underlying deficit in moral authority underscores Mandela's stated duty to protest rather than obey such laws. It should be noted that a racist political program of 'apartheid' legislation was formally introduced after the Nationalist Party assumed power in 1948. It is perhaps worth recalling the context that Abel usefully frames in this way:

Law has been a terrain of political contestation throughout South African history. Courts have oscillated between being compliant, even enthusiastic, instruments of white domination and erecting obstacles, if only temporary, to the apartheid project. . . . After its 1948 victory, the National Party lost no time in translating its racist ideology into law: the *Mixed Marriages Act* 1949, *Population Registration Act* 1950, *Group Areas Act* 1950, *Suppression of Communism Act* 1950, and *Immorality Act* 1951 (1995: 14).

For our purposes here, though, let us focus on one of the early enacted apartheid laws—the *Prohibition of Mixed Marriages Act*, 1949[1]—as a backdrop to key ideas in Fuller's and Finnis's formulations of natural law.

The intention of this act was bluntly stated: 'To prohibit marriage between Europeans and non-Europeans, and to provide for matters incidental thereto'. It declares that from the act's date of commencement, 'a marriage between a European and non-European may not be solemnized', and Section 3 made a 'presumption of race from appearance' that it qualified as follows: 'Any person who is in appearance obviously a European or a non-European, as the case may be, shall for the purposes of this act be deemed to be such, unless and until the contrary is proved.' Section 1(1)(a)(i) of the act rendered a marriage valid only if:

any party to such marriage professing to be a European or a non-European, as the case may be, is in appearance obviously what he professes to be, or is able to show, in the case of a party professing to be a European, that he habitually consults with Europeans as a European, or in the case of a party professing to be a non-European, that he habitually consults with non-Europeans as a non-European . . .

In an absurdity of colossal dimensions, the stated logic appears to be this: one is deemed to be 'European' or 'non-European' if s/he 'obviously' appears to be such! The act also made it an offence for anybody to give a false statement to a marriage officer, or for a marriage officer to solemnize a so-called mixed marriage. In addition, it decreed that, 'If any male person who is domiciled in the Union [of South Africa] enters into a marriage outside the Union which cannot be solemnized in the Union in terms of sub-section (1), then such a marriage shall be void and of no effect in the Union.' This extraordinary piece of legislation, with its racist and sexist wording, was introduced as a bill in parliament, voted on by an assemblage composed exclusively of white members, and followed the usual passage for legislation before being published as a statute. Despite its incongruous content, the statute was generated out of ordinary rituals and formalities (parliamentary readings, etc.) used to legitimize it as a genuine law. It was only repealed in 1990, with the transition to the new South Africa.

The act's diabolical effect on many people's lives has been documented in novels, histories, and various political analyses (e.g., Stone 2007; Worden 2007; Lewis 1986). Interestingly, in the context of our discussion of natural law, Moodie's (1975) classic text explains how apartheid legislation was enacted under a broader Afrikaner 'civil religion', in which legislators appealed to a supposedly 'natural' order enunciated by both Calvinist doctrines and a version of secular philosophy. Such laws, he argues, were legitimated by appealing to Calvinist doctrines of predestination (i.e., that some people were closer to God and would thus be amongst the saved rather than the damned), to a neo-Fichtean philosophy that believed happiness could only be achieved by living within a close communal fraternity, and to a racist ideology that deemed race to be the most basic 'community'. Apartheid law extended this civil religion, and was justified on the grounds that it followed a natural/religious order. No matter the details of Moodie's argument, it shows how apartheid's architects claimed that their laws were purportedly based on a (racially skewed) concept of the 'natural order'.

To be sure, this gives considerable pause for reflection on whether classical natural law's emphasis on a higher authority provides a way unequivocally to reject unjust laws. It also gave rise to a debate between two opponents of apartheid structures—both referred to natural law theory to make their respective cases (i.e., the Wacks (1984)-Dugard (1988) debate). The debate centred on whether judges should resign from an unjust apartheid legal system on the grounds that their presence simply perpetuates an unjust system (Wacks), or whether it is better to have opponents of apartheid sitting on its Bench and working for reform from within (Dugard 1990, 1978).[2] Given that both refer to natural law theory to make their cases, a question arises: is there a version of natural law theory that might allow us to differentiate between laws that are justifiable on moral grounds and those that are not? Let us now turn to Fuller's and Finnis's formulations of natural law to investigate this matter further.

Lon Fuller: The 'Internal Morality' of Law as a Craft

While Lon Fuller's (1902–78) natural law perspective held onto elements of classical natural law theory, it also departed from it in important ways. In his classic work, *The Morality of Law*, Fuller offered a natural law theory that focused explicitly on the rational dimensions of **lawmaking as a craft**, not unlike the crafts of, say, glassblowing or carpentry. For him, the moral authority of lawmaking (legislating, adjudicating, enforcing) never resides in abstract principles embodied in substantive law (statutes); it is found in the procedures through which people carry out the rule of law in a given context.[3] For Fuller, making law is a rational activity or 'craft' that has a distinct purpose and an internal logic. When that craft is practised according to the logic of its purpose, it flourishes (note the Aristotelian overtones). But if, in a given instance, members do not follow that logic, it breaks down as a lawmaking practice, and cannot rightfully be considered law. In other words, the craft of lawmaking has what he calls a unique 'internal morality' that allows us to identify it, legitimately, as law. If a given craft does not reflect that morality, then it may be called something else, but it is not law. Lawmaking, as with any 'craft,' is practised through distinctive, internal rules that its practitioners follow.

But what exactly does the craft of lawmaking involve? Fuller (1981: 211ff; 1975) argues that law can be used as both a coercive 'instrument' of social control and, just as importantly, to facilitate 'human interaction'. But he defines law generally as: 'the enterprise of subjecting human conduct to the governance of rules' (1969: 91). This pithy statement is worth emphasizing, because it highlights Fuller's understanding of law, not as a set of moral principles per se, but as a set of internally coherent and morally defensible practices that subject human actions to the 'governance of rules' (as opposed to, say, tyrannical, arbitrary decree). He thus views lawmaking as morally justified when its ways of subjecting conduct to rule governance follow a logic appropriate to its purpose. In other words, every legal system, by definition, is a way of making human conduct amenable to the regulation of particular kinds of rules, and always reflects an underlying morality. Or stated in another way, the process of 'subjecting human conduct to the governance of rules' raises questions about whether we are obligated to obey these rules and why. This is always a moral question, and hence the unbreakable tie between law and morality.

From this he argues that any lawmaking craft must conform to a basic 'internal morality' to be called 'law'. In short, this is 'the morality which makes law possible' (1969: 102–3). If a legal system's lawmaking practices do not conform to this basic internal morality, then the system is not a legal one, and hence has no authority to impose itself on subjects. Its decrees are then by definition not law, even if they are dressed in the guise of legal rituals, language, and formalities. But what precisely are the basic rules for the craft of successful lawmaking?

Fuller answers this question through a 'moral tale' that imagines the conditions under which lawmaking would fail. Then, he takes the opposite of these failures to indicate positive 'desiderata' for successful lawmaking. Specifically, he asks us to imagine a fictional king, *Rex*, who fails in every way to secure minimum moral standards for achieving law, for practising the craft of lawmaking. Fuller (1969: 38–9) offers eight such failures:

1. King Rex does not manage to formulate general rules, so his decisions are always made on an ad hoc basis;
2. He fails to inform subjects of the rules that apply to them;
3. He uses retroactive legislation that not only fails to guide action, 'but undercuts the integrity of rules prospective in effect, since it puts them under the threat of retrospective change' (1969: 39);
4. His rules are not understood by subjects;
5. He enacts contradictory rules;
6. His rules require subjects to behave in ways that are beyond their powers;
7. The rules are changed frequently, so subjects are not able to orientate their conduct;
8. The king fails to align the rules that are announced with their administration in reality.

Through this moral tale, Fuller alerts us to the idea that when legislators use such awful ruling practices, they do not actually have laws or work through legal systems that can rightfully expect obedience from their subjects.

At the same time, for Fuller, the opposites of each of these eight failures give us a sense of what is minimally required for the craft of lawmaking to achieve internal coherence, or the 'internal morality' required for valid law. In particular, he extracts eight 'desiderata' of effective lawmaking as direct opposites to the above noted failures: generality, promulgation, non-retroactivity, clarity, non-contradiction, possibility of compliance, constancy, and congruence between declared rule and official action (1969: 39). In concert, these desiderata allow us to grasp the internal morality of law. However, he is clear that not all of these will be applicable to every working legal system. Yet, to the extent that a system repeatedly pursues the failures represented by King Rex, it does not achieve even minimum moral requirements to be considered a legal system.

It is important to consider Fuller's sense of the kind of natural law theory he has hereby articulated:

Do the principles expounded in my [eight rules] represent some variety of natural law? The answer is an emphatic, though qualified, yes. . . . What I have tried to do is to discern and articulate the natural laws of a particular kind of human undertaking which I have described as 'the enterprise of subjecting human conduct to the governance of rules'. These natural laws have nothing to do with any 'brooding omnipresence in the skies' . . . they are not higher laws; if any metaphor of elevation is appropriate they should be called 'lower laws'. . . . What I have called the internal morality of law is in this sense a procedural version of natural law (1969: 96–7).

Here Fuller clearly reflects on his attempt to produce a procedural natural law theory predicated on actual human practices that fashion law (like Aristotle), rather than through some or other abstract moral principles (Plato). These practices must reflect an internal morality appropriate to the craft of lawmaking in order for law to exist. Only then can the legal craft expect a 'fidelity to law' from its subjects (Fuller 1957).

The significance of this point for a key debate between natural law and legal positivism will become clearer in the following chapter. But, for now, we might say that when a legal system no longer achieves a minimum degree of procedural moral legitimacy, when its ability to command fidelity from its subjects expires, then such a legal system has no claim to the obedience from subjects. The integrity of that legal system is compromised, and it ceases to be—in any meaningful sense—'the law'. In other words, the authority and legitimacy of law is, for Fuller, founded on morally guided practices of lawmaking that involve the consent of those whom it governs (1958: 642); that consent derives from the 'internal morality of law'.

In trying to better understand the philosophical status of Fuller's **procedural morality**, one could refer to a distinction he (1969: 5) makes between a 'morality of duty' and a 'morality of aspiration'. The morality of duty refers to basic moral edicts required to produce human interactions in an ordered society. This is a minimum level of morality required for any collective associations, and for a legal system to exist at all. By contrast, he separates out a 'morality of aspiration' in which we find 'the morality of the Good Life, of excellence, of the fullest realisation of human powers' (1969: 5). This is not a minimum criterion for ordered existence, but the highest aspiration of moral ideals. Having placed duty and aspiration as opposite poles on a moral continuum, Fuller then argues that law is largely concerned with matters of duty, or the basic requirements for creating an ordered society.[4] Indeed, when used to impose human aspirations, law risks becoming tyrannical. As such, one of law's key functions is to limit its own operations to a 'lower' morality of duty.

Clearly, for Fuller, it is not possible to consider law apart from its founding morality. Therefore, the previously noted fact-value distinction becomes superfluous:[5] facts and values always maintain a 'collaborative articulation of shared purposes' that makes the separation between them untenable (Fuller 1958: 74). All facts are tinged by value, and to deny this is to turn one's back on a central dimension of what it is to exist in ordered human societies. As such, he argues that, 'Good order is law that corresponds to the demands of justice, or morality, or men's notions of what ought to be' (1957: 644).

In sum, for Fuller, valid law is possible when lawmaking practices embrace a minimum internal morality reflected by the actions of legislators, judges, and lawyers, and are accepted by those whose conduct is subjected to the rule of law. With his approach in mind, how might we assess apartheid's prohibition of *Mixed Marriages Act*? In other words, does Fuller's account provide adequate ways to show the injustice of apartheid law? Framed in this stark way, it is not at all clear that Fuller's account could provide a litmus test of legislative morality; however, is this demand fair? Is it ever possible to provide solid guarantees in the context of human indeterminacy? History might suggest otherwise, but at least a Fullerian approach provides a way of assessing the internal morality of the lawmaking processes that produced the *Mixed Marriages Act* delineated above.

For example, Fuller might well ask whether or not the procedures used to create this law complied with the basic desiderata of all legal systems: generality (barely); promulgation (depends on how the laws were communicated to subjects, some of whom may have been illiterate); non-retroactivity (the act appears to contradict this by applying to existing marriages); clarity (one could question the absurd way by which 'Europeans' and 'non-Europeans' are defined, and 'other' identities constituted); non-contradiction (given the absurdity of the definitions, contradictions were inevitable; see Stone 2007); the possibility of compliance (complicated by arbitrary and changing definitions, e.g., 'Europeans'); constancy (impossible given the arbitrariness of enforcement arising from the definitions); and congruence between declared rule and official action (the bureaucratic arbitrariness of determining whether someone 'appears' non-European or not often challenged this requirement).

With this approach, Fuller could argue—if not in a compelling, then perhaps a rudimentary manner—that this apartheid act does not embrace a clear internal morality of lawmaking. However, an important deficit is the theory's failure to highlight the illegitimacy of the way in which the statute was written and passed in a 'whites only' parliament, even though it clearly applied to a vast majority who had no say in its creation, and for whom this law represented a thoroughly illegitimate political ruse (Lewis 1986). Perhaps this critique does not completely repudiate Fuller's approach, but it does suggest the need to expand the desiderata to include whether democratic patterns of representation exist when legislators make law (Wacks 2005, 1984). Regardless, for illustrative purposes here, suffice to say that Fuller's approach to natural law would assess the validity of the *Mixed Marriages Act*, 1949, not by turning to the content of the statute, but to the internal morality of the various ways it tried to 'subject human conduct to rules'.

John Finnis: Law and Flourishing Human Life

> Legal reasoning is, broadly speaking, practical reasoning. Practical reasoning moves from reasons for action to choices (and actions) guided by those reasons. A natural law theory is nothing other than a theory of good reasons for choice (and action) (Finnis 1990: 1).

If Fuller focuses on the 'internal morality' of law to develop his theory, Finnis's natural law scheme returns to Thomas Aquinas and Aristotle to rework classical approaches. He rejects the idea that morality (practical reasoning) can ever be deduced from one or other essential nature. His modified Aristotelian ethics champions **practical reasoning** as an 'objective'—but not natural—way to reveal moral ways of acting (Finnis 1980: 33). In other words, morality cannot be inferred from human nature, but can only be understood through a particular type of practical (i.e., moral) reasoning that is unique to human beings. Furthermore, this sort of reasoning is crucial not only to law, but more generally to how we live our lives, because 'acts of practical reasoning' allow us to 'grasp the basic values of human existence and thus, too, the basic principles of all moral reasoning' (1980: 59).

But what are these acts of 'practical understanding'? For Finnis, practical reasoning is grounded on a human 'moral substratum'. That is, each of us has the unique ability to recognize self-evident moral goods through introspection. We do so by using **intuitive methods** that work quite differently from either scientific disciplines (e.g., anthropology, psychology) or philosophy. Intuitive methods involve a distinctive logic of self-discovery (i.e., 'practical understanding') (1980: 81) that aims to uncover certain 'indemonstrable' and yet 'self-evident' values that lie at the heart of our human morality. That is, we all have a primordial sense of what is good for us as human beings, 'with the nature that we have' (1980: 34). And so he argues that 'practical reasoning begins not by understanding this nature from the outside, as it were, by way of psychological, anthropological or metaphysical observations and judgments defining human nature, but by experiencing one's nature, so to speak, from the inside, in the form of inclinations' (1980: 34). It is important to stress that such reasoning never involves inference: 'Rather by a simple act of non-inferential understanding one grasps that the object of the inclination which one experiences is an instance of a general form of good, for oneself (and others like one)' (1980: 34).

In other words, by using an introspective and intuitive analysis, individuals can identify certain common 'basic goods'. These goods are self-evident, requiring no metaphysical analysis to reveal them. We simply ask ourselves this question: 'what *are* the basic aspects of my well-being?' And in this very act of asking, ' . . . each one of us . . . is alone with his own intelligent grasp of the indemonstrable (because self-evident) first principles of his own practical reasoning' (1980: 85).

But what do his self-introspections reveal as basic goods? Finnis (1980: 86–90) gestures towards Aristotelian *eudaimonia*, and offers seven such 'basic forms of human flourishing' that he thinks each of us will arrive at were we left to contemplate the 'basic aspects of my well being':

1. the valuing and transmission (procreation) of life
2. knowledge for its own self (not as means to end)
3. 'play'
4. 'aesthetic experience'
5. 'sociability' and especially friendship
6. 'practical reasonableness' that 'seeks to bring an intelligent and reasonable order into one's own actions and habits and practical attitudes'—this structures the ways in which we pursue basic goods
7. 'religion' or the value of spiritual experience

As Finnis sees it, even though not exhaustive, these basic forms of human flourishing are essential to a fulfilling life. They are also, for him, universal to all human societies at all times, and intrinsically valuable (rather than the means to other ends). Although these ends are interrelated and combined in diverse ways, reflecting the heterogeneity and diversity of human being, we simultaneously aspire to all seven goods through a practical reasoning immediately available to all of us. Furthermore, he argues that, at base, human life cannot flourish without a community, led by an authority who pursues the interests of a 'common good' (note the Aristotelian overtones). If a ruler's law offends against the common good, it forfeits a moral right to govern its subjects. In Finnis's account, justice is always about securing and nurturing that common good—and this common good derives from his theory of universal human good, or moral principles that secure such good. The overriding rationale is to establish ways of being together that are good for all human beings. Hence, we do not aspire to basic goods simply as individuals; rather, we do so in the context of our interactions with other people—namely, in a community, with a common good.

How does law fit into this schema? As implied, Finnis argues that a healthy community requires a common code of conduct that orders and coordinates interactions (coercively and through regulation) to achieve a common good.[6] Law is precisely such a code of conduct, for it allows subjects of society to pursue and achieve the seven basic goods. Law, in short, orders social actions in ways that enable people to pursue basic goods. He argues that the great achievement of natural law theorists was 'to show that the act of "positing law" (whether judicially or legislatively or otherwise) is an act which can and should be guided by "moral" principles and rules' (1980: 290).

Furthermore, the 'basic forms of human flourishing', together with essential elements of reasonableness in moral matters, constitute the eternal 'principles of natural law'. As such, Finnis argues, it is never possible to have a 'value free description and analysis' of law (1980: 3). By expressly focusing on the moral dimensions of law, he argues that 'natural law theory tries to do openly, critically, and discussably, what most other analytical and descriptive theorists do covertly and dogmatically' (1986: 494).

In his version of natural law, then, the morality of law is examined via its practical reasonableness, and by ensuring that any study of law explicitly focuses on the values that give it any authority or legitimacy. As he puts it, 'it is the values of the Rule of Law that give the legal system its distinctive entitlement to be treated as the source of authoritative solutions' (Finnis 1984: 136).[7]

Presumably, then, were Finnis to examine the *Mixed Marriages Act* in South Africa, he would focus on its legitimacy and whether it serves the common good of a society, i.e., to what extent it enables subjects to pursue the basic goods that he has articulated. As well, he might look at whether it helps with society's 'coordination problems' in the interests of a common good (1980: 351).[8] The imposition of a prohibition on so-called mixed marriages, enacted by a partisan and exclusive parliament, clearly violates the requirement that law serve the common good of *all* people. The statute also clearly violates Finnis's basic value of sociability that requires 'a unity of common action' (1980: 138), and the formation of shared objectives that serve everyone.[9]

In short, Finnis's framework might be used to argue that the *Mixed Marriages Act* is unjust because it does not further the common good; it suppresses several forms of human flourishing, especially sociability and friendship, across a social body. He also notes that, 'stipulations made for partisan advantage, or . . . imposing inequitable burdens on their subjects, or directing the doing of the things that should never be done, simply fail, of themselves, to create any moral obligation whatever' (1980: 360). Equally in his discussion of justice, Finnis argues that practical reasonableness 'excludes arbitrary self-preference in the pursuit of good' (1980: 164), which may be applicable to some (though not all) of the self-identified 'Europeans' promulgating a law that confuses sectarian impositions with the common good. However, like Aquinas, he disagrees with the notion that unjust laws should be disobeyed with impunity because, he argues, there are times when an unjust law should be obeyed so as not to weaken the legal system overall (what he calls 'collateral obligation') (1980: 365). In this sense, Finnis may well agree with Aquinas's appropriation of St Augustine's famous *lex injusta non est lex*, but this twist certainly weakens his attempt to provide grounds for rejecting the validity of unjust laws, such as the *Mixed Marriages Act*, 1949.

Justice via Law and Society

In both Fuller's and Finnis's natural law theory, one detects a commitment to justice understood as the outcome of morally defensible procedures of law, or as a product of successful practical reasoning. For Fuller, the idea of justice appears to be a collective aim best understood through the procedures bearing its name: 'we can arrive at a better understanding of the aim we call justice if we discuss critically the various means by which it is imperfectly realized' (1981: 263). For Finnis, justice is about fostering the common good in a community: it concerns an individual's interactions and duties with others, and revolves around matters of proportionality and equilibrium (1980: 161–3). Justice is thus not defined through principle, but rather through proper practices of lawmaking or practical reasonableness. As we have seen, for Fuller, law is the activity that subjects human conduct to rules, whereas Finnis sees law as species of legitimate rules emanating from a rule-bound authority working in the common good of a society or community (1980: 276). For both, the law is seen as a way of justly coordinating, shaping, coercing, and ordering societies for a common good. In other words, the law is distinguished as an entity *sui generis* whose role is to shape and order human interactions in a morally proscribed and prescriptive fashion.

Such a view of law, in both cases, influences how each in turn conceptualizes society. Fuller (1981: 48, 68ff.) boldly declares two opposing 'principles of human association' as the basis for *good* social order: 'shared commitment' and 'legal principle'. He describes in some detail 'laws' governing the interrelations between these opposing principles of association, and distinguishes between customary patterns of associating and modern, law-based social forms. Unlike later sociologists and anthropologists, however, Fuller (1981: 213) does not consider customary law to be an inferior anachronism to modern law; instead he argues that the 'neglect of the phenomenon called customary law has . . . done great damage to our thinking about law generally'; he even emphasizes that 'officially declared or enacted law' cannot be understood without a sense of customary law.

Referring to sociologists like Parsons and Simmel, Fuller appears to be suggesting that with any spontaneous form of association there are 'complementary expectations' that help to constitute a customary form of legality. And modern law finds expression by referring to this customary base. Unlike many sociologists and anthropologists, he argues that customary patterns thus exist alongside legal principle. Indeed, the two may be interrelated in their bid to order a good society; however, law appears here as a distinct entity that may shape and be shaped by society, but it always materializes from its own foundations. Fuller sees the relationship between law and society in this way: 'law and its social environment stand in a relation of reciprocal influence; any given form of law will not only act upon, but be influenced and shaped by, the established forms of interaction that constitute its social milieu. This means that for a given social context one form of law may be more appropriate than another . . . ' (1981: 237). To force an unsuitable form of law on a social context could produce 'damaging results', but law has a distinctive being.

Finnis, for his part, has a somewhat different view of society. As he puts it, 'Who has not noticed the peculiar vagueness of the term "social"? Who has not felt slightly baffled about the "communities", and "societies", which are spoken of as (lots of) individuals, sometimes as if they were themselves individuals with interests, well-being etc., and sometimes extremely abstract "systems" (of what?)?' (1980: 135). He thus tries to offer a more concrete sense of community as a 'form of unifying relationships between human beings' (1980: 136) with various dimensions, including the ability to order actions by 'intelligently deliberating and choosing' (1980: 138). Society then emerges as an effect of 'unifying relations' between individuals (e.g., relationships of family and friends as well as other groups), and can only exist as such through the sustained coordination of activities by some members 'with a view to a shared objective' (1980: 153). For him, 'the "existence" of the group, the "existence" of social rules, and the "existence" of authority tend to go together' (1980: 153). Whatever else is implied, Finnis here argues that just laws coordinate human relationships well through a version of practical reason that aspires to further the 'common good'. His use of 'scare quotes' around the term 'existence' in the above quotation is instructive, because it shows that society is secondary to the unification of individual interactions and the coordinating functions of law.

Despite their differences, both Fuller and Finnis take for granted the existence of 'law' *sui generis* and its ability to order, structure, and set social relations free. Fuller's interest in legal anthropology and his version of customary law began, in a subtle and not always clear fashion, to make reference to society as a structure that might well have a foundational effect on law. But neither of these natural law theorists is yet prepared to predicate the existence of law wholly on an underlying, and more encompassing, society.

Concluding Reflections

The preceding discussion has explored two influential natural law theorists' approaches to law, society, and justice. In both, one notes the significance of morality to law, and the need to found any legal system on morally defensible grounds. Both also emphasize morality as a process in the real world rather than something to be captured through pure, abstracted principles. For Fuller, valid law must embrace an 'internal morality' that materializes through rules, practices, and procedures appropriate to the craft of lawmaking. For Finnis, law's morality can be derived from a wider morality that is available to all people who use an intuitive practical reasoning to grasp indemonstrable but indubitable values that allow us, by virtue of our unique nature as human beings, to flourish. Both also understand law to be an independent activity with social effects, and offer practice-based, moral accounts of how to differentiate between valid and invalid law. Their firm allegiance to the idea that law and morality cannot be divorced provides a useful point of entry into the next chapter, because there we will encounter the **legal positivists** who argue that whatever the connections between law and morality may be, those who study law scientifically must abandon moral questions to philosophers. For them, as we shall see, legal analysis ought not to dwell on moral matters.

Discussion Questions

1. Is Fuller right to insist that law must have an internal morality to be defined as such?

2. Does Fuller's moral tale of King Rex adequately explain failures of lawmaking?

3. Does Finnis's conception of the basic aspects of well-being really apply to all human beings? Does it exclude particular groups?

4. Which of the two approaches—Fuller's or Finnis's— provides a better way to challenge unjust apartheid legislation? Why?

Suggested Readings

Citron, R. (2006). 'The Nuremberg Trial and American Jurisprudence: The Decline of Legal Realism, the Revival of Natural Law, and the Development of Legal Process Theory'. *Michigan State Law Review*, 2006(2), 385–410.

Fuller, L. (1969). *The Morality of Law* (revised edition). New Haven: Yale University Press.

Murphy, M.C. (1996). 'Natural Law and the Moral Absolute against Lying'. *American Journal of Jurisprudence*, 41, 81–102.

Relevant Websites

www.disa.ukzn.ac.za/index.php?option=com_displaydc&recordID=l
    eg19490708.028.020.055
http://ivr-enc.info/index.php?title=Fuller,_Lon_Luvois
www.iep.utm.edu/natlaw/
www2.law.ox.ac.uk/jurisprudence/finnis.shtml

3 Positing Law

Questions to Consider

- ⊛ Can an unjust law nevertheless be considered as a valid law?
- ⊛ Is law nothing more than a command issued by a sovereign and obeyed by subjects?
- ⊛ What is the basic foundation of law?
- ⊛ When studying law scientifically, must we ignore its morality?

An enduring set of approaches to law over the past two and a half centuries has collectively come to be known as **legal positivism**. Several theorists are associated with this school of thought, but this chapter selectively highlights contributions from Hobbes, Bentham, Austin, Hart, and Kelsen. Is anything distinctive about legal positivism? Bix says 'yes':

> Legal Positivism is based on the simple assertion that the proper description of law is a worthy objective and a task that needs to be kept separate from moral judgments (regarding the value of the present law, and regarding how the law should be developed or changed). In the more precise terms of theorizing about the law, it is the view that a descriptive, or at least morally neutral, theory of law is both possible and valuable (2006: 33).

To better understand the 'simple assertion', it may be worth considering the example of a scientist investigating the mechanics of an airplane's jet engine. When trying to comprehend its nature, one might argue that it is unnecessary, indeed problematic, to focus on moral questions like, 'Is it ethical to fly long distances on planes, given the environmental impact?' One might acknowledge the importance of such questions, but not in the context of a scientific analysis directed to explaining the engine's workings. In an equivalent fashion, legal positivists call on legal theory and jurisprudence to analyze the nature of law impartially, and surrender moral discussions to philosophers, theologians, etc. The point is made sharply in a famous debate[1] between a natural law theorist (Fuller) and a legal positivist (Hart) regarding a Nazi-era case.[2]

In 1944, while at home on travel orders for a reassignment in the German army, a man confided a disdain for Hitler to his wife, regretting that a recent assassination attempt had failed. His spouse, who purportedly 'had turned to other men' and wanted to leave, denounced him to a local Nazi party leader for insulting Hitler (Fuller 1958: 653). She is reported as saying that 'a man who would say a thing like that does not deserve to live'. In consequence, the man was arrested and a military tribunal found him guilty of a crime under statutes that made it illegal to speak against the Third Reich or impair the military defence of the country. He was sentenced to death, and imprisoned for a short while. The death sentence was not carried out, and he was instead returned to fight on the front. After the war, in 1949, and after the new West German state was established, the woman was prosecuted in a new court. Specifically, she was charged for unlawfully procuring her husband's imprisonment under an 1871 statute of the German Criminal Code that made it an offence to illegally deprive a person of his/her freedom. The woman pleaded that she had not committed any offence, arguing that her husband's 'crime' and confinement were fully in accord with Nazi statutes of the day.[3] The case was eventually heard by a court of appeal, which found that she was in fact guilty of depriving her husband of his liberty; her denunciation had, it argued, led directly to his imprisonment. Furthermore, the court found that the statute to which she referred in her defence 'was contrary to the sound conscience and sense of justice of all decent human beings' (quoted in Hart 1957: 620).

This decision raises many issues, including the already noted problem of when a law can be considered valid, and whether an immoral statute can properly be called law. In dealing with such problems, the Hart-Fuller debate helps to locate key elements of legal positivism and its departures from natural law theory. By way of at least indicating bald contours of the debate, we might expect Fuller to have some sympathy with the appeal court's decision:

> To me there is nothing shocking in saying that a dictatorship which clothes itself with a tinsel of legal form can so far depart from the morality of order, from the inner morality of law itself, that it ceases to be a legal system. When a system calling itself law is predicated upon a general disregard by judges of the terms of the laws they purport to enforce, when this system habitually cures its legal irregularities, even the grossest, by retroactive statutes, when it has only to resort to forays of terror in the streets, which no one dares challenge, in order to escape even those scant restraints imposed by the pretence of legality—when all these things have become true of a dictatorship, it is not hard for me, at least, to deny to it the name of law (Fuller 1958: 660).

By contrast, Hart's legal positivist approach, discussed in more detail below, considers the court's decision to be erroneous. For Hart, even though the decision has ' . . . been hailed as a triumph of the doctrines of natural law and as signaling the overthrow of positivism', he bluntly states that:

The unqualified satisfaction with this result seems to me to be hysteria. Many of us might applaud the objective—that of punishing a woman for an outrageously immoral act—but this was secured only by declaring a statute established since 1934 not to have the force of law, and at least the wisdom of this course must be doubted (Hart 1957: 620).

So, Hart argues that whatever the morality of the laws at hand, they were in force at the time and should be considered valid. He does not agree with the retrospective rejection of past law by the appeal court; the undoubted immorality of Nazi laws is, for him, beside the point that they functioned in that society as laws. Why would he argue this? To better understand Hart's legal positivism, let us turn initially to key reference points that his work assumes.

Sociological and Legal Positivism

The concept **positivism** is commonly associated with a commitment to scientific methods to secure true knowledge.[4] Auguste Comte (1798–1857), considered one of the founders of sociology, proposed that positivist scientific methods be used to detect underlying laws of social progress, to budge societies from 'primitive' states of violence to 'civilized' states of peace and harmony. Only by observing facts, he believed, could we discover underlying social laws, and deduce law-like regularities; armed with the latter, one could manipulate social factors for the benefit of all, just as the laws of physics had been manipulated to benefit industry. Comte (1975) argued that social rules could equally be subjected to scientific study. As the 'queen of all sciences', sociology was tasked with discovering and manipulating social laws to achieve no less than eternal peace and prosperity for all. To achieve a higher state of being, Comte believed that human societies had to progress through three forms, or 'stages', of knowledge: a theological stage in which knowledge is revealed through a supernatural deity; a metaphysical (philosophical) stage that relies on reason to formulate abstract ideas and universal concepts (e.g., nature) to replace God; and, finally, the highest positivist stage of modern society where general laws of existence are discovered exclusively by close observations of facts, or 'positive phenomena'.

He considered the final stage to be the highest achievement that was born from theology and philosophy. At this stage, people embrace only **empirical** methods to find the truths of society. In simple terms, **empiricism** refers to the view that any statement is only true if it can be observed (verified, confirmed, etc.) through sensory experience (seeing, feeling, smelling, etc.). Only by impartially observing *positive phenomena*, or *facts*, through our senses can we ever arrive at true statements about the world, and only then can our explanations yield scientific laws that embody true knowledge of our existence.

In sociology, as we shall see, there is also a rival view arguing that because human beings are so different from the objects of natural sciences, on account of their ability to create subjective meaning, we need to use particular methods when studying them. Typically, qualitative sociologists call for what might be termed **hermeneutic** methods; these methods are designed to uncover the frameworks of meaning that people use to make sense of the world around them. As will become apparent, there is much that divides sociological and legal positivism, but they do share a view of knowledge; namely, the truth about 'positive' phenomena that can be observed (e.g., society, law) is accessible not through speculative reasoning, but by careful, empirical observation of their actual existence in the world (the 'is')—not as we think they should be (the 'ought'). Bearing this in mind, one may say that legal positivism seeks objective and morally neutral ways to study law as an observable fact in the world. Not all positivists wanted to replicate the methods of the 'hard' sciences, and most recognized law as a distinct, autonomous, human endeavour. Hence, Davies succinctly notes that:

> The idea behind 'positivism' as a legal philosophy is that legal systems are 'posited', that is, *created*, by people, rather than having a natural or metaphysical existence. Positivists emphasize that the law of legal systems is made by human acts, posited or imposed on people, and that the proper role for legal philosophy is not to speculate about the morality of the system or particular parts of it, but to come to an understanding about the nature of legal systems (2008: 100).

Before turning to Hart's and Kelsen's 'positivist' approaches, let us consider selected earlier theoretical trajectories.

The Leviathan's Law

Although some commentators read Thomas Hobbes (1588–1679) as a proponent of natural law, and so part of the natural law tradition,[5] he is more often allied with legal positivism. In his most famous work, *Leviathan*, Hobbes contends that human beings are naturally egoistic, rational, free-willed beings who pursue pleasure and are repulsed by pain. The story is well-known, and yet the conventional readings are now under review (Pavlich 2010; Fitzpatrick 2007; Martel 2007). Drawing on the 'mechanics' (science?) of the day, Hobbes considers this condition to be natural because 'vital motions' around the heart are accelerated through pleasurable sensations, and slowed by painful ones. Without boundaries, people are naturally inclined to pursue pleasure, regardless of consequence to others. But if everyone is free to follow egoistical pleasures, they may choose to steal, plunder, and even murder in pursuit thereof. In abstract terms, we could well imagine an insecure state of nature that is without industry, arts, letters, navigation, time, and society, and characterized by, 'worst of all, continuall Feare, and danger of violent death; And the life of man solitary, poore, nasty, brutish, and short' (1985: 186, chap. 13). In other words, those who live without a 'common Power' to keep them in awe, live in a potential condition of 'warre, as is of every man, against every man' (1985: 185, chap. 13). But a universal fear is evoked when people realize that they are all equal in one respect: 'For as to the strength of the body, the weakest has strength enough to kill the strongest, either by secret machination, or by confederacy with others . . . ' (1985: 183, chap. 13).

This 'Feare of Death' entices people to check 'unruly passions', and pursue those that 'encline men to Peace' and 'a desire for commodious living' through industry (1985: 188, chap. 13). They do so by forming a social covenant in which they agree to transfer some rights to an almighty *Leviathan*, who then exerts sovereignty over a 'civil commonwealth', and ensures that the covenant is upheld. Whatever form that sovereign takes, it appears as a redoubtable being with absolute power over subjects (1985: 259ff., chap. 21). Yet, Hobbes is clear, this sovereign is a relatively benevolent power:

> And though of so unlimited a Power, men may fancy many evill consequences, yet the consequence of the want of it, which is perpetual warre of every man against his neighbour, are much worse. The condition of man in this life shall never be without Inconveniences; but there happeneth in no Common-wealth any great Inconvenience . . . (1985: 260, chap. 21).

The mutual trust of the covenant creates society, and order maintained through a sovereign who enforces law for security, peace, and freedom.

In another of his works, *De Cive*, Hobbes explicitly formulates an early version of a positivist approach often referred to as **command theory**. This theory defines law as no more than a legitimate command from a sovereign that is obeyed by subjects. It is worth quoting the passage at length:

> Furthermore, since it no lesse, nay it much more conduceth to Peace to prevent brawles from arising, than to appease them being risen; and that all controversies are bred from hence, that the opinions of men differ concerning . . . *just* and *unjust*, *profitable* and *unprofitable*, *good* and *evill*, *honest* and *dishonest*, and the like, which every man esteems according to his own judgement; it belongs to the same chiefe power to make some common Rules for all men, and to declare them publiquely, by which every man may know what may be called his, what anothers, what just, what unjust, what honest, what dishonest, what good, what evill, . . . But those Rules and measures are usually called the civill Lawes, or the Lawes of the City, as being the Commands of him who hath the supreme power in the City. And the Civill Lawes (that we may define them) are nothing else but *the commands of him who hath the chiefe authority in the City, for direction of the future actions of his Citizens* (Hobbes 1651: chap. 6, x).[6]

Law: Sovereign Command, Sanction, and Habitual Obedience

All this talk about nature, natural rights, natural justice and injustice proves two things and two things only, the heat of the passions and the darkness of the understanding (Bentham 1970: 84).

Jeremy Bentham (1748–1832) developed Hobbes's basic sense of law, but he did so—as is evident in the above quotation—in strong reaction to natural law theory, and to versions of English common law theory. In particular, he ridiculed Blackstone's *Commentaries* for their unscientific, moralizing, and preaching quality that legitimized unfounded prejudices under the guise of law. A staunch Enlightenment thinker, Bentham criticized the ideas of English common law theorists and the doctrine of precedent, proposing 'rational' reforms to correct their 'dog's law' (which he took to be akin to a person who punishes a dog *after* it has done something that this person decides is wrong). For him, undeclared law is unclear and vague, and cannot be held up as an unequivocal public standard to guide human behaviour. He thus championed a rational, easy-to-understand code of laws that would severely limit judicial discretion and render lawyers irrelevant. He especially disliked lawyers, believing them to be 'impotent to every enterprise of improvement' (1988: 13). Bentham defined law as an 'assemblage of signs declarative of a volition conceived or adopted by the *sovereign* in a state' (1970: 88). This is a roundabout way of saying that law is the command issued by a sovereign (state) over subjects, and he adds further that this command must be based on the 'expectation of certain events'—i.e., a sanction.

Although Bentham's work develops Hobbes's foundations of a command theory of law, it was a self-proclaimed disciple, John Austin (1790–1859), who offered a clearer, if less politically charged, formulation.[7] In *The Province of Jurisprudence Determined*, Austin proposed a general theory of jurisprudence (i.e., to explain all legal systems), and famously stated his positivist commitment to study law as a distinct entity:

The existence of the law is one thing; its merit or demerit is another. Whether it be or be not is one enquiry; whether it be or be not conformable to an assumed standard, is a different enquiry. A law, which actually exists, is a law, though we happen to dislike it, or though it vary from the text, by which we regulate our approbation and disapprobation (1995: 157).

With this conception of 'law as fact', Austin defines jurisprudence as a subject concerned with humanly created law ('posited' laws) that does not refer to morals (1995: 112).

For him, positive law possesses four overriding characteristics. First, law is posited by a sovereign, and in modern society that usually means a nation-state that authorizes certain agents (e.g., judges) to act on its behalf. The sovereign is thus a commander of law, and the sole source thereof. Secondly, positive law takes the form of a 'command', which signifies a sovereign's desire that something be done. Thirdly, unlike other commands, law is accompanied by ' . . . the power and the purpose of the commanding to inflict an evil or pain in case the desire be disregarded' (1995: 21). Positive law is thus a command backed by a sanction, or the threat of this, to enforce obedience from subjects (1995: 22). Finally, law, as a sovereign command accompanied by a sanction, nurtures a certain 'habitual obedience' from subjects, and this makes sure that there is regularity or consistency to legal systems. These concepts provided important departure points for Hart's and Kelsen's legal positivist approaches.

Hart: Rules, Rules, and more Rules

Although sympathetic to Bentham's and Austin's non-moral approach,[8] Herbert Lionel Adolphus (H.L.A.) Hart's (1907–92) most famous work, *The Concept of Law*, criticizes many of their key claims—including the definition of law as a command backed by realizable sanction, the idea of a sovereign as the source of law, and the matter of habitual obedience. To illustrate the point, he contrasts two people demanding money: a 'gunman' who orders a bank clerk to hand over loot, and a tax collector compelling tax from a citizen. In both examples, there is a command backed by the threat of sanction, but the gunman lacks legitimate authority. This example clarifies that in some cases we have a duty to obey ('being under an obligation'), regardless of the sanction, whereas in others we are merely obliged to do so. Hart concludes that duty is thus essential to law—as such, it emanates from multiple sources, and not just from a central sovereign (1994: chap. 3). He also challenges Austin's 'habitual obedience', which was meant to explain how law persists over time. Hart explains this idea instead by referring to a certain '**internal aspect of rules**', which he explains in the following way. Legitimate social rules are accompanied by a basic, if implicit, sense that they set 'a general standard to be followed by the group as a whole' (1994: 56). In chess, for example, players may share the habit of moving the queen in similar ways, but they also share a more basic 'internal aspect' in that they regard this rule as 'a standard for all who play the game' (1994: 57). This state of mind is, for him, much more basic than habit.

Through this critique of command theories, Hart introduces a concept that will be central to his version of legal positivism: **rules**. Rules, for him, occupy a central place in legal theory—without them, ' . . . we cannot hope to elucidate even the most elementary forms of law' (1994: 80). Therefore, he envisages law, not as a sovereign command, but as a multifaceted and integrated system of rules that he thinks will enable 'an improved analysis of the distinctive structure of a municipal legal system and a better understanding of the resemblances and differences between law, coercion, and morality, as types of social phenomena' (1994:17).

Rules, therefore, are pivotal to his analysis of law, and he distinguishes between two elements of all rules. On the one hand, there is an external dimension apparent to any observers, whether they accept that rule or not. On the other, an internal aspect of rules is discernible only to those who use them as guides to action (1994: 147). In a gesture that resembles Max Weber's approach to law,[9] which we shall encounter later, Hart argued that to capture both these dimensions of rules, jurisprudence cannot simply import the 'objective', empirical methodologies of the 'hard' sciences. To do so would unduly limit its study to empirically observable 'regularities of behaviour', and ignore 'the way in which the rules function as rules in the lives of those who normally are the majority of society' (1994: 90). In such statements, as Bix usefully notes, Hart recognized that 'the social sciences require an approach distinctly different from that used in the hard sciences, an approach based on understanding not merely the actions that occurred, but also the meaning those actions have to the participants in the practices or institutions being studied' (Bix, 2006: 36). In other words, jurisprudence must understand not only *that* people obey rules (the external aspect), but also *why* they do so (the internal aspect).

With this in mind, Hart detected many different types of rules in any social context. Specifically, he emphasized the distinction between **rules of obligation** and all other kinds of rules (e.g., rules of sports, games, 'correct speech', social etiquette). For Hart, the obligation rules are unique because of the 'serious' social pressure employed to encourage conformity to them. They are also different from other rules because they deal with highly valued facets of social life, and often involve 'sacrifice and renunciation' on the part of subjects who comply with them (1994: 87). Having made this distinction, he separated two types of rules of obligation: **rules of law** and **rules of morality**. The rules of law differ from the rules of morality because they can mobilize coercive, physical punishment to achieve conformity—an option not available to rules of morality (Hart 1994: 167ff.). In sum, he distinguished rules of obligation from other rules in society, and views the rules of law and morality as two types of obligation rules.

But what types of rules may be considered specifically 'legal rules'? Hart identified two basic legal rules of obligation, primary and secondary rules. **Primary rules** of legal obligation are basic rules found in all societies— they specify directly what people ought to do. By themselves, such rules are insufficient to constitute law, and are pervasive in what Hart (revealingly) calls a 'pre-legal world' of tightly-knit, kinship-based, 'primitive' communities (1994: 92, 94). Leaving aside the patronizing, if imperialist, tone of his claims here, Hart's basic position is that primary rules are unstable, because they are often challenged, especially as a society diversifies. In such contexts, **secondary rules** emerge to control the operation of primary rules. Thus, he argued, 'while primary rules are concerned with the actions that individuals must or must not do, . . . secondary rules are all concerned with the primary rules themselves. They specify the ways in which the primary rules may be conclusively ascertained, introduced, eliminated, varied, and the fact of their violation conclusively determined' (1994: 94).

Secondary rules that govern primary rules tend to be of various kinds: *rules of change* (which authorize particular agents to create new primary rules); *rules of adjudication* (which empower 'individuals to make authoritative determinations of the question whether, on a particular occasion, a primary rule has been broken'; 1994: 97); or *rules of recognition* (which determine the rules that legitimately form part of the legal system, i.e., they 'recognize' and isolate specifically legal rules).

Hart (1994: 100–1) ascribed great importance to rules of recognition because of their gatekeeping role: they determine which rules are to be defined as 'law', and so are basic to the very existence of law. They may be written down as criteria, or standards, in official texts (such as constitutions); they sometimes take the form of rules that official agents must follow to produce law (e.g., rules that define the appropriate passage of a bill through parliament). In other circumstances, however, the criteria that judicial agents follow can only be determined *ex post facto*, once a decision has been made (e.g., 'judicial precedents'). In all cases, rules of recognition specify how officials do, in fact, determine which rules qualify as law, and which do not. However, as he notes, 'In the day-to-day life of a legal system its rule of recognition is very seldom expressly formulated as a rule . . . its existence is *shown* in the way in which particular rules are identified, either by courts or other officials or private persons or their advisers' (1994: 101).

Clearly, the 'internal' aspects of rules are integral to the way that rules function, even when the rule in question determines the validity of law. Here, Hart reaffirms this point: the validity of law is not determined by referring to morality, but by examining how the conventional and internally appraised rules of recognition function in a given society. This is a crucial matter because here he clarified that the appropriate objects of legal theory are the day-to-day rules used by those who make up a given legal system. Following this, as indicated before, he insisted that one cannot simply use the methods of the natural sciences to study law; it is necessary to use hermeneutic methods to fully grasp the ways rules work.

Hart then argued that two minimum conditions must be met for law to be valid: citizens must accept the primary rules within a society, and the officials of the society must accept the secondary rules of change, adjudication, and recognition as ' . . . critical common standards of official behaviour' (1994:

117). Without the widespread acceptance of, and conformity to, both sorts of rules, there can be no legal system. For him, these rules provide a way to determine whether apartheid's *Mixed Marriages Act*, or the Nazi laws noted above, can be considered valid law. [10] We are now able to see why, for Hart, Nazi laws—as immoral as they might have been—operated in a legal system that appears to have, to some degree at least, met the basic criteria for validity: primary rules were followed, and legal officials presumed and followed rules of recognition. It is important to note that Hart was not hereby endorsing Nazi law, or the woman's actions; instead he argued that Nazi law operated on the basis of conventional legal rules (primary and secondary), and so was valid in context. Elsewhere Hart does argue that some 'minimal moral' content is required (1994: 193–9), but his overall assessment is that the key indication of valid law lies in its factual, rule-based presence in a given society.

Hart's work has been deeply influential in Western jurisprudence, and has engrossed both supporters and critics (see Davies 2008; Wacks 2006, 2005). Perhaps most famously, Dworkin (1986, 1978) contested various elements of his work, including one that we have not yet addressed here, namely, so-called hard cases. [11] In these cases, Hart argued that judges use discretion and caution, but nevertheless create new rules. This 'open texture' to law has them walking a tightrope between formalism and rule skepticism, and yet 'performing a rule producing function' (1994: 135). The implication is that judges in these cases create law, but Dworkin argues that judges merely interpret the law using established ways of doing things; for him, this is 'Law's Empire'. Hart (1994: 238–76) offers a very helpful 'postscript' that describes, and responds to, Dworkin's critiques. But, given the focus of the present book, it is perhaps most useful to focus on a challenge to Hart's claim that he provides an 'essay in descriptive sociology'.

On this score, Cotterrell (2003: 90ff.) takes issue with Hart's tendency to wander naively into sociological terrains. As noted, Hart does not conceive of law as a 'purely behavioural social science' that would focus on external aspects of rules or rulers; rather, the law must be understood through a hermeneutic, internal understanding of those to whom the (primary and secondary) rules apply. In this process, one detects a kind of 'sociological drift' where the internal aspects of the rules of obligation appear to be pivotal for his study of law. But as Cotterrell points out, there is a fundamental problem because Hart merely speculates about the sociological dimensions of rules and rule-following without providing an actual sociological study that might confirm his theory. As such, Hart simply offers a 'speculative philosophy not grounded in any systematic consideration of actual social conditions' (2003: 91). In other words, for Cotterrell, the problem is that Hart's theory of law rests foundationally upon 'internal aspects' of rules, which would require an analysis of the 'actual experience' and 'observation' of legal rules. It should, that is, involve a careful look at how people talk, think, and act in the context of law; this moves the approach away from a study of legal doctrine to 'sociology or social psychology' (2003: 91). And yet Hart provides no such analysis. Stated differently, Hart's approach demands an empirical study of how people obey primary rules, and a hermeneutic analysis of how legal officials act or think within a given legal system. Recall that both of these dimensions enable us to make statements about the validity of law. Yet, as Cotterrell rightly observes, Hart's work is weakened because it never engaged any substantive work of this kind.

Kelsen: Law, Norm, and Revolution

With his rather different legal positivist approach, Hans Kelsen (1881–1973) considered law to be a **normative system**; i.e., it is based on norms rather than rules. From that trajectory, he (1967) called for a **pure theory of law** that focuses on a precise idea of law as its object of study. A proper science of law is, for him, directed to ' . . . that part of knowledge which deals with the law, excluding from such knowledge everything which does not strictly belong to the subject-matter law. That is, it endeavours to free the science of law from all foreign elements. This is its fundamental methodological principle (Kelsen 1934: 474).'

But how does he conceive of law? Against the command theories previously noted, and, indeed, Hart's emphasis on rules, Kelsen defined law as a particular kind of **norm**. Conventionally, norms may be considered as social expectations regarding particular behaviours, which means that:

> there are different kinds of norms, norms of thinking, that is, logical norms, and norms of acting, that is, moral and legal norms. . . . According to a legal norm, men ought to behave under certain conditions in a certain way. That a man ought to behave in a certain way means that this behavior is prescribed or permitted or authorized (1959: 107).

In this sense, the word 'norm' refers, 'primarily, though not exclusively, to a command, a prescription, and order. Nevertheless commanding is not the only function of norms: norms also empower, permit, and derogate (1991: 1).'

What differentiates specifically legal from other norms is the threat of, or actual, sanction.[12] But as with all norms, legal norms can only claim to be valid by referring to other norms (not to morals, or even facts).[13] Thus a positive law is nothing other than a norm located in a dynamic legal 'system of norms', and that system has a particular hierarchy (1961: 110).

Returning to the robber and the tax collector example, we might recall that both command you to pay up. However, for Kelsen, only the tax collector's norm may be considered valid because its claim to validity refers to other, higher norms. The robber's demand is no more than a 'subjective will' that cannot appeal to higher norms for legitimacy, and is not (for him) part of a wider system of norms. By contrast, the tax collector's demand is 'objective' because it appeals to a hierarchy of norms (e.g., tax statutes, Supreme Court decisions, Parliament, and eventually to the founding of Canadian law through, say, the *Constitution Act, 1982*). At some point, law's appeal to higher norms stops, and here we reach a **basic norm**, or *grundnorm*—a norm that founds all other norms in a given legal system. That basic norm is the authorizing limit of all law; it is the 'unmoved mover' of legal norms in a specific society with no higher norms of appeal. Moreover, it is never posited, for 'it is not a positive norm, but a norm presupposed in our thinking' (1959: 108). It is also not a law because it is the ground of all law. In other words, a basic norm is simply presupposed by the norm regime that it authorizes; it is that which determines the validity of law. As Kelsen put it:

> No norm of a positive legal order created in conformity with the constitution can be considered as non-valid. . . . The basic norm of the Pure Theory of Law is the reason of the validity of a democratic as well as of an autocratic law, of a capitalistic as well as of a socialistic law, of any positive law, whether considered to be just or unjust. This is the essence of legal positivism, in contradistinction to the natural-law doctrine. And the Pure Theory of Law is the theory of legal positivism (1959: 110).

From this we see that valid law is always relative to specific societies and their basic norms. Furthermore, changing the basic norms of legal systems has massive effects. It usually involves replacing one constitution with another—typically through a revolution by extra-legal forces that disturb existing normative hierarchies and establish new legal norms. However, a basic norm always has the final say on legal validity:

> If we ask for the reason of the validity of a positive legal order, we arrive finally at a historically first constitution, which authorizes custom or a legislative organ to create general norms, which, in their turn, authorize judicial and administrative organs to create individual norms. The assumption that these norms are valid presupposes a norm authorizing the Fathers of the Constitution to create the norms instituting legislation or custom as the basis of all the other legal functions. This norm is the reason of the validity of the Constitution and hence the basic norm of the legal order established in conformity with the Constitution (1959: 108).

Interestingly, as with Hart's rules of recognition, we run up against the ultimately unjustifiable quality of all posited law, beyond its operation and acceptance in context. In Kelsen's work, however, revolutionary 'law creating activities'[14] assume particular prominence as they establish the basic presumptions (basic norms) that subsequently legitimize a legal system's norms. Paradoxically, the *grundnorm* is both inside and outside of law, suggesting, as Davies usefully points out, the 'artificial nature of legal closure, and the impossibility of drawing absolute limits to law' (2008: 111).

Were Kelsen to enter the Hart-Fuller debate, he might have considered the validity of Nazi law, and so the requirement for people to obey it, from the perspective of whether applicable legal norms referred to other norms, ultimately supported by a basic, law-constituting norm (even if this: 'a sovereign issues laws'). He would likely have agreed with Hart that the law in question, though immoral, is valid. He would also have agreed that the science of law must use hermeneutic and conceptual analysis. Unlike Hart, however, Kelsen would likely also have considered the West German Appeal Court's decision to be valid, since its law presupposed a democratic basic norm (a postwar constitution) and appeals to different norms. Kelsen and Hart would not dispute the immoral nature of Nazi law, but their legal positivist quest for a science of law that explains all legal systems prevents them from repudiating Nazi law by referring to a moral authority, as natural law theory tends to do. Their basic position is this: a legal system is valid to the extent that it is deemed legitimate and understood by the subjects who form it as well as those that it serves, and who thus comply with its rules or norms. And in the end, the ways that subjects reflect on, or respond to, legal rules and norms are decisive in determining a law's validity.

Concluding Reflections

As we have seen, both Hart and Kelsen regard the validity of law as less a moral than a factual matter. Hart's recognition of minimal moral considerations suggests a kind of 'soft' positivism, whereas Kelsen's 'pure science' distinguishes more sharply between law and morality. Another prominent legal positivist, Joseph Raz (1979), echoes a related positivist approach by arguing that the very existence of law needs to be determined by an empirical enquiry into the conventions, institutions, and intentions of those who participate in a given legal system. He also underscores the idea that any analysis of the question 'What is the nature of law?' is only ever a factual— not a moral—one. But all three thinkers, like the command theorists before them, consider law to constitute an autonomous field of distinct institutions, with their own rules or norms, purposes, rituals, and logic, and with a unique authority to execute state-authorized violence. Law as an object *sui generis* is both assumed and defined as requiring unique methodologies to reveal its essence.

At the same time, a non-moral science of the law assumes that social processes associated with rules and norms always determine valid law. But neither is prepared to subsume their definitions of 'law' under sociological concepts of 'society'. On the contrary, they consider social order to be dependent on law's function in securing collective order. Indeed, Hart dismisses Durkheim's (see Chapter 5) suggestion that law be used to indicate the implicitly more primordial concept of society: 'Somewhat fantastically Durkheim thinks that the law can be used as a measuring instrument' (1967: 6). Kelsen's more sustained analysis makes clear that 'What we call society or community is either the factual coexistence of individuals or a normative order of their mutual behavior' (1960a: 628). To the extent 'society' is of scientific value, it is concerned with order, and here we enter the domain of law. To underscore the point that society is foundationally reliant on law, Kelsen argues that the sociology of law derives from legal science's conception of law:

> The sociology of law cannot draw a line between its subject—law—and the other social phenomena; it cannot define its special object as distinct from the object of general sociology—society—without in so doing presupposing the concept of law as defined by normative jurisprudence. . . . To this extent, sociological jurisprudence presupposes normative jurisprudence. It is a complement of normative jurisprudence (1941: 53).

In both cases, law constitutes the base upon which social superstructures may emerge. Even Raz (1979), who argues that law can be identified only through its efficacy, institutional character, and sources—all of which are social facts—does not thereby surrender the concept 'law' to 'society', insisting that law is autonomous. He too argues that social processes rely on law. The fact of law that operates in the real world, independent of moral considerations, may be indicated by social facts; but law, in essence, is primordial. In all cases, the 'sociological drift', to which Cotterrell refers, is therefore a strictly limited one, making overtures towards social factors as a way of conceptualizing law without reference to morality, without privileging virtues like 'justice' (see Hunt 1993).

The legal positivists claim to focus on fact, declaring the quagmires of moral debate as irrelevant to a science of law. What determines a valid law has to do, ultimately, with the efficacy of a legal system within a given society, not extraneous moral codes. In such positivist frameworks, a moral value like 'justice' is literally beyond the scope of their analyses. In a reductive gesture, Kelsen even suggests that the idea of 'justice' can be studied scientifically, concluding thus: 'If the idea of justice has any function at all, it is to be a model for making good law and a criterion for distinguishing good from bad law (Kelsen 1948: 383).' But, for Kelsen, this is not a moral statement; it is a factual claim about the ways in which justice as a norm operates in a given system. In a pure science of law, moral attributions of justice must remain silent. They may, appropriately, be studied in philosophy or ethics, but for the legal scholar, law lies in the fact of its manifestation in specific contexts.

Discussion Questions

1. Is law no more than what a sovereign decrees?

2. Can we ever justify law beyond the mere fact of its existence in context?

3. Does Hart adequately study law as a social fact? How might a sociologist approach the study of legal rules?

4. If Kelsen's 'basic norms' are ultimately unjustifiable, does this mean that the source of law is arbitrary?

5. Are legal systems usually born from violence? What does this mean for the study of law?

6. What ultimately is the difference between the laws of a tyrant and those of a democratic ruler?

Suggested Readings

Bix, B. (2006). *Jurisprudence: Theory and Context*. London: Sweet & Maxwell.

Frank, J. (1955). 'A Conflict with Oblivion: Some Comments on the Founders of Legal Positivism'. *Rutgers Law Review*, 9(2), 425–63.

Wacks, R. (2005). *Understanding Jurisprudence: An Introduction to Legal Theory*. New York: Oxford University Press.

Relevant Websites

http://plato.stanford.edu/entries/comte/
http://oregonstate.edu/instruct/phl302/philosophers/hobbes.html
www.philosophypages.com/ph/hobb.htm
www.ucl.ac.uk/Bentham-Project/info/jb.htm
www2.law.ox.ac.uk/jurisprudence/hart.shtml
http://plato.stanford.edu/entries/lawphil-theory/

4 Realizing Sociological Jurisprudence

Questions to Consider

- ⊛ What is the difference between an abstract view of 'law on the books' and real 'law in action'?
- ⊛ Are judges rule-driven, or do they make pragmatic decisions that maximize social interests to advance society?
- ⊛ Can we predict how judges will decide by identifying the socio-cultural and psychological factors that determine their decisions?
- ⊛ Is law no more than what judges decide in particular cases?

If natural law theorists saw valid law as reflecting a higher morality, and legal positivists turned to rules and norms, the two perspectives discussed in the current chapter—**sociological jurisprudence** and US **legal realism**—viewed law as inextricably connected to the social and psychological processes judges use to decide what law is in a given context. In general, and simply stated, judges do not adjudicate the law through a neutral application of legal rules; rather, extra-legal factors (social, cultural, psychological) determine how they will decide. This approach to law achieved considerable prominence in the late nineteenth and early twentieth centuries, during the **progressive era** in the US, with its enthusiasm for rational management to achieve an end, such as progressive social reform. (Henry Ford's invention of the automobile assembly line provided somewhat of a model here.) In this context, many thought it possible to engineer social progress, to produce advances in society through focused, practical, and rationally managed reform. Hence, Roscoe Pound's sociological jurisprudence explicitly wanted to engineer a better society through prudent legal decisions, while legal realists like Oliver Wendell Holmes, Karl Llewellyn, and Jerome Frank thought that law could be used pragmatically to reform society for the better. For them, the view that judges decide cases by applying neutral rules is a myth that masks the social, cultural, and psychological factors that really explain how they arrive at judgments about what the law is in a particular case. The importance of this seemingly innocent statement is far-reaching. Law continues to be the focal point for jurisprudence, but now its essence is relayed to the everyday social interactions of human beings involved in legal decision-making. What does this all mean?

Focusing specifically on law as a process, both sociological jurisprudence and legal realism actively called for the significant reform of existing legal practice, particularly a dominant nineteenth-century approach referred to as **legal formalism**. Most commonly associated with Christopher Langdell (1826–1906), the dean of Harvard Law School between 1870 and 1895, legal formalism defined law as no more than the formal legal rules, doctrines, and principles underlying high court decisions; law could only be discovered by careful and systematic analysis of this case law. Langdell's approach literally defined law as decisions judges make when they apply pre-established rules (the Charter, statutes, or precedents) to a set of 'facts', and arrive at decisions in a predictable, mechanical way. He thought that when judges impartially follow legal rules, and actively eschew any 'extra-legal' biases (created by prejudices, social standing, gender, etc.), they will arrive at predictable judgments. With this in mind, Langdell defined 'law' as an empirically discernible set of doctrines and principles employed by (especially higher) court decisions: 'Law, considered as a science, consists of certain principles and documents . . . to be traced in the main through a series of cases; and much the shortest and best, if not only, way of mastering the doctrine effectively is by studying the cases in which it is embodied' (in Twining 1973: 11).

For Langdell, legal science, like any other natural science (e.g., physics, zoology), could discover what is essential to law; he believed this is what law schools should teach through a so-called **Socratic method** in which students are expected to memorize and regurgitate on demand in the classroom the key arguments and rebuttals of judges in given cases (Milovanovic 2003: 110).

Followers of sociological jurisprudence and legal realism explicitly rejected the idea that decisions predictably follow from the formal application of paper rules, and that law could be studied much like objects of 'hard science'. As a complex set of relations, law is an unfolding human process that is centred on real, acting people making concrete decisions—it is not simply a mechanistic application of abstract rules or principles. Most turned to **pragmatism** (e.g., William James and C.S. Pierce) to support their view that the real effects (practical consequences) of law on people's lives are very much part of the truth about law. They echoed pragmatic philosophies that largely dismissed *abstraction* as irrelevant to the *real* truths people use to cope with everyday life (James 2000: 25). For pragmatists, the only 'test of probable truth' is whether an idea actually makes a practical difference: 'what works best in the way of leading us, what fits every part of life best and combines with the collectivity of experience's demands, nothing being omitted' (James 2000: 40). In short, this empirical, common sense pragmatism rejects unnecessary abstraction and only accepts as truth those meanings that make sense of, and are practically useful for us in, our everyday lives.

Anchored in such pragmatic thinking, sociological jurisprudence and realist movements called for practically useful analyses of law, which they understood to mean a focus on those who actually decide the law (Cardozo 1960). To advise clients effectively, realists tried to predict how a judge might decide in a given case by focusing on the decision-making processes of real law in action. Specifically, they focused on the extra-legal, informal, unspoken, social, cultural, institutional, and psychological factors affecting judicial decisions. Their aim was to understand law in a new way, but also to indicate how legal decisions might pursue progressive social reforms. They drew on various social science approaches—sociology, anthropology, and psychology—to facilitate their endeavours.

One of the founders of the movement—Oliver Wendell Holmes (1841–1935)—served as Supreme Court judge in the United States and defined several of its key ideas (Holmes 1879; Holmes 1982). Let us turn to one of his famous judgments (namely, *Buck v. Bell*, 274 US 200 [1927]) to illustrate how a founder of realism would later become a realist judge in action.

Holmes Decides 'Three Generations of Imbeciles Are Enough'

> The law is the witness and external deposit of our moral life. Its history is the history of the moral development of the race. The practice of it, in spite of popular jests, tends to make good citizens and good men (Holmes 1897: 992).

Holmes's view of the law is evident—warts and all—in the Supreme Court judgment in *Buck v. Bell*. In this case, an appellate decision of the State of Virginia endorsed an earlier circuit court verdict against Carrie Buck, an 18-year-old institutionalized 'feeble-minded white woman . . . the daughter of a feeble-minded mother in the same institution, and the mother of an illegitimate feeble-minded child'. Holmes summarized the opinion of the Supreme Court, which (with one judge dissenting) affirmed as lawful the order to sterilize Carrie by 'salpingectomy' under a Virginia act. Reflecting the eugenic thinking of this time, the act portrays sterilization as a means of 'containing' or 'eradicating' social problems for the 'benefit' of society (see Rafter 1997; McLaren 1990; Pick 1989). Endorsing this dangerous view, Holmes wrote that 'experience has shown that heredity plays an important part in the transmission of insanity, imbecility, etc.'; moreover, the statute allows for the 'superintendents' of some institutions to have patients with 'hereditary forms of insanity, imbecility, etc.' 'sexually sterilized'. And he judged as fact that Carrie meets these requirements because she 'is the probable potential parent of socially inadequate offspring, likewise afflicted'.

Perplexingly, he further asserted that 'she may be sexually sterilized without detriment to her general health and that her welfare and that of society will be promoted by her sterilization. . . . ' Detecting no breach of due process in this case, he declared his view of 'practical common sense' of the time: 'sterilization of mental defectives, under careful safeguard, etc.' can be of 'benefit to themselves and to society'. The written opinion rejects various constitutional arguments, declaring that it is 'better for all the world, if instead of waiting to execute degenerate offspring for crime, or to let them starve for their imbecility, society can prevent those who are manifestly unfit from continuing their kind'.

Quite extraordinarily, he likened this to 'compulsory vaccination' before reaching this appalling conclusion: 'Three generations of imbeciles are enough.' Remarkably, and reflecting the prejudices of his day, Holmes deals with the objection that this law is unfairly applied only to those in institutions (not to 'the multitudes outside') by asserting, with pragmatic resignation, 'the law does all that is needed when it does all that it can, indicates a policy, applies it to all within the lines, and seeks to bring within the lines all similarly situated so far and so fast as its means allow.'

This is a disturbing case for many reasons, and has been rightly challenged by a Canadian Supreme Court decision (*E. [Mrs.] v. Eve*, [1986] SCJ No. 60 [SCC])[1] as well as in the famous Leilani Muir case (*Muir v. Alberta*, [1996] AJ No. 37). Even if Holmes's opinion echoes a wider eugenic view of the day, one might question the auspices of a reform movement that unquestioningly parodies, as a basis of reform, the 'practical' common sense of its day. The dangers of this stance are clear from the above decision. However, in the context of his times, Holmes appeared as a progressive thinker, and this case highlights key elements of a realist position and of the dangers attendant upon that. For example, the judgment does not proceed, as a legal formalist might, by linking up abstract, general rules or legal doctrines. Rather, it refers practically to the statute at issue, straightforwardly insisting that it applies to Carrie, and that due process in its application was followed. Skeptical that general laws could ever solve specific problems, Holmes then makes pragmatic sense of the local issues and offers a concrete ruling on the practical 'problem' before him. That he should consider 'imbecility' and 'feeblemindedness' as 'problems' to be eradicated reflects the dangers of social engineering that progressive pragmatists espoused. For such eugenic thinking he offers neither critique nor apology, because he swam well within, not against, prominent intellectual tides of his day. Moreover, he pragmatically declares that the 'life of law has not been logic: it has been experience' (Holmes 1982: 1). Here Holmes openly recognizes that 'extralegal factors' best account for why judges (including himself) make the decisions they do; law is not based on logic, but rather the experiences of very real people who live out their lives as both creatures and creators of law.

As is clear from the decision, his judgment is affected by his perception of public morals, his politics, and his prejudices. Indeed, Holmes notes, 'The very considerations which judges most rarely mention, and always via an apology, are the secret route from which the law draws all the juices of life. I mean, of course, considerations of what is expedient for the community concerned (1982: 35).' The premises that judges seldom articulate are often the most significant elements in determining the outcomes of specific cases (e.g., Holmes's endorsement of eugenics). If this is so, then judges make law; they do not simply follow or apply neutral rules. For Holmes, this is neither good nor bad; it is simply inevitable. Judges confront real-life problems that require solutions in the present, and no simple rule-following will suffice. Judges must and do learn a craft that involves practical knowledge of how to decide, passed down through generations.[2]

For Holmes, then, jurisprudence is a practical science that must attend to extra-legal factors to predict how judges will decide (and so determine the 'law' in context). In somewhat turgid terms, Holmes asserts that, 'The object of our study . . . is prediction, the prediction of the incidence of the public force through the instrumentality of the courts' (1982: 35). From this he offers a famous definition of law: 'The prophesies of what the courts will do in fact, and nothing more pretentious, are what I mean by the law' (Holmes 1897: 994). Interestingly, he suggests that the best way to predict how judges will decide is to ask the 'bad man'. For him, law professors with noses in books do not have the depth of understanding of those who face law's processes directly, empirically, and with the great consequence. In parentheses, one wonders how Carrie might speak of her experience in his court; though obviously no 'bad man', she might frame the decision through the suffering that followed from the dangerous prejudices held by the judge of her case.

Roscoe Pound's Sociological Jurisprudence: Against 'Legal Monks'

> Legal monks who pass their lives in an atmosphere of pure law, from which every worldly and human element is excluded, cannot shape practical principles to be applied to a restless world of flesh and blood (Pound 1907: 611–12).

As the quotation above makes clear, Roscoe Pound's (1870–1964) sociological jurisprudence clearly rejected legal formalism. His work tended to be a synthetic exercise, working with other people's ideas and reflecting a tedious tendency to imagine that 'all trends lead to Pound' (Hunt 1978: 12). The decision to call his approach 'sociological jurisprudence' is based less on content than on an opportunistic use of sociology's reputation for championing progressive changes to society (Hull 1989). As dean of Harvard Law School, Pound championed both sociological jurisprudence and the realism of his foremost students (e.g., Llewellyn). He always held law in high regard, and never wavered from his view that it could be used to advance society (Pound 1968: 32–4).

In a multi-volume work, *Jurisprudence*, Pound identified three different ways 'law' had previously been defined: as a legal order; as a body of authoritative discussions that enable us to predict the law; and as a system of judicial or administrative processes. However, he thought it possible to unify these three definitions into 'one subject of one science', merely by defining law as social control (1959: 15), or, more specifically, as a 'highly specialized social control in the modern state' (1959: 346). Pound simply understood society to be a collection of individuals, or groups, each pursuing different interests. Sometimes their interests were shared, sometimes not. To preserve the equilibrium of a given society, various forms of social control were required to manage both subjects and their interests. As a key form of control, law could be studied empirically (he adopted a version of Comte's positivism) with an eye to improving society (Hunt 1978: 15). Unlike the 'sociology of law', which he dismissed as a purely 'theoretical' endeavour, sociological jurisprudence was to be an empirical, pragmatic science that used law to solve real social problems.

E.A. Ross (1866–1951), a sociologist who studied various forms of social control, notably influenced Pound's approach. In broad terms, Ross targeted the 'regularities' of 'social phenomena'—events where one person's actions affect another. Because these phenomena are complex, he argued that ' . . . some of the precision and absoluteness of physical and chemical laws must be renounced' (1905: 41). The focus on social phenomena led him to view sociology's object as neither the individual, nor group, nor institutions, nor even beliefs. All these objects, he argued, were mere outcomes of a more basic focal point: social processes. Furthermore, he considered social control to be a basic element underscoring all social processes—shaping individual 'feelings and desires to suit the needs of the group' (Ross 1969: iv). Such control helps to integrate society, but we should always avoid situations in which one group institutes social controls to further its own interests.

These brief references to Ross are enough to grasp the source of Pound's (1959: 293) 'social process' approach, and his specific critique of Langdell's formalism. Although he alluded to the 'what is law?' question (1968: chap. 2), Pound was more concerned with—as Hunt (1978: 20) usefully notes—responding to this issue: what are the social purposes of law? His response was predictable. As a process of social control, law's main purpose is to ensure the survival and advancement of a society. To play this vital role, law could not simply operate by mechanically applying rules that, at best, serve as general guides. Without denying the importance of applying law equally, Pound argued that justice requires judges to use discretion carefully to the benefit of society (1954: 70). To illustrate the point, he considered the case of people at a packed concert rushing out of a burning hall. If their exiting were not controlled in some way, many people would be trampled in the rush and fewer would likely escape. In such situations there are competing interests that must be assessed and ordered to preserve the welfare of the whole—a sensitive contextual evaluation requires thoughtful discretion that cannot be achieved by mechanically abstract rules. This example illustrates how 'social control makes it possible to do the most that can be done' (1968: 64).

So it is with law; it must prioritize diverse interests in a given set of circumstances.[3] In that role, law should strive to maximize both public and private interests, with the overall aim of securing a better society. Law may thus be characterized as a form of 'social engineering' that uses highly specialized forms of social control to maximize interests and improve society (Pound 1954: 47; 1959: 346–7).[4] On the question of social improvement, Pound offered a version of evolutionary theory,[5] and described how law advances through various stages—from 'primitive' forms solely concerned with public peace, to more 'mature' processes concerned with individual rights, to the socialization of law dealing with social interests. He also anticipates another stage as being 'a law of the world' (1959: vol. 428ff.). This evolutionary approach animated his gentle reformist agenda, which sought to maintain social 'equilibrium' while urging change in the name of 'civilization'.

With this in mind, one could speculate whether Pound might have approached the *Buck v. Bell* case differently from Holmes. I think not, for his commitments to social engineering and social improvement through the eyes of privileged judges swim well within the tides of progressive era thinking that sanctioned the eugenic thinking behind the decision (Willrich 1998: 67). His cautious reformism was unlikely to have led him far beyond the status quo; this became a point of theoretical and personal conflict between sociological jurisprudence and more reform-minded realists like Llewellyn and Frank (see Hull 1989). As Hunt usefully explains,

> Sociological jurisprudence failed, or more accurately failed to realise its potential, because in its Poundian articulation, it was very heavily oriented towards the 19th century philosophical currents of juristic thought. It's programmatic content, as symbolised by the call for 'social engineering', was very loosely formulated and it did not offer any concrete line of action or research, despite the fact that Pound had explicitly advanced a 'programme' to be undertaken under the banner of sociological jurisprudence (Hunt 1978: 41).

It was precisely in search of an explicit, forward-looking and active reform program that more youthful legal realists considered themselves to have outpaced sociological jurisprudence.

Two Figures in the Legal Realist Movement: Llewellyn and Frank

> What, then, *are* the characteristics of these new fermenters? One thing is clear. There is no school of realists. There is no likelihood that there will be such a school. There is no group with an official or accepted, or even with an emerging creed. . . . There is, however, a *movement* in thought . . . (Llewellyn, 1931: 1233–4).

In so declaring the dynamic quality of a movement, rather than a static and homogeneous school, Llewellyn signalled the nebulous connections between scholars who considered themselves to be active legal reformers (Twining 1973).[6] Like Holmes, they rejected nineteenth-century legal formalism, endorsed a pragmatic approach, and saw law as no more than the complex processes by which judicial decisions are made. The differences between thinkers in the movement are not always clear-cut, but they did focus on various processes of law in different ways and with different ends in mind—as indicated by the approaches taken by Llewellyn and Frank respectively.

Karl Llewellyn (1893–1962)

> The doing of something about disputes, this doing of it reasonably, is the business of law. And the people who have the doing in charge, whether they be judges or sheriffs or clerks, or jailers or lawyers, are officials of the law. *What these officials do about disputes is, in my mind, the law itself* (Llewellyn 1930: 3).

In his study of the Supreme Court, Llewellyn noted with some dismay how earlier in the century justices would 'write an appellate opinion as if the conclusion had followed of necessity from the authorities at hand and as if it had been the only possible correct conclusion' (1960: 11). If one accepted their premises, then a 'well-reasoned' opinion might show not only why the decision was right, but also 'the process by which the decision was arrived at'. Yet it was exactly these premises that Llewellyn contested. Echoing Holmes, he argued that findings in psychology indicated that when faced with a 'problem-situation out of life'—especially if it is a real 'puzzler'—people seldom use 'accurate deduction' or 'formal logic' to deal with the matter. Instead, they typically apply a more intuitive approach to arrive at solutions; only afterwards do they look for a 'reasoned justification'. Once a decision is made, people (judges) then test 'the decision against experience and against acceptability, buttressing it and making it persuasive to self and others' (1960: 11). The conceptual shift to social science is worth noting—indeed, by studying law as an institution Llewellyn turned especially to sociology and anthropology (Llewellyn and Hoebel 1941).

As has been documented elsewhere, Llewellyn and Pound had a rather erratic, though long-standing, relationship (see Hull 1989). Llewellyn considered Pound to be one of the 'shrewdest' observers of law, and commended him for focusing attention on the living people who exercise social control through law (Llewellyn 1949: 1288). Indeed, he noted that, 'Pound has moved "law" out of the world of the purely normative, the world of words and meanings, and into the world of action, of human behavior, of patterns and ways of actually getting things done; and, what is more, of the people who get things done (1949: 1289).' In so doing, Pound focused attention on 'the legal order', which he left somewhat undefined, but which Llewellyn argued could have been better formulated more precisely:

All you have to do is to borrow a concept from sociology: Institution, and to make explicit that you include therein the relevant going practices and the relevant specialists and the relevant physical equipment and the manner of organization of the whole; and Pound's picture of law—the institution of law—becomes forthwith a something which any social scientist can look at, understand, make friends with, learn from, and comfortably contribute to. The central aspect of an institution is organized activity, activity organized around the cleaning up of some job (1949: 1289).

Following from this, Llewellyn defined law as an **institution** that performs **'law-jobs'**; in other words it is a group of practices, specialists, equipment, and organizations that perform functions specifically tied to a society's survival. Although he develops the idea of law-jobs over time, he initially identifies two of these: conflict resolution and moulding the actions of a community to prevent conflict (Twining 1973). Such law-jobs are both universal and necessary to ensuring that people behave in ways that enable a society to function as such (1940: 1373). As he and Hoebel—in an anthropological study *The Cheyenne Way*—note, these law-jobs are brought into clear relief by **trouble cases**, or cases that challenge the very integrity of a group's social cohesion. These cases highlight the manner in which law repairs social ruptures, and so indicate how crucial law is for the survival of any group.

Llewellyn initially identified four (1940: 1373), and later five (Llewellyn and Hoebel 1941: 293), basic law-jobs—some are required directly for group survival, while others organize the justice system itself.

1. First, the law disposes of trouble in society by dealing with mostly minor cases and eliminating disputes and conflict (i.e., 'the disposition of trouble cases').
2. Second, law regulates conflict by dealing with opposing interests; here the role of law is to produce and maintain order in society by sorting out 'a disordered series of collisions' (1940: 165). It either prevents conflict by 'channelling' behaviour and expectations, or by 're-channelling' behaviour when it results in conflict.
3. Third, the law helps to decide and regulate institutions of governance and to allocate 'authority' through procedures that 'legitimate' actions to be 'authoritative' (1940: 165).
4. Fourth, law is involved with the 'organisation of society as a whole' and helps it remain 'integrated, directed and provides suitable incentives' (this law-job integrates 1–3 above, 1940: 165).
5. Finally, there is a law-job involved with the 'juristic method' that maintains, trains, and regulates the materials, tools ('law-stuff'), and people ('law-people') charged with performing other law-jobs (Llewellyn and Hoebel 1941: 293).

When considering the 'craft' of law associated with these five functions, Llewellyn claims, ambitiously, to offer a 'general theory of the nature and function of law-stuff and the law-jobs with which any group is faced in the process of becoming and remaining a group. The theory applies to groups of any size or complexity' (Llewellyn and Hoebel 1941: 273).

In other words, by studying law as a craft with various social functions, Llewellyn (1960: 19–51) considered it possible to regulate how judges will decide; he even advanced several 'steadying factors' that would make appeal court decisions more consistent. For example, he called for such pragmatic reforms as life tenure for justices (who should all be experienced lawyers), the use of **frozen records** (i.e., agreed-upon records from lower courts to ensure common agreement on facts), and the creation of a professional office (an office of justice) for judges.

His overall aim was to make the craft of law more predictable—but not one that, formally or mechanically, applies general rules. Instead, he advocated for legal institutions to recognize the complexity of human processes when executing their basic social functions, and to encourage pragmatically informed decisions that would ensure the survival of a social group. Such pragmatic realist reforms, he thought, could increase the predictability of case outcomes, and so allow law to perform its key social functions. How might Llewellyn have responded in *Buck v. Bell?* While he recognized that his pragmatic relativism could not secure absolute principles to guarantee just findings, he thought it could, nevertheless, realistically seek just outcomes: 'The pragmatic way is no way to reach an ultimate or absolute, but it is the only sound way to apply an ultimate, however reached. The finest common-law tradition sums up the manner in which the parties, the generations, the clashing groups of a democracy must work their way to wisdom' (Llewellyn 1940: 265).

So, he may have a different sense of a just outcome from Holmes, but in the end he echoes Holmes's pragmatic fatalism: 'One does his best' (Llewellyn 1940: 265).

Jerome Frank (1889–1957)

Pound has done magnificent work of permanent value. But he mangled his work because he compromised the heritage from Holmes, because he refused to recognize its essentially revolutionary character, its sharp break with the past; because he tried to cover up the true nature of that break. Pound was the right wing of the Holmes' movement (Frank 1931: 18).

The tone of Frank's statement reflects his commitment to political change. Regardless of whether his description of Holmes as a revolutionary is even vaguely credible, Frank's commitment to a more critical way of thinking is underscored by his crusade to '*rescue Pound's lasting contributions from Pound and his uncritical adulators*' (1931: 18). In that attempt, he drew on modern psychology, especially Freud and Piaget, and emphasized the 'subjective' dimensions of legal processes. This approach led him to the view, derived from psychology and echoing both Holmes and Llewellyn, that the process of judging never works syllogistically from premise to conclusion. Instead, 'Judging begins rather the other way around—with a conclusion more or less vaguely formed; a man ordinarily starts with such a conclusion and afterward tries to find premises, which will substantiate it (Frank 1970: 108).'

This kind of thinking led him to an extreme **relativist** position (i.e., one that denies there is any independent, objective truth, but rather that truth is always relative to context), leading to an internal debate between so-called **rule skeptics** (Llewellyn, Pound, Holmes) and **fact skeptics** (Frank).

Both sorts of skeptics agree that we cannot predict how judges will decide in specific cases by simply examining the formal rules (the 'paper rules') used in context. As noted, rule skeptics accept that pragmatic predictions of judgments are available once we have the extra-legal rules that govern how judges actually decide in given cases. Thus, by looking at patterns of appeal court judgments, rule skeptics thought it possible to identify unwritten rules of conduct to predict judicial decisions. By contrast, Frank positioned himself as a 'fact skeptic' who emphasized the radical uncertainty of all judicial decisions. He argued that even if one could uncover 'real rules' behind judges' decisions, the 'facts' on which those decisions were made were in constant flux. In other words, different judges perceive a case's facts differently; quite literally, they are deciding on incommensurable grounds. There are no facts that provide a firm foundation for judicial decisions. As Frank puts it,

> The 'facts', it must never be overlooked, are not objective. They are what the judge thinks they are. And what he thinks they are depends on what he hears and sees as the witnesses testify—which may not be—often is not—what another judge would hear and see . . . since those 'facts' are only what the judge thinks they are, the decision will vary with the judge's apprehension of the facts (1931: 35–6).

In short, the 'elusiveness of the facts on which decisions turn' makes it impossible 'to predict future decisions in most . . . lawsuits' (Frank 1970: xi).

This subversion of traditional legal thinking certainly challenges predictability in law, but it also challenges other realists for focusing on appeal court decisions. If judges literally work from different perceptions of 'facts', it is important to confront the 'upper court myth' that portrays higher courts as the 'heart' of legal systems (Frank 1949: 222ff.). Equally important, Frank argued, is the way lower court judges perceive facts, for it is these that are often 'frozen' in texts as they move up to appeal; thus, he emphasizes the importance of studying lower court decisions. In this, Frank opposed Llewellyn, for the former felt that it was precisely the 'frozen records' of trial judges that need to be opened to greater scrutiny because:

> A trial judge's reaction to a witness, and thus the judge's decision, may be the consequence of an unconscious bias, a bias unknown to the judge himself, for or against persons with red hair or black hair; for or against women or old women or pretty young women; for or against Irishmen, priests, Jews, Negroes, policemen, etc. The decisional process in trials is at the mercy of such hidden prejudices (1953: 187).

Here Frank offers a critique of law's replication of wider societal inequities and prejudices, which critical legal studies (see Chapter 8) used for socially framed assaults on liberal images and forms of law. Frank, however, did not see that potential in his own work, though he did propose institutional reforms (e.g., better pre-trial discovery practices with a neutral official tasked with unearthing facts). His inclination was more often than not psychologically framed (1949). Hence his pragmatic remedies tended to emphasize self-exploration, personal development through effective legal education, judicial self-analysis, improving a jury's ability critically to reflect on cases, and so on. One gets the drift of his thinking in the following: 'Must we not, in our law schools, educate future trial judges, through fairly intensive self-explorations so that they have some acquaintance with their own idiosyncratic, buried prejudices, and so that, with such acquaintances when they become judges, they will have at least a chance to overcome those biases?' (1953: 187).

He recognizes the resource implications for 'psychoanalytic treatments' that would enable such 'self-exploratory voyages', but thinks they may be necessary for the reforms he had in mind. Precisely through such self-exploration Frank might want to approach Carrie Buck's case—what prejudices enabled the lower and review court judges to accept a eugenic logic as uniform 'fact'? By opening such prejudices to review, Frank's realism suggests how his approach might have led to a different judgment. And that speaks highly in favour of his call for significant reform.

Realist Reflections on Law, Society, and Justice

> Justice is never a thing, but a quest,
> Among our folk, as among the nations
> (Llewellyn 1960: 214).

In the above statement, Llewellyn offers a view of justice that resonates with other pragmatic realists; justice as an ongoing practical quest is an 'aspect of the Good', regulates conflict between people, is concerned with fairness, and involves the distribution of scarce resources (1960: 203). He distinguished between a broad social justice, and a more specific legal justice. On a related note, Pound (1959: II, 351ff.) had argued for an evolution from 'justice without law' to more advanced contexts with its pursuit of 'justice through law'. Through such formulations, he considered justice as a contextually-specific matter to be worked out through legitimate social and legal processes appropriate to a given phase of a society's development. There are no absolute principles, and no founding rationality; but that does not mean—*contra* legal positivists—that justice is irrelevant to modern law. Rather, the quest for justice through law is a highly refined, specialized way that progressive, modern societies deal with the issues of justice noted above.

Implicit in these formulations is a recognition that law, while performing distinctive functions, exists only because of underlying social, psychological, and cultural forces. Law is even defined as a specialized form of social control; as such, the 'movement' emphasizes the importance of referring to external factors to study law appropriately. At the same time, however, realists focus on 'social forces of law' only, as Hunt notes, 'insofar as it is a determinant of the internal dynamic of the legal order itself' (Hunt 1993: 38). That is, law is assumed to have an internal dynamic that, while not completely closed, may be distinguished as a viable object for legal analysis. In such formulations, moreover, society tends to be conceived as a set of group relations and interactions made possible through ordering processes like social control. In modern societies, law emerges as the most specialized form of control, concerned, especially for Llewellyn, with the very survival of groups. Given the privilege accorded to law, it is perhaps unsurprising that sociological jurisprudence and legal realism should elevate that object, and approach social sciences (like sociology) as subservient to the study of law.

This emphasis on the law and legal analysis is underscored too by the way that Pound rejects the sociology of law for being too 'theoretical', and proposes his pragmatic sociological jurisprudence as a remedy for this (see above). As well, he distinguishes the specialized internal dynamics of the legal order from general social controls: 'While the sociologist looks at social control through all manner of groups and associations and relations, the jurist has to do with a specialized phase of it' (Pound 1959: II, 352).

As a specialized phase of social control, law has a unique 'internal dynamics', even if generated by surrounding forces. Frank (1949: 190ff.) echoes the point, as does Llewellyn, who posits law as a distinctive 'craft' with specific social functions. Llewellyn goes further to argue that approaching law as a craft serves as a sort of model for sociological analysis. In rather sweeping terms, he (1949: 1302) asserts that, 'Sociological concepts have tended to be too vast, too vague for convenient daily use', adding that, 'No discipline is healthy in which the practical-arts side is not in steady interplay with the theoretical: providing problems, providing experience and insight, testing and retesting theory (1949: 1302).' Legal realism can greatly benefit sociology: 'I find it not queer, but natural, that the resulting light on the institution of law, by simultaneously illuminating the whole problem of the crafts and of the team-work phase of all institutions, should give fresh perspective on all of social science. As between disciplines, as between persons, as between nations: it pays to be neighborly' (1949: 1305).

In other words, as Hunt astutely observes, the realist movement declares the internal dynamic of law as a proper domain of legal analysis; in the process it enables the development of a field of 'law and society', with multidisciplinary perspectives, and where 'social scientists subserve the interests of the jurist who is, if not the leader of the team, its link pin' (1993: 38).

Concluding Reflections

The preceding discussion has outlined the approach of sociological jurisprudence and several realist scholars who—over a period of time—offered various pragmatic, reform- minded approaches to law. Despite their differences, they all rejected the idea that law be understood as a technical process with internal rules that only specially trained judges (especially of higher courts) are able to detect and apply to given facts when adjudicating particular cases. As we noted, for legal formalists, to predict how judges will decide is to know the formal rules they will use in their decisions, and this is what defines law. By contrast, for Pound and legal realists, this is a self-serving myth that should be overthrown in favour of a more pragmatic approach. Pound understands and defines law as a social process that performs particular functions in society. To predict how the judges will decide in particular cases is to understand the extra-legal factors that shape how all human beings decide on the strength of their experiences, and to recognize the social, cultural, and psychological determinants shaping decisions. In this sense, the law is best understood through the practices, institutions, socio-cultural factors, and psychological dispositions that shape the decisions that define its limits in context. The direct relevance of social sciences is thus clear. However, even with their close proximity to such sciences, none of the approaches considered in this chapter is yet prepared to yield the idea of law as an essential being to notions of society. To get a better sense of a contrasting approach in the sociology of law, Part II turns to the work of three key social theorists—Émile Durkheim, Karl Marx, and Max Weber—who anchor their varying sociological discussions of law in another object: the social, *sui generis*.

Discussion Questions

1. What does the *Buck v. Bell* case tell you about how judges actually make decisions?

2. Do you think law professors, or people who come before judges, are most able to predict what the law will be in a given case? Why?

3. Does the law serve dominant interests in society? What does this mean for Pound's sociological jurisprudence?

4. If Frank is correct, the facts of a case are always differently perceived. What implications does this have for cases as they move from lower to higher courts? Are the 'same' cases being heard?

5. Can a legal decision ever be neutral? What does this say about law?

6. If law performs the basic function ('law-job') of preserving a social group, can it ever be an effective instrument for social change?

Suggested Readings

Llewellyn, K.N. (1931). 'Some Realism about Realism: Responding to Dean Pound'. *Harvard Law Review*, 44(8), 1222–64.

Lucey, F. E. (1942). 'Natural Law and American Legal Realism: Their Respective Contributions to a Theory of Law in a Democratic Society'. *Georgetown Law Journal*, 30(6), 493–533.

Twining, W.L. (1973). *Karl Llewellyn and the Realist Movement*. London: Weidenfeld and Nicolson.

Wacks, R. (2006). *Philosophy of Law: A Very Short Introduction*. Oxford: Oxford University Press.

Relevant Websites

www.roscoepound.org/
www.nebraskahistory.org/lib-arch/research/manuscripts/family/poundroscoe.htm
http://law.jrank.org/pages/8336/Llewellyn-Karl-Nickerson.html
http://online.wsj.com/article/SB124346735555660341.html
www.let.rug.nl/usa/B/oliver/oliverxx.htm

PART II

Society *Sui Generis*

5 Durkheim Socializes the Law

Questions to Consider

- Is law a product of more basic societal relations?
- Do independent societies create individuals?
- What societal functions does law perform?
- Do specific systems of law correspond to particular types of society?

Consider the following events:

> Shortly before midnight on 5 April 1994, three young black men burst through the doors of an upscale, midtown Toronto café called Just Desserts and held 20 patrons and staff at gunpoint. The assailants demanded money and jewellery, and, after encountering some resistance, one of the gunmen pulled the trigger of a sawed-off shotgun, mortally wounding a young, white woman named Georgia 'Vivi' Leimonis. The assailants escaped in a waiting car driven by a fourth suspect (*R. v. Brown*, [1999] OJ 486, Appendix B, 3).

The case, with its racial overtones, attracted wide media coverage, prompting an application to the Ontario Court of Justice for an order permitting two of the accused to challenge prospective jurors on the grounds that there would be a 'reasonable possibility that they would not be indifferent between Crown and defendants'. The application was granted, but of interest to the present chapter is the testimony of a 'criminologist and sociologist with special expertise on the perception of race and the correlation between race and crime'. His statement refers to a sociological study of the incident that was used by the judge as part of the reason for the decision (Appendix B). This study analyzes media reports that define the event as indicative of a 'social crisis' that has provoked reactions united in sympathy for the victim's family and anger directed towards the perpetrators. By allowing the application, the judge accepted that such public reactions could skew jurors' mindsets; but the authors elaborate further: 'On the surface, such narratives seem to support Durkheim's idea that public reactions to crime can bring a community closer together and subsequently reinforce social norms and increase social consensus' (Appendix B).

Here, within a court judgment, we find an oblique reference to Durkheim's view that crime is a normal part of any society because it performs important collective functions (e.g., reinforcing social norms, increasing consensus). This approach implicitly identifies 'society' as an independent entity that helps to explain why phenomena like crime, the actions of offenders, and the reactions of bystanders occur in a given context. Moreover, using criminal courts to deal with these events in individual terms (i.e., the accused are separately charged) could be seen as the outcome of a given society (i.e., law is not defined as an independent entity with its own essence). In sum, law is conceived of as the product of a given society, and Durkheim specifically reverses the jurisprudential view of law as an a priori being and predicates law upon the 'social'. To study any given system of law will thus ultimately mean studying the essence of the society to which it is born, and which calls upon 'legal institutions' to perform specific social functions. Consequently, Durkheim's sociology is primarily directed to an analysis of society, and his statements on law are secondary to that.

Durkheim's Socially Constituted Individual

Émile Durkheim (1858–1917) was born near Strasbourg in France and assumed various appointments in provincial high schools before he was offered, in 1887, a professorship in sociology and education at the University of Bordeaux. Here, he wrote three of his major works, *The Division of Labour in Society* (1893), *Rules of the Sociological Method* (1895), and *Suicide* (1897). He later accepted a prestigious position at the Sorbonne in Paris, where he completed *The Elementary Forms of the Religious Life* (1912) and founded a leading journal entitled *L'Année sociologique*.

Reflecting on the broad themes in his work, Hunt concludes that Durkheim was mostly concerned with **social solidarity**, or how society is held together: 'What is it about human society with its ever more complex interrelationships, structures and institutions which ensures not only its continuity and cohesion, but also its transformations?' (Hunt, 1978: 61). To address this question, Durkheim rejected the prevailing **methodological individualism** of such disciplines as economics, biology, and psychology that assumed the 'individual' to be a basic starting point for the study of groups—any group (e.g., society) was simply taken to be the sum of its individual members. Durkheim not only contested this claim, but insisted that collective, social being should serve as the starting point.

As if that were not enough of a controversial statement, he went on to claim that society is—indeed, must logically be—independent of the individuals that it moulds and shapes. The social whole is, in this sense, more than the mere sum of its parts, and so deserves to be studied on its own terms. Durkheim's approach understood society as prior and external to individuals, exercising a 'power of constraint' over them. Consequently, social being may be studied as a 'thing' (much like any other scientific object), and society offers a unique object for sociological inquiry that now focuses on **social facts,** or 'ways of acting, thinking, and feeling, external to the individual, and endowed with the power of coercion, by reason of which they control him' (1938: 3). He understands such social facts as collective, not individual, phenomena: unlike biological facts, they involve 'representations' and 'actions', and *contra* psychological facts they do not derive from any particular individual. As such, social facts constitute 'a new variety of phenomena' and ' . . . since their source is not in the individual, their substratum can be no other than society' (1938: 3). More specifically, Durkheim regarded **society** as an independent, ritual-based order that is a composite of all consciousnesses[1]— a kind of fusion of all individual consciousness that is created out of social interactions in a given historical context. For him, the collective consciousness may be defined as:

> The totality of beliefs and sentiments common to the average members of society forms a determinate system with a life of its own. It can be termed the collective or common consciousness. Undoubtedly the substratum of this consciousness does not consist of a single organ. By definition it is diffused over society as a whole, but nonetheless possesses specific characteristics that make it a distinctive reality . . . individuals pass on, but it abides (1984: 38–9).

This totality appears as a moral grid[2] that shapes and allows individuals to exist as historical beings. That moral substratum is, for Durkheim, the 'proper domain of sociology' and can be objectively studied in its own right, distinct from how it appears to any individual consciousness.

As strange as this may sound to some, Durkheim *is* deliberately making a strong claim: society has a life of its own, quite independent of the members, or groups, that it shapes. For him, 'it is the whole that, in a large measure, produces the part'; a society can exist, therefore, 'only if it penetrates the consciousness of individuals and fashions it in its "image and resemblance" (1973: 149)'. Or, stated more bluntly,

> . . . society has its own nature, and, consequently, its requirements are quite different from those of our nature as individuals: the interests of the whole are not necessarily those of the part. Therefore, society cannot be formed or maintained without our being required to make perpetual and costly sacrifices. Because society surpasses us, it obliges us to surpass ourselves (1973: 163).

Individuals and their consciousness are thus largely created through social forces because 'there is nothing in social life that is not in the consciousness of individuals. Yet everything to be found in the latter comes from society. Most of our states of consciousness would not have occurred among men isolated from one another and would have occurred completely differently among people grouped together in a different way' (1984: 287).

As such, individual consciousness only emerges when people 'associate together' and 'exert a reciprocal effect upon one another'. Since the group produces them, only it— the group—can explain 'states of consciousness': 'society does not find ready-made in the individual consciousness the bases on which it rests; it makes them for itself' (1984: 287). Therefore, the 'determining cause' of any social fact should never be sought from 'states of individual consciousness'; rather, the cause of one social fact should be found in another. Durkheim considered various examples of social facts, including family, kinship, the division of labour, religion, magic, ritual, crime rates, and suicide rates. He felt that sociology should always study societies through social facts, accepting that one social fact should be explained by referring to other social facts, not individual phenomena. Let us specifically turn to his *The Division of Labour in Society* to further explore Durkheim's sociological perspective and his study of law.

Science, Morality, and Social Solidarity

Given the serious upheavals of then contemporary French society, Durkheim did not share Comte's (and later Herbert Spencer's) faith that modern society was assuredly evolving and developing in a progressive direction. Nor did he accept conservative views that hankered after old orders, or, by contrast, the radical socialists' sense that capitalist society was inherently destructive. Instead, Durkheim supported a republican France, and understood scientific knowledge as a way to guide possible social improvement. His **science of society** was thus drawn to the cause by empirically analyzing social facts, and particularly the moral frameworks that arise from, and shape, various kinds of social interactions. The object of his science (society) becomes especially exposed—as indicated by *R. v. Brown*—when people join together in a common purpose, or around events that they denounce in unison. In such circumstances, emotions and opinions are exchanged in ways that sometimes strengthen into a collectively constraining force that is greater than any one individual. To take another example, people singing the Canadian anthem after an athlete wins an Olympic gold medal sing individually, but most recognize they are participating in a force that is greater than each one of them—this 'force' is the moral order that is independent of, yet partially constitutes, each individual. Durkheim's later work emphasized how rituals and symbols of sacred objects allow individuals to grasp, concretely, that whole.

In *The Division of Labour in Society*, Durkheim highlights two contradictory moral tendencies in modern societies. On the one hand, society members value increased individualism (e.g., developing unique individual personalities); on the other, they value efforts collectively to follow the 'same ideal' in concert with others. He tries to explain the seeming contradiction between individual and collective through a sociological analysis of the **division of labour**. Briefly stated, and with an admitted degree of oversimplification, Durkheim argued that early societies are small, cohesive groups that have a strong, uniform, and repressive collective conscience. These societies divide up tasks between members in relatively simple ways. As these societies' populations increase (and members interact more frequently with strangers), their survival demands that members become more specialized in the type of labour they perform. And as labour is divided into more specialized tasks, differentiated 'individuals'—who now are geographically more dispersed—are required to perform these. In the process, the collective conscience diversifies and its contents become less tangible, coalescing around abstractions like 'justice' and 'fairness'. For Durkheim, these societies, which are now more advanced, with complex divisions of labour, come to depend on individuals; far from eroding solidarity between members, this reliance on each other actually binds them closer together. A differentiated division of labour in fact strengthens society because socially produced individuals depend on the specialized tasks performed by others to survive (e.g., think of all the people involved in bringing supper to hungry tables!). There is, as such, greater functional interdependence between individuals in complex modern societies.

Durkheim was influenced by the social evolution theories of his day (e.g., Herbert Spencer) that envisaged simple organisms evolving into complex ones with internal specialization of function. We should note that there are far-reaching dangers associated with this evolutionary view as grafted onto society, including the exclusionary imperialism that effectively imagines 'primitive' societies through European eyes, and casts them as simple others to complex, modern societies (Pavlich 2009a, 2000). Regardless, Durkheim analyzed the organizational structure of 'traditional' societies by comparing them with more 'advanced' societies, focusing on the different ways in which each achieves 'social solidarity'. Yet, for him, we cannot directly measure social solidarity (like other moral concepts): 'Social solidarity is a wholly moral phenomenon which by itself is not amenable to exact observation and especially not to measurement. . . . We must therefore substitute for this internal datum, which escapes us, an external one which symbolizes it, and then study the former through the latter' (1984: 24).

What precisely could that symbol be? 'That visible symbol is the law', because, 'Life in general in a society cannot enlarge in scope without legal activity simultaneously increasing in proportion. Thus we may be sure to find reflected in the law all the essential varieties of social solidarity' (1984: 24–5).

So, as a measure of social solidarity, law offers a general indicator of moral feelings within a society—these are not exact indicators because they sometimes lag behind, or run ahead of, collective morals. But they do, for Durkheim, provide a useful way to understand social change.

The Evolution of Morality, Social Solidarity, and Law

Durkheim argued that there are two basic kinds of law, **repressive** (penal, criminal) and **restitutive** (civil, administrative, commercial, procedural); each is associated with a particular kind of sanction, and each reflects an underlying kind of social solidarity. Penal law is dominant in contexts where a strong, homogeneous collective conscience exists, and is associated with 'repressive' sanctions that require an individual be punished (by infliction of pain, incarceration, etc.) for transgressing universally approved morals within a given society. In societies of this type, the experiences of each individual consciousness are relatively similar, and internalized to a large degree. Individual differentiation is discouraged, and transgressions are violently punished through repressive sanctions. In short, these societies are structured through a **mechanical solidarity** that is denoted by penal law: 'a social solidarity . . . which arises because a certain number of states of consciousness are common to all members of the same society' (1984: 64). While mechanical solidarity and penal law are common in traditional societies, Durkheim argues that they persist in contemporary contexts where punishment to avenge offenders is used to protect and reaffirm the collective consciousness. Increasingly, however, penal law and punishment come to be replaced by notions of deterrence rather than vengeance.

As such, restitutive forms of law are more common in 'advanced' modern societies, and they point to a new kind of social cohesion that Durkheim calls **organic solidarity**. This sort of solidarity operates much as a body does (hence 'organic'): namely, as a composite of several interdependent systems (e.g., circulatory, breathing, neural). The normal functioning of each system ensures the normal functioning of the whole. Restitutive law presupposes a complex division of labour that generates disputes around individual property rights, commercial transactions, torts, administrative regulations, and so on. In these contexts, criminal matters become a smaller part of an expanded law concerned increasingly with civil–administrative matters in which 'offenders' are required to make amends, or pay fines, rather than be punished. The aim here is to restore a status quo, or a normal state, using new administrative agents (legislators, magistrates, administrative boards, industrial tribunals, etc.). In short, the specialization required by restitutive law mirrors the increasingly differentiated division of labour of modern societies, and indicates a complex organic solidarity.

If, in the context of mechanical solidarity, the collective consciousness embraces individual consciousness, organic solidarity—with its differentiated division of labour— requires differences (rather than resemblances) between individuals. Whereas mechanical solidarity absorbed individuals into a collective personality, organic solidarity demands that each of us have

> . . . a sphere of action that is peculiarly our own, and consequently a personality. Thus the collective consciousness leaves uncovered a part of individual

consciousness, so that they may be established in it those special functions that it cannot regulate. The more extensive this free area is, the stronger the cohesion that arises from this solidarity (1984: 85).

This argument is in part a polemical attack on methodological individualism, but it also explains how modern individuals are integrated into societies. Rampant individualism, for Durkheim, neither annuls collective being, nor leads to anarchism: 'Not only is individualism not anarchical, but it henceforth is the only system of beliefs which can ensure the moral unity of the country' (1973: 50). From this vantage, one can better understand why he should say that: 'Not only does mechanical solidarity generally bind men together less strongly than does organic solidarity but as we mount the scale of social evolution, it becomes increasingly looser' (1984: 105).

Before moving onto a more detailed discussion of Durkheim on law, it may be useful to mention in passing three further claims in his work. First, he argues that the expansion of the division of labour is caused by the increased amount and range of social contacts—what he referred to as **dynamic density**—which is related to the growth of populations (1984: 201). Secondly, he implicitly relied on a **functionalist** approach (in which a phenomenon is studied through its functions in an overarching system) to explain the integration of organic solidarity. Thirdly, all is not well with modern society, and so he described three of its 'abnormal forms': the 'anomic', 'forced', and 'unnamed' divisions of labour (1984: pt. 3). The first refers to situations where the economic functions required by a new division of labour outpace moral rules, yielding insufficient normative regulation (anomie). The second arises when moral regulations do not develop spontaneously and contractual relations are coercively imposed to order society. In many ways this is Durkheim's version of class (and one might add gendered) conflict, in which the spontaneous distribution of natural talents is thwarted by the power of a monopolizing group—leading one group to seize an 'unjust advantage' over others. His implicit quest is for a meritocratic, spontaneous division of labour that demands equal opportunity to mobilize natural talent appropriate to a given function. The third unnamed abnormal form has to do with the lack of coordination among functions, producing dysfunction and inefficiencies that cause 'the pores of the working day to contract' (1984: 327). In sum, as Milovanovic (2003: 36) notes, these abnormal forms of the division of labour 'go against the movement towards cooperation, mutual fulfillment, and happiness that inhere in the spontaneous forms'.

Durkheim's Law

As can be gleaned from above, Durkheim regarded law as a 'social fact' that concretely embodies a society's morals and norms—a 'visible symbol' of social solidarity. In a review of Gaston Richard's work on the origin of law, Durkheim notes that the 'philosophy of law cannot be separated from its sociology', and insists that investigation into the origin of law should take this form: 'What are the social influences which gave rise to the idea of the law and in terms of which it has evolved historically?' (1983: 147). In other words, to repeat, law is always premised on social influences, and so its origins are necessarily sociological. We must therefore return to early societies to understand how the idea of law emerges out of their 'intervention in the settlement of conflicts; from there come arbitration and the guarantee' (1983: 150). Even though Durkheim (e.g., 1938, 1983) repeatedly studied law, he always regarded it as a predicate of prior social functions. He treated it as a social fact, and, in line with his method, used it to explain other social facts (like social solidarity). But this social fact is rather unique in that it is both an index, and a specific expression, of underlying social morals; it is also directly tied to the evolution of a society and its changing forms of social solidarity. With this overall sense of law in mind, let us turn to Durkheim's more specific discussions of criminal law and punishment, as well as contract and property law.

Criminal Acts and Punishment

Durkheim initially approached the concept of crime through discussions of mechanical solidarity. In a well-known reversal of conventional thinking about crime as an unambiguous violation of societal norms (laws) that must be eradicated from normal society, he defines crime in this way: 'We may state that an act is criminal when it offends the strong, well-defined states of the collective consciousness', but he insists,

> . . . we should not say that an act offends the common consciousness because it is criminal, but that it is criminal because it offends that consciousness. We do not condemn it because it is a crime, but it is a crime because we condemn it (1984: 39, 40).

Unlike common individually centred conceptions of crime and criminals (e.g., Lombroso's criminal anthropology), Durkheim insisted that crime is always tied to particular types of societies. In this sense, as his response to Gabriel Tarde highlights, crime may or may not be useful, but it is 'normal because it is linked to the fundamental conditions of all social life; such is the case because there cannot be a society where individuals do not diverge more or less from the collective type and because, among these divergences, there are no less inevitably some which exhibit a criminal character' (Durkheim, 1983: 95–6).

Considered as a social fact, then, crime is a 'normal' element of any society because it is both *universal* and *necessary* to the functioning of given social types. It is universally present in 'all societies of all types' (1938: 65), and indeed, 'a society exempt from it is utterly impossible' (1938: 67). At the same time, he argues, crime is necessary because it is 'fundamental' to social life, and is 'indispensable' to 'the normal evolution of morality and law' (1938: 70). Without crime, he seems to be saying, there can be no sense of what is normal and what is not. Thus, crime is relative to, and functions within, a specific moral framework of a given society. It performs both direct and indirect social functions: 'indirect because crime could only cease to exist if the *conscience collective* dominated individual *consciences* with such an ineluctable authority that all moral change would be rendered impossible; direct, in that occasionally, *but only occasionally*, the criminal has been a harbinger of a morality to come' (1983: 96). Here one might again think of Nelson Mandela, whose anti-apartheid activism was branded criminally treasonous by the apartheid state, but turned out to be a 'harbinger' for a future morality.

However, even with crimes that appear to be common to all types of society, Durkheim maintained that we must be attentive to the different ways they operate. His (1957) analysis of homicide, for example, echoes the mechanical–organic solidarity argument discussed above, showing how this crime was initially understood through collective and, later, individual moralities. Briefly, in 'primitive' societies, homicide was considered to be the worst kind of offence because it was seen to attack the 'sacred' social order directly; as such, repressive attacks on offenders and kinship groups were widespread to avenge collective emotions. In modern society, as the 'cult of the individual' becomes established in organic solidarity, homicide may continue to be viewed as one of the worst offences, but for different reasons; now the individual is considered sacred, not society (1984: 338). As an affront to the individual body that society renders sacred, homicide enables the collective reactions of the kind alluded to in *R. v. Brown*—but it licenses less severe, less spectacular forms of punishment than those of earlier social forms.

Clearly, for Durkheim, punishment, though central to defining crime, is also one of its consequences; thus, the evolution of punishment is closely tied to the evolution of crime (1983: chap, 4). With this in mind he proposes two scientific laws governing the development of punishment from its early to modern forms. His first, quantitative law, asserts (rather unsurprisingly by now) that punishment is more intense in less developed societies where 'the central power assumes an absolute character' (1983: 102). Even if the quantitative analysis he provides is less than compelling (Hunt 1978: 80), he distinguishes between punishments associated with religious versions of crime versus a 'human criminality' in which acts injure a newly developed sense of 'the individual'. The latter crimes are different because they offend against different parts of the collective consciousness, and so are punished in different ways. Religious criminality attracts coercive and repressive sanctions because it is considered to be an offence against the collective body.

By contrast, human criminality emerges against the backdrop of a receding religious criminality and emerging humanism that emphasizes the individual. In this context, offences against the individual do not attract the same harsh demand for vengeance, and therefore a reliance on coercive punishment.

Durkheim offered a second qualitative scientific law governing the evolution of punishment: '*Deprivations of liberty, and of liberty alone, varying in time according to the seriousness of the crime, tend to become more and more normal means of social control*' (1983: 114). This law seeks to explain why it is that prisons become the dominant form of punishment in modern contexts when they were unknown in 'primitive societies'. We will have reason to return to a version of this matter when dealing with Foucault's work, but Durkheim argued that incarceration was absent from early societies because responsibility for crime rested not with an 'individual' but with a collective entity—hence it made sense to substitute family members for punishment. Imprisonment became meaningful with the growth of individual criminal responsibility and the development of a more centralized form of authority, reflected by the development of public buildings. The early prisons tended to be found at the outskirts of other public buildings (e.g., palaces), which he sees as part of the development of city-states. Over time, and appropriating the mentality associated with devices for humiliation (e.g., the pillory, stocks, dunking stool), prisons were developed as uncomfortable places of detention designed to punish individuals. Here a 'pure' form of imprisonment arose as essentially individual deprivation of freedom; this technology permits gradations of punishment on a flexible scale, and adds a new intensity to punishment. It also nurtures 'individuality', even if only to 'make individual consciences aware of the force of collective constraint' (1983: 128).[3] Durkheim then observed—again of direct relevance to Foucault—that, 'although social discipline, of which morality properly so-called is only the highest expression, progressively extends its field of action, it loses more and more of its authoritarian rigour. Because it becomes more human, it leaves more room for the spontaneity of individuals; it even solicits it. It has therefore less need to be violently imposed' (1983: 128).

The Evolution of Contract and Property Law

Replicating his general sense of law, Durkheim approached contract and property law as social products, and ties their evolution to the rise of modern society. Regarding contract law, he emphasized the social bases that regulate a given contract: ' . . . a contract is not sufficient by itself, but is only possible because of the regulation of contracts, which is of social origin' (1984: 162).

This may seem like an odd opening gambit, for contracts are usually considered as expressions of individual will—if an individual does not voluntarily consent to a contract, then typically it is null and void. However, Durkheim asserted that society generates the prior conditions within which it is possible for two individuals to form a contract; it also provides the enforcement mechanisms for any breaches thereof. As such, the formation of contract law is directly linked to the evolution of a society; that is, he argues, contractual relations materialize when a division of labour diversifies and multiplies commercial transactions requiring reliable commercial exchange. Thus, for him, contract law emerges at a time in history when modern society requires a way to facilitate the reliable acquisition and transfer of property. In short, 'The contract is the supreme instrument by which transfers of ownership are carried through' (1983: 194), and yet the contract relies on the development of legal entities who are capable of forming individual, freely chosen agreements. Durkheim took the rise of contracts to be an important part of the **meritocratic** societies (i.e., societies based on merit, where the most capable person is allowed to perform societal tasks without discrimination) he championed, and approved of their potential to thwart the inequities generated by archaic practices of inheritance (1983: 230ff.).

With this broad sketch, Durkheim filled in more details regarding the evolution of contract law from 'status-based' contracts to those more familiar to us, i.e., based on individual will and 'mutual consent'.[4] A status-based contract, common in 'primitive societies', was usually shrouded in sacred or religious content to symbolize the mandatory nature of the deal. He described, for instance, how **blood covenants** were literally sealed through the sharing of blood, or communal eating, to symbolize close family ties and the binding nature of a given agreement (1983: 197). Here, he notes that 'real contracts' were only formed 'by the actual delivery or handing over of a thing' (1983: 198). With these, we are still worlds apart from contracts understood as individual 'wills in agreement', which begin to occur when persons involved in status contracts are required to make fixed declarations with all 'due and solemn formality' (1983: 199). The solemn contract is expressed in words and guaranteed through sacred references to a divine authority that, say, a party possesses a particular thing. The promise here is directed both to various gods and to other people.

However, as modern society advances, so divine links weaken and the promise to others strengthens. Even so, without the 'solemn ritual', Durkheim noted, 'there is no contract' (1983: 200). This more mobile form of contract becomes more evident as the social conditions for the development of modern will-based forms of contract are cemented. For him, however, 'the consensual contract amounts to a revolutionary innovation in the law. The dominant part played in it by consent and the declaration of will had the effect of transforming the institution' (1983: 219).

In other words, the law as an institution was radically transformed by will-based contracts that emerged alongside novel forms of trade and industry where the older rituals, symbols, and sacred promises of status-based societies appeared outmoded. In turn, this opened the way for understanding contracts not in terms of status, but as individual wills freely, and by mutual consent, entering into agreements guaranteed with new judicial mechanisms. It is worth noting that this new image of contract presupposes the existence of persons (individuals) capable of having free will—a product, in part, of a rising 'cult of the individual' associated with organic solidarity.

Yet, Durkheim cautioned, 'The old institutions never disappear entirely; they only pass into the background and fade away by degrees (1983: 234).' He also insisted that there is no necessity about this development; it is a historically contingent matter because:

> The mere fact that an institution is required does not mean it will appear at a given moment out of the void. There must be something to make it of . . . existing institutions must not oppose it but, rather, supply the material needed to shape it. So it was not enough for the consensual contract to be demanded by the advance of economic life: the public mind, too, had to be ready to conceive it as possible. . . . a change had to be made in the region of ideas, that would allow of the having a different start (1983: 208).

Changes both to institutions and the collective consciousness propelled the contingent evolution of contract law. In the event, evolving will-based contracts in modern society often occurred through structural inequalities, revealing the unfair and forced basis of 'mutual consent' and free will (1983: 226ff.). But Durkheim pointed to a rising intolerance of 'unjust and immoral' contracts, especially those based on structural unfairness, and an emerging consensus that society is not bound to enforce unjust contracts (1983: 227).[5] This intolerance signals the praiseworthy prospect of a new stage in the evolution of contract beyond the putatively 'free will' of 'consensual' contracts. This new contractual form—a 'contract of equity'—recognizes the public interests involved in not only the nature of contracts, but their social effects.[6] One detects in Durkheim's writings here a preference for a society based on social justice, where all legal contracts are to be collectively assessed rather than framed around individual free will.

Durkheim's parallel analysis of property law as an inherently social process assumes that society allocates property and revolves around notions of sacredness (1983: chap. 7). He begins by asking how **private property rights**[7] were established. To answer this, he argued, property is better 'defined negatively than in terms of positive content, by the exclusion it involves rather than the prerogatives it confers' (1983: 164). Understanding property thus allows one to show how it arose from certain 'religious beliefs'; in earlier societies, priests (and the like) were granted exclusive abilities to decide what was sacred and what was not. They alone were permitted to differentiate between the sacred and the profane. Sacredness thus initially fell under the exclusive ability domain of priests (and the like), but gradually selected objects were taken to be intrinsically sacred. In a related way, clans used stones to mark out boundaries of cultivated fields, from which non-family members were excluded. Elaborate rituals were used to render such fields sacred, and these rituals integrated clans into common bonds with their god and established early images of collective property.

But how did this more communal sense of property transform into individual, private property rights? As we might now expect of Durkheim, he tied this transformation to a rising individualization of modern societies, and argued that certain individuals were accorded greater status than others; e.g., when a family patriarch emerged as the 'head' of a household. Through such developments, land was no longer deemed to be a sacred entity—sacredness was now transferred to the head of the family. As he put it, 'The family's centre of gravity thus became displaced . . . [the family's centre of gravity] passed from the things it was vested in to a given person. Henceforward an individual came to be an owner, in the full sense of the word, since the things were subject to him, rather than he to them' (1983: 187).

At the same time, personal or movable property, as opposed to 'landed property', became more crucial to a diversifying division of labour that moves from agriculture to trade and industry. Through this diversifying process, the idea of property was distinguished from the moral and sacred connotations of earlier societies, becoming far more flexible than was the case with real property. In other words, the earlier communal understandings of property were fragmented, and with the rise of landed and movable forms, so new laws arose. All such developments were nurtured by shifts from mechanical to organic solidarity. Again, one hears the Durkheimian refrain, but now individual rights and private property are seen as combining to weaken sacred and religious bonds that lay at the heart of earlier understandings of communal property.

Concluding Reflections

> The task of the most advanced societies may therefore be said to be a mission for justice. . . . Just as the ideal of lower societies was to create or maintain a common life as intense as possible, in which the individual was engulfed, ours is to inject an even greater equity into our social relationships (1984: 321).

For Durkheim, as we have seen, moral values (such as justice) and the social world are inextricably connected. Society is a necessary condition for morality; individuals do not simply bring to society innate conceptions of, say, justice. On the contrary, people become 'individual' moral beings capable of grasping notions of justice only because of their socialization into a given society. 'Let all social life disappear, and moral life will disappear with it, since it would no longer have any objective' (1973: 137). Morality is therefore impossible without the collective preconditions that emerge with specific social forms. In other words, morality is always tied to the solidarity of a given social form, and, consequently, it varies with the kind of solidarity at hand. With such views in mind, one can better understand why Durkheim argues that justice can never be understood as an abstract idea, but must always be tied to the development of a particular kind of society, and a concomitant collective consciousness.

As implied by the quotation at the beginning of this section, Durkheim saw justice responding to key social problems (the 'abnormal forms of the division of labour') that have emerged with the unprecedented pace of change from mechanical to organic solidarity. In particular, this rapid social change has left in its wake a moral vacuum; the morality corresponding to early societies has lost its influence,

> but without its successor developing quickly enough to occupy the space left vacant in our consciousness. Our beliefs have been disturbed. Tradition has lost its sway. Individual judgement has thrown off the yoke of the collective judgement. . . . The new life that all of a sudden has arisen has not been able to organise itself thoroughly (1984: 339).

In such a context, society requires new forms of organization that will satisfy a 'need for justice that has been aroused even more passionately in our hearts' (1984: 339). In that quest to organize society justly, we should not expect remedy from a revival of past moralities that 'no longer correspond to present-day social conditions'.

Instead, Durkheim calls on us to pursue social justice by seeking to ameliorate the structural inequities that generate the problems outlined by the forced division of labour: 'Just as ancient peoples had above all need of a common faith to live by, we have need of justice. We can rest assured that this need will become ever more pressing if, as everything leads us to foresee, the conditions that dominate social evolution remain unchanged' (1984: 322). And that 'need of justice' involves organizing the consciousness, rituals, and moral frameworks that comprise collective being in society in ways that promote fairness, meritocracies, and forms of social life based on equity of opportunity. Law, as one of society's means for pursuing such justice, must (as indicated above) evolve appropriate forms of contract, property, criminal, and penal law to enhance just and fair social forms. By so formulating justice and law, Durkheim made absolutely clear the subservient ontological position of both to a primordial 'society'. In this, one sees a sociological move to understand law and justice through notions of society *sui generis*. No longer is society to be drawn upon to help explain certain aspects of law understood as a distinctive terrain; now, law is no more than what a given society fashions for its own independent purposes and requirements. Society is now the moving mover!

Discussion Questions

1. Is society the creator of your (individual) consciousness?

2. What is wrong with assuming that 'modern' societies are 'more advanced' than 'traditional' societies?

3. Do contract and property laws help or hinder the development of modern society?

4. Do you agree with Durkheim that crime is a normal part of any society?

5. How does Durkheim's sense of morality differ from that of classical natural law approaches?

6. Does law ever function in ways that stifle, rather than promote, collective solidarity?

Suggested Readings

Alexander, J.C., & Smith, P. (2005). *The Cambridge Companion to Durkheim*. Cambridge: Cambridge University Press.

Giddens, A. (1971). *Capitalism and Modern Social Theory: An Analysis of the Writings of Marx, Durkheim and Max Weber*. Cambridge: Cambridge University Press.

Milovanovic, D. (2003). *An Introduction to the Sociology of Law*. Monsey: Criminal Justice Press.

Relevant Websites

www.emile-durkheim.com/
www.sociosite.net/topics/sociologists.php#durkheim
http://durkheim.itgo.com/

6 Law, Ideology, and Revolutionary Social Change

Questions to Consider

⊛ To understand the foundations of any society, do we have to look at the ways it produces things (food, shelter, etc.) that enable its members to survive?

⊛ Is the development of society based on conflict and revolutionary struggles?

⊛ Is law little more than an ideology that serves the ruling interests of dominant classes?

⊛ Can law ever bring about consequential social changes?

If, for Durkheim, modern society had reached a stage in the division of labour that required the urgent pursuit of justice and social reform beyond law centred on individuals, Karl Marx (1818–83) framed a more radical form of socialism, or communism. Durkheim appears to have been aware of Marx's work[1], and both agreed that society shapes individuals, that justice should be conceived socially, and that law is the historical outcome of wider social forces. However, Durkheim rejected Marx's insistence on economic relations as the basis of power in society, and preferred an evolutionary, progressive, reformist approach to Marx's *revolutionary* socialism. This difference has proven consequential, and is, perhaps, one of the main reasons that Marx's thought is popularly considered, by turns, explosive, seditious and even traitorous, or inspiring, liberating, and revolutionary. Either way, Marx's legacy continues to provoke strong reactions; it has profoundly influenced global politics generally, and Canadian socialism specifically.[2] It is commonly associated with radical threats to capitalist societies, and its adherents have been subjected to various 'security' measures. During the 1950s, with 'Cold War', anti-communist, and 'Iron Curtain' politics peaking, US Senator Joseph McCarthy of Wisconsin led a quasi 'witch hunt' to identify and blacklist 'communists', and to put a stop to what he perceived as a 'communist subversion' of US society. His slanderous claims against many people (including the Truman administration) were never substantiated; yet they destroyed many lives (Lattimore 1971), and eventually led to the Senate taking the unprecedented action of censuring him.

Within this context, we might read the following Canadian case—*Martin v. Law Society of British Columbia*, [1950] 3 DLR 173—as indicating how Marxism and communism were perceived by prominent Canadian justices over a century after Marx's early writings, and the negative consequences for those who openly championed its precepts. According to the facts presented, a Mr Martin had applied to the Law Society of British Columbia for admission to the bar as a solicitor. The benchers, claiming authority under the *Legal Professions Act* (1948), denied his admission on the grounds that he was a self-confessed communist—even though he was never convicted of a subversive act, and overtly rejected 'subversive activity or use of force against governmental institutions'. The decision was challenged, but upheld, and then brought before the British Columbia Court of Appeal, which dismissed the appeal. The various ratios provided to support this decision reveal contemporary attitudes towards Marx, and those who declared themselves to be communists. In his argument, for example, Chief Justice Sloan says this of Marx and the Society's decision: 'The Benchers, considering the ideological values and motives and loyalties of an adherent of that alien philosophy, reached the conclusion that such a person was unacceptable for the reasons given refusing his application to become a member of the Bar of this Province' (6).

His colleague, Justice O'Halloran, is rather more explicit:

> The appellant having admitted he has been a Marxist Communist for some time, the Benchers came to the conclusion that the Marxist philosophy of law and government, in its essence, is so inimical in theory and practice to our constitutional system and free society, that a person professing them is *eo ipso*, not a fit and proper person to practise law in this Province, and hence cannot be of 'good repute' within the meaning of the Legal Professions Act (9).

He rejects Mr Martin's argument that 'an avowed Marxist Communist' can be a good citizen so long as that person is not involved in sedition or force against the state ('such as [to give an extreme example] blowing up the Parliament Buildings'). Justice Bird gives more of a sense of the appellant's argument by noting that Mr Martin rejected any form of subversive act and 'declared that he would not follow the Marxian doctrines to the extent of using force if necessary to overthrow constituted authority' (9). Moreover, the court was aware that Mr Martin would leave the party if told to commit a subversive act, but had, in any case, 'always felt free to disagree with the application of such doctrines and in lieu to advocate social change by means of education and social organization' (11).

However, Justice O'Halloran insists that

> Marxism exercises a strange power over its adherents. The moral needs of man which Marxism forbids to be expressed in terms of human ideals, are injected instead into a mechanistic conception of politics to which they impart the force of a blind passion somewhat like that which inflamed the minds of Nazi youth during the Hitler regime. Communism is a complete philosophy of life. It wishes to be not only a state but a church judging the consciences of men (17).

This seemingly ad hominem assertion is coupled with the claim that 'Marxist philosophy' is potentially dangerous, even in 'mildest appearing of its adherents'.[3] He therefore dismisses the appeal, arguing that 'a Marxist Communist cannot be a loyal Canadian citizen' because 'the Communist leadership outside Canada' is 'engaged ideologically through him (whether he knows it or not)' in 'promoting disruptively in Canada and other countries what *Lenin* called "the class struggle of the proletariat" for the world revolution' (56).

This judgment is affirmed by Justice Robertson, who refers to other cases to argue that 'Communists' protestations of loyalty are not to be accepted' because their 'first obligation' is to the Communist Party, which adheres to the 'principles' articulated 'in the Communist manifesto, viz., that their ends can be attained only by the forcible overthrow of all existing social conditions; coupled with a warning to the ruling classes to tremble at a Communist revolution' (67). Such provocative language contrasts with Justice Smith's more reserved view that the appellant's membership in a Communist organization, 'prepared to overthrow existing Governments by force if necessary', is the issue; this leads him, also, to dismiss the appeal. The unanimous agreement by the court, and the openly expressed critiques (even if narrow interpretations) of Marx's 'alien philosophy', a century after Marx first developed some of his ideas, signal its legacy and influence. But what kind of thinking could resound so loudly through the ages, and what did it actually have to say—for our purposes in context—about law and society? To respond to these questions requires some detail on his overall approach before attending to the rather more fragmented comments he (and Engels) offered on law.

Marx's 'Alien Philosophy', Alienation, and Real History

The truncated interpretations of the justices above certainly give very little indication of the breadth, scale, and development of Marx's ideas over the course of his life. They also betray superficial understandings of Marx's work, and give no recognition of the close collaboration between Marx and his life-long friend, Friedrich Engels, in writing many 'Marxist' texts, including *The Communist Manifesto*. Engaging philosophers like Kant, Hegel, and Feuerbach (Hirst 1972), Marx's early work urges, as a member of a student group called the 'Young Hegelians', the development of Hegel's images of democracy and right to nurture a 'reform of consciousness' against the stultifying decrees of contemporary religion and politics.

In the British Columbia case, the chief justice's allusion to Marx's 'alien philosophy' is ironic, for Marx (1964) talked of the **alienation** of capitalist workers from their **species being**, a condition in which capitalist society makes people think and act in ways that counter their true nature as human beings. For example, he noted how in capitalist societies workers lose control over the things they create, are alienated from the very activity of creating products, and begin to incorporate instrumental logics into their relationships with other people. Capitalists exploit workers to the detriment of all: 'The more the worker produces the less he has to consume; the more value he creates the more worthless he becomes' (1964: 122). In this early work, Marx argued that a future **socialist**, or **communist**, society should seek to overcome alienation, ensure that everybody shares equally from the things they produce, supersede private property, and return people to their truly 'social' nature (1964: 155). Many of the basic tenets of this early work are carried through into his later work (e.g., in *Capital*), but he also reworked Hegel's understanding of history that focused on how new ideas are the mid-wives to better social life by embracing a **materialist** image of history focused on the matter, the real conditions, that shape our lives. In other words, it is not ideas, but tangible material things in the world that shape our history. One may refer to three important themes to help understand what he means by these concepts, especially as developed in a work with Engels, *The German Ideology* (1965).

First, Marx insisted that what we think, or how we *choose* to act, does not move history along its course. Ideas do not create history. Rather, our interactions with others in the context of the real world shape our consciousness and, consequently, what we think. The foundation of our ideas lies in the real world, and so too does the movement of history. Marx arrives at a more specific understanding of history through a rather basic assumption: to survive, we must eat; to eat, we must produce; but how we produce is conditioned by the ways that we associate; thus, the foundation of social being and history is predicated on something entirely necessary for our survival; he calls this the **mode of production**. Stated another way, the way we produce to survive is the foundation of our history; it is 'a fundamental condition of all history, which today, as thousands of years ago, must daily and hourly be fulfilled merely in order to sustain human life' (1964: 147). In another famous statement, he clarifies further, ' . . . the mode of production of material life conditions the general process of social, political and intellectual life. It is not the consciousness of people that determines their existence, but their social existence that determines their consciousness' (1970: 21).

Perhaps more realist than materialist, Marx in any case insists that the concrete ways we produce things—and not the ideas that we harbour about them—are the basic, founding moment that pushes social history along.

Secondly, Marx rejected an evolutionary approach to understanding the march of social history; rather, he takes from Hegel a **dialectical logic** as the basis for social progress. In brief, Hegel had posited the development of history not in causal terms (i.e., A causes B which causes C), or in evolutionary terms of the kind we have encountered with Pound and Durkheim. Rather, he argued that history proceeds through a unique logic of the negation and synthesis of ideas. Hegel's logic begins with an idea (a thesis), a subsequent negation of that idea (an antithesis), and the unifying overcoming of both (a synthesis). In turn, the synthesis becomes the thesis for the recurring developmental process. So, for example, Hegel might begin with a thesis, say, 'a King is a sovereign'; let us say that the idea is challenged (negated) at a given moment in history by its antithesis (e.g., 'that people, not the King, are sovereign')—the ensuing outcome could be a synthesis that takes bits from both (e.g., a 'parliament is sovereign'). Marx saw considerable value in the logic of this approach to history, but forcefully rejected Hegel's focus on ideas (i.e., his idealism). Consider the following words:

> My dialectic method is not only different from the Hegelian, but is its direct opposite. To Hegel the life process of the human brain, i.e., the process of thinking, which, under the name of 'the Idea', he even transforms into an independent subject, is the demiurges of the real world, and the real world is only the external, phenomenal form of 'the Idea'. With me, on the contrary, the ideal is nothing else than the material world reflected by the human mind and translated into forms of thought (1959: 145).

Marx here turned Hegel 'on his head' so that material, real conditions of production— not ideas—become vital to historical development. That is, a society's mode of production is negated through revolutionary struggles that enable a synthesis of past forms to radically reorganize society around a new mode of production. From this vantage, consequential social change is never gradual, or evolutionary; it is dramatic, large-scale, and revolutionary.

Thirdly, he incorporated both the above dimensions to develop a **materialist conception of history**. Here he understood modern society through an analysis of its mode of production and the changing forms of social divisions of labour. But note, Marx conceptualized the division of labour very differently from Durkheim—'The various stages of development in the division of labour are just so many different forms of ownership; i.e., the existing stage in the division of labour determined is also the relations of individuals to one another with reference to the material, instrument, and product of labour' (1964: 33).

Hence, for Marx, the division of labour develops out of struggles to own and control the ways given societies produce necessities to secure their survival. The formation of societies is thus not a matter of tidy consensus; rather, society is always the outcome of ongoing struggle and conflict. One gleans that for Marx, human societies develop dialectically from pastoral, hunter-gatherer societies to the slave societies of the ancient Greek and Roman worlds (he also discusses oriental versions of this development), which eventually lead to feudal societies and then to the emergence of modern capitalism. Scattered throughout his work, Marx provided some detail on each society,[4] but for our purposes here, suffice to detect that his materialist sense of history describes interrupted (not linear) social change through dialectical upheavals and conflicts that propel one mode of production to its revolutionary negation—revolution seeds the foundations of another mode of production. He and Engels put it thus:

> The history of all hitherto existing society is the history of class struggles. Freeman and slave, patrician and plebeian, lord and serf, guild-master and journeyman, in a word, oppressor and oppressed, stood in constant opposition to one another, carried on an uninterrupted, now hidden, now open fight, a fight that each time ended, either in a revolutionary reconstitution of society at large, or in the common ruin of the contending classes (2004: 9).

In all these epochs, one finds different orders and 'gradation of social rank'—from the 'patricians, knights, plebeians, slaves' in ancient Rome to the 'feudal lords, vassals, guild-masters, journeymen, apprentices, serfs' of the Middle Ages. The modern capitalist, or **bourgeois**, rises out of 'feudal society' and establishes new 'class antagonisms' with 'new classes, new conditions of oppression, new forms of struggle in place of the old ones' (2004: 9). Here, the idea of private property emerges, and the bourgeoisie become the exclusive owners of the means of production, while the **working class (or proletariat)**, as non-owners, have to work for wages in order to survive—thus becoming utterly dependent on owner capitalists.

Modes of Production, Class Struggle, and the Future of Capitalism

From his realist, historical method, and out of his concrete studies, Marx (1970) later outlined a specific model through which to analyze all kinds of societies. In particular, as we have seen, the mode of production is the primordial point of departure for history. This mode of production comprises both the **productive forces** (e.g., technology, tools, labour power)[5] required to produce something in a specific way, and the **social relations** through which people organize themselves in order to produce in a particular way: 'In the social production of their existence, people inevitably enter into definite relations, which are independent of their will, namely relations of production appropriate to a given stage in the development or their material forces of production . . . ' (1970: 20). These forces and social relations together form the mode of production, and also the basis of society: 'The totality of these relations of production constitutes the economic structure of society, the real foundations, on which arises a legal and political superstructure and to which correspond definite forms of social consciousness . . . ' (1970: 21). Much has been made of the latter statement, and is often referred to as Marx's **base-superstructure** model of society—akin to a building that arises from a particular foundation.

Referring to this analogy, one might say that the mode of production forms the real foundation from which arise more or less elaborate ideological, political, legal, and cultural superstructures. Three issues are worth noting: classes emerge as part of social relations of production once the division of labour diversifies in early societies; revolutions occur when the forces of production surge ahead of productive relations, rendering a given mode of production no longer sustainable; and, for our purposes, state and law are considered by Marx to be located in the superstructure. As we shall see, how one conceptualizes the relationship between the base and superstructure is important for how one will treat law and state (i.e., does the base determine, provide limiting conditions for, or loosely shape the superstructure? Does the superstructure have the ability to influence the base? etc.).

Marx's later work 'scientifically' studied the basic structure, dynamics, and effects of modern capitalist societies using the concepts noted above. Although partly responding to political economists of the day (Adam Smith, David Ricardo), Marx offered an ingenious theory of capitalist development in *Capital*, beginning with a close analysis of the product of labour in capitalism, i.e., the **commodity**. From that one concept he exacts a unique way of approaching and understanding all capitalist societies. The details of his argument are complex and intriguing (Giddens 1971: chap. 4); however, it will suffice here to sketch some key points in his discussion of capitalism. To begin with, he clarified that a capitalist mode of production is unique because of the new technologies (industrialization) that it uses, and the idea that the ways by which we produce can be privately and individually owned (hence, property law). As such, capitalist society emerges around struggles between those who own the means of production and those who do not. The former (capitalists or the bourgeoisie) have great leverage over the lives of the latter (the working class or proletariat), who must work, as noted, for wages in order to survive. They are the people that produce commodities. These commodities have both a **use value** (how useful they are to us as human beings) and an abstract **exchange value** (a numerical value for transactions, e.g., five dollars). Their value (both use and exchange) arises not from supply and demand, as liberal economists commonly assert, but from the **labour power** that workers invest to produce them.

However, in a capitalist mode of production, this labour power is expended at the behest of the private owners of production—the capitalists—who pay workers less than the amount of value they generated by producing commodities. Let us assume, for example, that a worker is paid $10 for a day's work, but produces commodities that sell for $100 as they leave the factory. In this case, the **surplus value**—taking account of other production costs —is $80; it is born largely out of the worker's toil, but capitalists claim it as their rightful **profit**. Marx argued that the rate of **exploitation** of workers in any such context is directly proportional to the rate of surplus value that the capitalist creams off as profit. In the above example, the rate of profit is high, and so is the sheer exploitation (and consequent misery) of the worker who produces it. As such, the interests of bourgeoisie and proletariat are directly opposed because the more capitalists exploit workers, the wealthier the capitalists become; by contrast, workers' interests are mostly in direct opposition to capital—the more they produce for themselves, the less is available to capital. Consequently, Marx and Engels argued, 'Our epoch, the epoch of the bourgeoisie, possesses . . . this distinct feature: it has simplified class antagonisms. Society as a whole is more and more splitting up into two great hostile camps, into two great classes directly facing each other—Bourgeoisie and Proletariat' (2004: 61). So, for Marx, capitalism develops around **class struggle**, and is the outcome of conflict between bourgeoisie and proletariat.

The details of Marx's analysis are beyond our remit here, but he envisages a falling rate of profit, an increasing **pauperization** (i.e., people become impoverished) of the working class, and a growing concentration and centralization of capital in the hands of a few; he predicts that all such tendencies will generate fundamental contradictions and crises for capitalism, bringing the class struggle to a head. In their *Critique of the Gotha Programme*, Marx and Engels showed how the revolutionary overthrow of capitalism might take place, focusing on the transition from capitalism to the first stage of **socialism**. Marx predicted that with the centralization of markets, private property would end and production would be socialized, rendering everyone part of a new humanized working class. This transitional period would also contain many of the features of bourgeois capitalist society, except that this proletariat would seize centralized capital and power from the bourgeoisie, becoming the dominant class. The state, in this phase, would not necessarily disappear, but its purpose would change dramatically: 'Between capitalist and communist society there lies the period of the revolutionary transformation of the one into the other. Corresponding to this is also a political transition period in which the state can be nothing but the revolutionary dictatorship of the proletariat' (2001: 32).

Marx had rather less to say about a future, perhaps communist, society, since we cannot fully conceptualize what it would look like through the concepts that are available to us today; but he does indicate that the worker will eventually be replaced by a 'fully developed individual, fit for a variety of labours' (1976: 488). Though vague, we get a better sense of what Marx and Engels have in mind when they call for the division of labour to be overthrown. They argue that it separates 'the particular and the common interest' and makes human activity 'an alien power opposed' to people, becoming a yoke rather than a source of expression:

> For as soon as the distribution of labour comes into being, each man has a particular, exclusive sphere of activity, which is forced upon him and from which he cannot escape. He is a hunter, a fisherman, a herdsman, or a critical critic,

and must remain so if he does not want to lose his means of livelihood; while in communist society, where nobody has one exclusive sphere of activity but each can become accomplished in any branch he wishes, society regulates the general production and thus makes it possible for me to do one thing today and another tomorrow, to hunt in the morning, fish in the afternoon, rear cattle in the evening, criticise after dinner, just as I have a mind, without ever becoming hunter, fisher-man, herdsman or critic (1965: 53).

And there we have it—the dream of egalitarian socialists seeking more for all than the productive or consumptive demands and human costs of capital-ism. Of course, many will cry that this is totally unrealistic, and Marx would probably agree—but with an ironic rider that it is unrealistic only from the vantage of current contexts and the social consciousness, ideologies, they en-able. The unadulterated call for revolution, coupled with a 'realist' assessment of achieving that call, may suggest why the justices in *Martin v. Law Society of British Columbia* appear agitated by Martin's Marxist inclinations, especially given the elevated social position of lawyers in capitalist societies. And on this note, let us return to Marx (and Engels) on law.

Marx on Law in Capitalist Society

The laws enacted are as innumerable as the interests which they outwardly deter-mine. They have an ominous tendency to multiply. The law is a fetter forced on me from without (Marx 1965: 58).

Much ink has been spilt tracing and debating Marx's version of law[6] and crime[7] in various contexts.[8] This is somewhat remarkable because Marx no-where develops a theory of either law or crime, leaving many scattered re-marks that others have taken as a context for developing such theories (e.g., Pashukanis 2002; Fine 1984; Bonger 1967). Even so, in the 1970s, radical challenges to conventional approaches to crime and deviance theory turned to Marx's work to develop 'new deviancy' theories and a new critical criminol-ogy that was to have considerable impact over the next decade (Pavlich 2000; Taylor et al. 1973). Here debates raged around exactly how Marx viewed criminals—were they proto-revolutionaries (see Taylor et al. 1975), unreliable and undisciplined reactionaries, a class of 'social scum' or 'lumpenproletar-iat', or dispersed individuals created by structural capitalist forces (Quinney 1980; Spitzer 1975)? Others rejected the very attempt to apply Marx to crime as 'reactionary', arguing that 'there is no "Marxist theory of deviance", either in existence, or which can be developed within orthodox Marxism. Crime and deviance vanish into the general theoretical concerns and the specific scien-tific object of Marxism' (Hirst 1972: 29).

The call to Marxist orthodoxy may have contoured some debates of the time, but a more influential 'socialist realism' found its way into criminology and the sociology of deviance (Pavlich 2000; Young and Mathews 1992). This work was partly fuelled by Althusser (2005), Gramsci (2001), and Poulantzas (1978), who variously argued that the ideological frameworks that allow current practices of law and state to persist can, at times, achieve some distance (and degrees of autonomy) from the economic foundations of society. These ideologies, in other words, may become 'relatively autonomous' from the underlying economic base at particular moments in history. The importance of such revisions was to allow for a somewhat less rigid interpretation of Marx's ideas—ideologies may well emerge from underlying economic (material) conditions, but they often develop in ways that are not fully determined by a given mode of production. This point was significant because it challenged a **determinist** or **reductionist** reading of Marx that reduced everything to the economy, allowing that in certain circumstances it might be useful for Marxist activists to engage law and state as part of a working-class struggle for revolutionary change. What does this mean specifically for law?

As noted, Marx did not focus on this question, but Cain and Hunt (1979) have usefully collected and interpreted many of his and Engel's writings on the subject. Although fragmented, it is possible to extract some key themes about law that have influenced socio-legal studies. Cain (1974) offers an older, but still insightful, way to frame his sense of law.[9]

Law as Ruling Ideology

The first theme revolves around the previously noted view that law (and state) reflect the dominant ruling ideas. Marx used the concept of **ideology** to reference how material conditions of production produce ideas that tend to perpetuate rather than resist existing modes of production. Specifically, then, ideology is associated with ideas about how legitimately to rule and resolve conflicts within, and so to preserve, capitalist societies. Ideology is superstructural (a concept or idea based on others) to material bases, and law can be regarded as an important ideological instrument used to perpetuate capitalist modes of production. While, say, specifically criminal and civil laws may be prevalent in capitalist societies, they are simply the most recent historical expressions of how a dominant class manipulates ideas to support, and give legitimacy to, its domination (Reiman 2004; Thompson 1975). Thus, for Marx and Engels, juridical structures are 'an expression whose content is always determined by the relations of this [ruling] class, as the civil and criminal law demonstrates in the clearest possible way' (1964: 61). Moreover,

> The ideas of the ruling class are in every epoch the ruling ideas, i.e. the class which is the ruling material force of society, is at the same time its ruling intellectual

force. The class which has the means of material production at its disposal, has control at the same time over the means of mental production, so that thereby, generally speaking, the ideas of those who lack the means of mental production are subject to it (1964: 61).

With this in mind, they argued that law provides a justification for the bourgeois state. This helps to make law and state appear as absolute, independent forces, but both are products of bourgeois attempts to structure people's consciousness in ways that legitimate an underlying capitalist mode of production.

Does this mean that the law (and state) are chimera, completely determined by capital? Those who read Marx reductively might argue yes: ideologies, like law and state, are simply instruments at the disposal of capitalists who determine their contextual forms. This unconvincing reductionist reading assumes that any law must perform a function for capitalism, even if that may initially not appear to be the case. Hence, laws that appear to challenge individual bourgeois interests are taken to work for wider capitalist interests (Quinney 1980; Miliband 1973). A more nuanced 'structural' interpretation reads Marx as saying that economic foundations provide only the outer limits for many different kinds of ideology to develop. Such ideologies may (as referenced above) become relatively autonomous from the economic base, and may even achieve limited changes to the economic foundations from which they arise (see Milovanovic 2003; Collins 1982). In effect, this position allows that the law can be used to bring about progressive social change and, indeed, enlisted to help socialist struggles (Poulantzas 2000; Fine 1984; Hay 1975; Thompson 1975). But there are some who question even this more open formulation, challenging Marx's idea that everything can, in some or other way, be reduced to the economy (see Albrow 1981).

Law's Functions in Capitalist Society

In addition to the law as ideology theme in Marx and Engels's work, Cain (1974: 142) detects another, having to do with three subtle functions they see law playing within capitalist society. First, they suggest that the state comes into existence when class conflicts become irreconcilable, providing a context for it to position itself as an external arbiter of such conflicts. Although the capitalist state is ultimately a creation of the ruling class, developed to secure its overall interests, that real power needs to be obscured and legitimated. Here law plays an important role: it obscures that power by extending rights equally and universally to all—but it does so within a fundamentally unequal social context. To make this point clearer, many commentators refer to Anatole France's famous adage: 'The law, in its majestic equality, forbids rich and poor alike to sleep under bridges, to beg in the streets, and to steal their bread.'[10]

The point? Granting equal and universal rights within structurally unequal societies often perpetuates, rather than alleviates, the inequalities (who is most likely to be begging, or sleeping under bridges?). But the law also legitimates state rule through a higher-order ideology—jurisprudence. As seen in previous chapters, jurisprudence formulates various approaches to decide on the validity of the law, as well as when rulers legitimately exercise power. But in its general operation, as indicated by *Martin v. Law Society of British Columbia*, law also decides in ways that support the capitalist state—in this instance even peaceful Law Society applicants who *potentially* threaten the capitalist order by adhering to Marxist views are judged unfit to work within the legal framework.

Secondly, Marx and Engels (1964) recognized that the bourgeoisie are by no means a homogenous group, for there are many different interests within this class. Thus, in some of their writings, they contend that law represents the ruling class's 'average interests'; that is, 'the interest of the class conceived as a whole rather than of particular sections or individuals' (Cain 1974: 143). Therefore, law reflects the common interests of the ruling group and may, on occasion, appear to work against the interests of particular capitalists. Carson's (1982) careful study of safety regulations and the politics on North Sea oil rigs illustrates the complexities of law as a harbinger of ruling class interests, having to negotiate common interests within that group and at the same time having to appear as a neutral force. A masterful study of nuances around health and safety legislation, which at times works against the profit motive of ruling interests, reflects how law is ambiguously positioned in a relatively autonomous position, enabling it to serve certain working-class interests, yet ultimately striving to benefit capital.

Thirdly, and following from the above, Marx and Engels noted the duplicitous face of law (and state): its repressive coercive (material) functions are obscured by its ideological (symbolic) functions that portray it as equal, universal, and just. Yet the enduring Marxian problem, to which we have alluded several times, is to examine whether or not law (and state) can ever do more than simply replicate the interests of capital—even in the 'last instance'. Pointing to this enduring problem, Cain (1974) detects four 'sub-themes' that highlight Marx and Engels's view of the role capitalist law plays.

1. They discuss, for instance, its role in helping to define and institute private property as something so self-evident that it becomes difficult to think about life without notions of privately owned property. In particular, Marx and Engels consider property as a social phenomenon that has, under capitalism, developed into a perverted private (individualized) version thereof. People emerge as 'individuals' who own things, and are pitted competitively against one another. At the same time, however, Marx and Engels understand the development of private property as a dialectical phenomenon—property law shapes 'external reality, develops with it,

and is developed by change within the new external world thus created' (Cain 1974: 145). As such, various forms of law are generated out of the vortex of dialectical change, and can, in certain instances (as noted), assume degrees of autonomy; however, law is always ultimately founded upon the real relations of production.

2. From the above, one might interpret that law may, in some cases, help to change society, but it cannot override its fundamentals, which are located in an underlying mode of production. The law, in other words, can bring about limited social change, but it cannot alter the foundations of capitalist society. Marx and Engels, in their analyses of various class struggles, therefore suggest that law is most likely to bring about change when a significant proportion of the ruling class supports its reforms.

3. It is difficult to determine in advance the value of law to working-class struggles. However, at certain moments in history, the average interest of the capitalist class can be fraught with conflict—in such contexts the proletariat can effectively exploit conflict through law. In other words, for Marx and Engels, the working class is likely to be most effective when it forms united and effective class alliances to resist ruling interests—law can sometimes form part of those struggles. However, when the bourgeoisie are united around an issue, law is not likely to bring about effective change.

4. Finally, Marx and Engels often caution us not to expect law to do much more than reform surface issues—as they put it, 'the law gives us nothing but only sanctions what we have' (1964: 70).

With these diverse themes in mind, we could return to *Martin v. Law Society of British Columbia* to reflect on how the content of law is dialectically forged out of historically specific ideological struggles. For instance, 'Marxist communism' at that time was considered a far greater 'threat' to society than is perhaps currently the case, and hence the unanimous ruling. At the same time, the appearance of judicial 'neutrality' could be taken to mask the way in which this decision works in favour of bourgeois interests, thereby serving the dominant mode of production that founds legal structures. The decision clearly supports, and legitimates, the state by eliminating the potential for lawyers to subvert its rule; hence Justice O'Halloran claims that any lawyer holding Marxist beliefs is '*eo ipso*' not a 'fit and proper person' to become a lawyer. The 'Marxist communist' allegiance renders that person not one of 'good repute', because, ironically, he regards these beliefs as 'inimical' to a 'free society'. Given the unanimity of the justices, Marxists might argue that their opinions reflect an average of ruling class interests and confirm that law is there to prop up capitalism. The case also could perhaps provide fodder for those who would argue that law is an ideology unlikely to change society fundamentally, especially when the ruling classes are united around a particular issue.

Concluding Reflections

One could evoke the foundational 'spectres' of Marx to understand his diffuse influence on many areas of contemporary life (Derrida 1994). However, it is worth noting that even if one were to disagree with Marx's specific theory of capitalist society, and the, at times, disastrous ways in which his ideas found expression (e.g., Stalin), his work is attractive to many because it attempts to overcome elements of our current histories. And justice often provides a promise for that possibility. At base, Marx distinguished his sense of justice from bourgeois images of 'eternal justice' (which he takes to be another attempt to legitimate its rule), or the view that bourgeois law is, or produces, justice. Instead, he has a wider 'social justice' in mind—one that is never divorced from the historical conditions, conflicts, and struggles that produce it as an idea or promise. This social sense of justice is one that may be framed around fairness and equity, but realizes its dialectical relation to a given context; unlike Hegel (and Feuerbach), Marx believed justice could never be framed as an eternal, abstract principle. In this sense, he viewed justice as a product of concrete (class) struggles in real contexts—a kind of praxis in which historically specific subjects and objects engage dialectically, through struggle, to fashion new forms of consciousness.

On the question of society, unlike Durkheim, Marx considered moral norms and social relations to be predicates of prior relations that develop out of, and always in tandem with, given economic conditions. As such, society is anchored in social relations of production; his aim was to pursue a communal mode of production with an attendant communist society that restores human beings as fully social beings, in accord with their basic nature.[11] Here, some might hear echoes of natural law theory (Taiwo 1996), but Marx's main point is to emphasize that individuals are social creations and beings, most fittingly located in 'socialist' patterns of association. In short, for Marx, the idea of society is closely related to historical context, and the underlying mode of production that contours—in a dialectical way—the relations amongst people, as well as between people and things. This sort of approach enables a historically invested socio-legal study that frames society not as a consensually produced set of relations that evolve; rather, society is based on concrete class struggles, conflict, and the revolutionary overthrow of past forms. No doubt there remain images of social progression, but now progress occurs through dialectical revolution, not (as with Durkheim) reformist evolution. Society is granted a historically determined essence that Marx's careful methods are meant to unearth.

In this scheme, as seen, law is clearly a secondary entity, predicated upon social relations as they rise out of struggles within a given mode of production. And on this point one might refer directly to Marx:

. . . society does not depend on the law. That is a legal fiction. The law depends rather on society, it must be an expression of society's communal interests and needs, arising from the material mode of production, and not to the arbitrary expression of the world of the single individual. I have here in my hands that Code Napoleon, but it is not the code which created the modern bourgeois society. Instead, it is bourgeois society, as it originated in the 18th century and underwent further development in the 19th century, which finds its merely legal expression in the Code. As soon as the code ceases to correspond to social relations, it is no more than a bundle of paper. (Marx, quoted in Phillips 1980: 187).

In this quotation, Marx betrays a particular view of law; his rejection of the various approaches discussed in Part I that assumed law to exist *sui generis* is marked. If these approaches enabled discourses centred on law, Marx's contributions have spawned socio-legal critiques of capitalist law as a historical predicate of specific class struggles that along with the state could simply outlive its use; under new forms of (socialist, communist) production, it could simply 'wither away'.

Discussion Questions

1. In what ways does law perpetuate the dominant economic patterns of capitalist society? Are there any examples where it resists such patterns?

2. Do you agree with Marx that all social relations can be explained by referring back to underlying modes and social relations of production?

3. Can you think of any examples where law has helped to bring about consequential changes to Canadian society? What does this mean for Marx's approach?

4. Do you think it would ever be possible, or desirable, for state and law to 'wither away'?

Suggested Readings

Collins, H. (1982). *Marxism and Law*. New York: Clarendon Press.

Milovanovic, D. (1988). *A Primer in the Sociology of Law*. New York: Harrow and Heston.

Spitzer, S. (1975). 'Toward a Marxian Theory of Deviance'. *Social Problems*, 22(4), 638–52.

Sumner, C. (1979). *Reading Ideologies: An Investigation into the Marxist Theory of Ideology and Law*. New York: Academic Press.

Relevant Websites

www.historyguide.org/intellect/marx.html
www.marxists.org/archive/marx/works/cw/index.htm
www.absoluteastronomy.com/topics/Anatole_France#encyclopedia
www.radicalacademy.com/philmarx.htm
www.marxists.org/archive/marx/bio/index.htm

7

Max Weber, Modern Disenchantment, and the Rationalization of Law

Questions to Consider

- ⊛ Has modern society, and its laws, become overly rational, regimented, and bureaucratized?
- ⊛ What does it mean to say our societies are 'disenchanted'?
- ⊛ Is law simply a particular kind of social action that involves an order to be obeyed, backed up by a staff of people tasked with ensuring compliance?
- ⊛ To understand law sociologically, do we have to interpret the meanings of actors involved with legal institutions?

The fate of our times is characterised by rationalization and intellectualisation and, above all, by the 'disenchantment of the world' . . . (Weber 1994: 302).

Against a jurisprudential assumption that the law exists *sui generis*, with society obliquely drawn into its orbit, Durkheim and Marx had privileged ideas of society over law. Max Weber (1864–1920) echoes a version of that refrain, emphasizing the role of subjective interpretation and meaning in our social relations with others. For him, law might be considered a historically situated type of 'social action'; it is not, therefore, an absolute object, independent of the socio-historical contexts from which it derives. Importantly for him, as suggested by the epigraph above, as rational thinking steadily contours social action in modern societies, so associated legal forms become increasingly rational. However, unlike Durkheim or Marx, he does not view law as the product of one determinant, be it a division of labour or mode of production.[1] Weber is often credited with initiating the sociology of law,[2] and his early training as a lawyer suggests an enduring interest in legal systems, from the time that he completed a doctoral thesis in 1889 until his untimely death from pneumonia at 56 years of age. Yet, those seeking a clearly spelt out sociology of law will likely be disappointed by Weber's segmented oeuvre, partly because his *Rechtssoziologie (Sociology of Law)* was still in draft form when it posthumously appeared in the 1921 edition of *Economy and Society*.[3] At times, the perspicacious analyses are embedded in seemingly nonchalant description, requiring, appropriately enough for his type of sociology, considerable interpretive work on the part of readers.

Weber's analysis of law is silhouetted against a wider sociological reach. Like Marx, and perhaps responding to him, Weber saw capitalism as the unique and exclusive form of economic activity in the West (the 'Occident'), distinguishing it from all other societies. Capitalism was also accompanied by **rationally** ordered ways of thinking and acting that shape how societal members understand their worlds, live out their lives, and obey legitimate forms of authority. This rationality has all but stripped the West of erstwhile magical enchantments, placing it under a spell of cold, instrumental, rational calculation that is capable of great technical achievement, but at significant cost; specifically, it has trapped us in an 'iron cage' of reason of our own making. This is perhaps why Weber repudiates the West's 'convulsive' sense of self-importance and its 'specialists without spirit, sensualists without heart'. His consequent assessment is blunt: 'This nullity imagines that it has attained a level of civilization never before achieved' (2003: 182). Weber's analysis of law should be approached through his version of sociology,[4] which considers how various political, economic, legal, administrative, social, and cultural institutions have rationalized modern society—with both negative and positive effects.

Rational Social Action, Sociology, and Modern Western Society

Weber proposed a certain **elective affinity** (i.e., close association as opposed to causality) between the rise of capitalism and rational forms of thought. In an essay entitled *The Protestant Ethic and the Spirit of Capitalism*, Weber examined how certain religious beliefs (i.e., Protestantism and, especially, a puritanical form of Calvinist doctrine) fostered ways of thinking that complemented capitalist ideology (e.g., as enunciated by Benjamin Franklin). The Puritan performed good deeds to still anxieties about being saved or damned, and this translated into a determination to work ascetically—a mindset that aligned well with the spirit of capitalism. Never mind the intricate complexities of this argument, and indeed its debated flaws (see Giddens 1971); one detects an attempt to show how ideas of a specific religion were central, rather than peripheral (as Marx alleges), to the development of capitalism.

More specifically, Weber's approach to sociology defines its object as both the *behavioural* and subjectively *meaningful* elements of human activities. **Social action**, the target of sociology, is only a subset of all possible behaviours, for it refers exclusively to those that take another individual's behaviour into account (i.e., are *socially* orientated). Suppose I randomly waggle my hand in the air; the movement may indeed constitute behaviour, but it is not a *social* action unless it is performed as a response to meanings that I, or others, ascribe to it. By contrast, suppose I see friends approaching and wave my hand to greet them; the subjective meaning behind that behaviour is orientated towards others, and so may be considered a social action. In short,

Not every type of contact between human beings is of a social character, but only where the individual's conduct is meaningfully orientated towards that of others.

Thus a collision of two cyclists is merely an isolated event comparable to a natural catastrophe. On the other hand any attempt by any one of them to avoid hitting the other, with the ensuing insults, a brawl or even a peaceful discussion, would constitute a form of 'social behaviour' (Weber 1980: 56).

Therefore, social action comprises both behaviours and meanings that take account of others—it is also the basic object of sociology.

Thus, Weber famously defined **sociology** as

> . . . a science which attempts the interpretive understanding of social action in order thereby to arrive at causal explanations of its course and effects. In 'action' is included all human behaviour when and insofar as the acting individual attaches a subjective meaning to it . . . action is social insofar as, by virtue of the subjective meaning attached to it by the acting individual (or individuals), it takes account of the behaviour of others and is thereby oriented in its course (1994: 228).

In a nutshell, sociology not only describes objective behaviours but, equally importantly, uses interpretive (hermeneutic) methods to gain an empathetic understanding of the meanings associated with socially orientated behaviours (he calls this *Verstehen*), and to trace causal explanations of their development. Weber also distinguishes between fact and value:[5] values may shape the kinds of questions that sociologists ask, but, once defined, their scientific responses should proceed on the basis of fact. He is aware that there are shades of differentiation between these concepts, but Weber (2005: 69) urges sociologists to neutralize their value commitments when studying things scientifically, calling for a sort of 'detached empathy' on their part. Following this formulation, Weber's sociology of law seeks a **value-free** (i.e., devoid of moral judgments) description of the legal social actions, or behaviours, that are meaningfully orientated by various understandings of 'law', and relations with others framed by notions of 'law'.

Given its subjective dimensions, social action must necessarily be 'qualitatively heterogeneous', which raises this question: is it apposite to use statistical averages to describe social patterns? Weber thinks not; instead, he proposes his well-known concept of **ideal types** (sometimes also referred to as 'pure types') as a way for sociologists to formulate 'type concepts and general uniformities of empirical process' (1994: 245). But the 'abstract character' of sociological concepts, dealing as they do with changing subjective meanings, means they lack the 'concrete content' of objects in, say, physics, or even history. In order to 'compensate for this disadvantage, sociological analysis can offer greater precision of concepts . . . by striving for the highest possible degree of adequacy on the level of meaning' (1994: 245).

That is, to achieve conceptual precision, 'it is necessary for the sociologist to formulate pure ideal types of the corresponding forms of action'; indeed, 'theoretical analysis in the field of sociology is possible only in terms of such pure types' (1994: 246). So, for him, ideal types enable precise, conceptual, and value-free analyses of social action. They are heuristic creations, never actually found in reality: 'An ideal type is formed by the one-sided accentuation of one or more points of view and by the synthesis of a great many diffuse, more or less present, and occasionally absent concrete individual phenomena, which are arranged according to those one-sidedly emphasised viewpoints into a unified analytical construct' (1994: 264).

For example, and pertinent to his study of law, Weber (2005: 28) distinguished between four ideal types of social action: **traditional social action** proceeds from settled customs (e.g., the behaviour of elders at tribal rites of passage); **affective social action** is determined by emotional states or impulses (e.g., religious conversions); with **value rational action**, an actor believes in the intrinsic value of an ethical, aesthetic, or religious value, and then rationally tries to realize it; **instrumentally rational action** organizes behaviour by treating objects and other human beings as means to achieving particular ends. The difference between the two rational forms of social action can be understood in the following ways. Suppose a student is asked why s/he is attending university. If that student views his or her behaviour as furthering the noble cause of education, the behaviour of attending classes, etc., is meaningfully conditioned by his/her value of education for its own sake. In this case, realizing that value by attending university reflects a value rational type of social action. By contrast, someone who attends university simply to get a good job, or earn more money, reflects an instrumentally rational type.

Working with these types, Weber developed the thesis that modern society has increasingly turned away from traditional and affective social action towards more rational types (even if traces of the former persist). As more actors understand and frame their behaviour in rational ways (especially instrumentally), so societies—and their legal, political, and social institutions—become rationalized.[6] He detects a similar pattern in rational forms of *power* and politics in Western modernity. **Power** is, for him, 'the probability that one actor within a social relationship will be in a position to carry out his own will despite resistance, regardless of the basis on which this probability rests' (1994: 23). Apparently nodding in the direction of command theories of law (e.g., Austin), Weber also notes that power implies 'imperative control', or the probability that a *command* will be obeyed. It also implies (as we shall see in Foucault), 'discipline', or, 'the probability that by virtue of habituation a command will receive prompt and automatic obedience in stereotyped forms, on the part of a given group of persons' (1994: 23). When power and discipline are incorporated into forms of authority, we are dealing with the probability that 'specific commands . . . will be obeyed by a given group of people' (1994: 28).

Such authority can assume various forms, but let us consider the case of **legitimate authority.** When authority claims legitimacy on the basis of 'the sanctity, heroism or otherwise impressive character of an individual', it reflects a **charismatic type of legitimate authority** (1994: 31). By contrast, **traditional forms of legitimate authority** stake a claim on the basis of existing traditions that specify who an 'appropriate authority' may be. Finally, a **rational-legal type of legitimate authority** works on the basis of 'a common belief in the legality of rules and the right of those empowered to exercise authority (i.e., legal authority)' (1994: 31). Here, again, Weber detects a rationalization of modern society, and a growing tendency towards *rational-legal authority*. At the same time, the development of **bureaucratic authority**, as a rationalized form of administration with hierarchical 'offices', official duties governed by rules, and so on,[7] has become a significant part of Western (and indeed many other) societies.[8] He accentuates the role of bureaucratic authority in the development of all rational forms of law:

> In particular, in the sphere of the administration of justice, it is normally the bureaucracy which first creates the basis for the introduction of a conceptually coherent and rational legal system, founded on 'statute', of the kind first created in a technically perfect form by the later Roman Empire. In the Middle Ages, the acceptance of Roman law went together with the bureaucratisation of the administration of justice: the gradual introduction of rationally trained specialists to replace the earlier procedures tied to tradition or irrational preconceptions (2005: 352).

With this sociological approach in mind, let us now turn specifically to Weber on law.

Weber, Law's Orders, and 'Flying Tackles'

One might consider Weber's approach to law through a case like *R. v. Collins*, [1987] SCJ No. 15. On appeal from British Columbia, the case facts are depicted thus:

> Appellant had been under surveillance by two members of the RCMP Drug Squad. A police officer approached her in a pub, laid hold of her identifying himself by saying 'police officer', grabbed her throat and pulled her to the floor. (The 'throat hold' is used to prevent someone from swallowing drugs contained in a condom or balloon and recovering them later.) The officer directed her to let go of an object clenched in her hand—a balloon containing heroin.

At trial, the search was judged unlawful, but the evidence was allowed anyway because the accused 'did not properly establish that s. 24(2) of the

Charter[9] would exclude it'. The decision was appealed, but dismissed by the BC Court of Appeal.

On a further appeal, the Supreme Court of Canada did not consider the justness of the decision; rather, at issue was whether the 'evidence should be excluded under s. 24(2) of the Charter'. Consequently, it determined that 'a civil standard' was required to assess whether admitting this evidence would, as per s. 24(2), 'bring the administration of justice into disrepute'. It argued further that such disrepute could occur from either allowing the evidence (and perhaps not giving the accused a fair trial), condoning 'unacceptable conduct by the authorities', or excluding the evidence. Later cases would discern a three-pronged 'test' requiring them to: (1) determine if the admitted evidence would render the trial unfair; (2) consider the seriousness of the breach; (3) decide, on balance, if the administration of justice might be brought into disrepute.[10] In this case, however, the majority (with one dissenting opinion) argued that the greatest threat to the reputation of the 'administration of justice' would occur ' . . . if this Court did not exclude the evidence and dissociate itself from the conduct of the police'. The officer's actions constituted a 'flagrant and serious violation of the rights of an individual. Indeed, we cannot accept that police officers take flying tackles at people and seize them by the throat when they do not have reasonable and probable grounds to believe that those people are either dangerous or handlers of drugs (45).' The appeal was allowed and a new trial ordered.

There are, as we have seen, many ways to approach and understand the 'law' reflected by this case. Within the context of natural law theories, for example, one might evaluate the decision using extra-legal, moral criteria; we might say this is a good decision because it protects human rights, or, equally, a bad decision for preventing police from doing their job. Weber's value-free sociology differs from this line of thought (1954: 26). But it also rejects what he calls 'legal dogmatics', which appears to be much like Langdell's legal formalism, previously discussed in Chapter 4 (1954: 11). Legal formalists might scour the above ruling to detect underlying principles, rules, and tests to determine a 'correct' reading of the court's decision (e.g., *R. v. Rutten*, [2006] SJ No. 65). For Weber, this juridical approach privileges existing law, taking a value-based stance in favour of its precepts. Against both approaches, his sociological understanding of law focuses on how the behaviour of all the participants in this case (the accused, police, judges, witnesses) is causally shaped by their subjective understanding of, and commitment to, law, together with their beliefs about how others understand the law (Weber 1954: 8–9). Value-free descriptions of such 'law-oriented behaviour' thus constitute the proper domain of the sociology of law. From this perspective, Weber asserted that a 'thief's' illegal behaviour—or, in our case, drug dealing—is a legal matter to the extent that such behaviour is somehow affected by understandings of law (1954: 4).

At base, Weber considers the law as a kind of social action that involves an **order** to be obeyed.[11] An order is only valid when people perceive it to be legitimate, and obligatory; obedience thereto can be secured subjectively (through emotions, or ethical/religious beliefs), or it may be guaranteed, 'by the expectation of certain external effects' (1954: 5). If the order is obeyed because an individual anticipates the 'external' disapproval of a group for non-compliance, then we are dealing with 'convention' or 'custom'. What differentiates law from custom is the following: 'An order will be called *law* if it is externally guaranteed by the probability that coercion (physical or psychological), to bring about conformity or avenge violation, will be applied by a *staff* of people holding themselves specially ready for that purpose' (1954: 5).

In other words, for Weber, the pivotal difference between customary controls and legal orders is simple: the presence of a *staff* of people who have exclusive powers to coerce compliance to a legal order.[12] In the above case, one might think of an order from, say, an outraged regular at the pub ordering Ms. Collins to stop her actions as opposed to the 'flying tackle' and threat grab by the officer (although this may present too dramatic a contrast). By focusing on how legal rules are *administered*, in all the details, Weber's approach overlaps somewhat with legal realists, but he views the 'process of law' in broader terms. This allows him to focus on all levels of enforcement, from police, legal bureaucracies, legal administrators, and prosecutors, to defence lawyers—not only the decisions of judges. It also prioritizes 'social action' as the basis of any legal action.

Weber: 'Basic Categories of Legal Thought'

In keeping with his overall approach, Weber's analysis of law begins with the observation that the modern West has developed a distinctive, rational way of understanding and acting in law, not found in any other contexts—what he, at times, calls **logical formalism**. Although this work was still incomplete when he died, several texts give some sense of his approach to law.[13]

He starts by noting two fundamental activities in the field of law: creating law, and finding law once it is created (adjudication). Both activities operate either in formal or substantive ways. **Formal systems of law** tend to be self-sufficient and use internally specified rules and procedures to make decisions. By contrast, **substantive systems of law** usually refer to external criteria (e.g., religious, political, ethical values)—these can be emotional or reactive—that either make or adjudicate laws. In addition to being either formal or substantive, legal systems are either **rational** or **irrational**. As Kronman (1983: 75) indicates, Weber considers systems to be rational if they are rule-governed, systematic, 'use logical interpretations of meaning', and are intellectually framed. Irrational systems are exact opposites of this. Table 1 below provides a not uncommon way to represent Weber's implicit typology visually.

TABLE 7.1 **Weber's Typology of Law-making and Law finding**

	Irrational	Rational
Substantive Criteria	Substantively Irrational	Substantively Rational
Formal Criteria	Formally Irrational	Formally Rational

Reflecting back on history, Weber notes that, 'Law has always developed first through legal oracles, precedents of charismatically qualified bearers of legal wisdom (Weber 1967: 84).' The charismatic nature of early forms of law tends toward the irrational side of this typology.[14] When lawmakers and law discoverers do not follow general rules or norms, and proceed in an ad hoc way, leaping to conclusions based on emotional evaluations that differ widely from case to case, they operate substantively but in irrational (i.e., *substantively irrational*) ways. Here, adjudication works in a purely ad hoc manner (1954: 229ff.). Not unlike the law of Fuller's King Rex, such legal systems reflect unpredictable ethical, emotional, and political considerations—Weber refers here to examples of justice in Attic Greece—'Khadi-justice'—or the justice dispensed by some English justices of the peace (1954: 229, 231). These systems are 'irrational' for him, because they do not follow clearly articulated rules, and make no effort to link decisions to general precepts. They are 'substantive' because they do not distinguish systematically between legal and extra-legal ways (e.g., ethics, religion) of grounding decisions. Consequently, their jurisdiction is vast, without clearly defined images of a legal point of view.

According to Weber, examples of lawmakers and adjudicators with *formally irrational* understandings of law include those endorsing prophetic revelations and oracular verdicts. In these contexts, there is a fastidious adherence to complex rules that specify how to reveal an oracle's decision, or prophecy. Such understandings are formal in the sense that even minor deviations of protocol annul the process; they are irrational because they rely on magic, prophecies, etc., beyond reason-based thought. On this note, Weber points to the way in which early stages of English common law embraced formal procedure but called on a mystical 'customary' law as a guiding auspice. These irrational types remain embedded in, and so are never completely transcended by, the move towards rational law (e.g., 1954: 224ff.).

Substantively rational law-making and adjudication systems make decisions by following clearly defined and specified principles within ethical frameworks, religions, or even from 'reason of state' discourses. However, no boundary between law and ethics is recognized in a 'priestly approach to law' or in a 'patriarchal system of justice'.[15] Both systems use law to secure ethical, political, and religious beliefs, or ideologies. Law may be rationally framed in context, but these systems are not 'juristically formal' because they appeal to external (i.e., extra-legal) criteria (1954: 205–23).

Finally, *formally rational* systems of law-making and law finding are characterized by systematic, rule-governed, self-sufficient, closed fields that explicitly differentiate themselves from ethics, religion, and politics (1954: 198–205). They base themselves on the 'logical analysis of meaning' within a 'gapless system of legal propositions'; in both substantive and procedural law, facts are ascribed determinate meanings in a generic fashion rather than on a case-by-case basis. For Weber (1954: 222ff.), this kind of law emerges out of Roman law as enunciated through the 'legal science of the Pandectists', a jurisprudential school that emphasized formal, rationally conceived, and self-sufficient law. But given his predilection for types, Weber distinguishes between two kinds of formally rational law.

First, there is an **empirical type** of formally rational law where facts considered significant to establishing legal relationships are found outside of law. For example, a piece of land is deemed to have been properly transferred if a visible symbol, or formal, written instrument, is delivered in a specified manner and in the presence of specified agents, witnesses, etc. Had the arresting officers in *R. v. Collins* strictly followed demarcated procedures, including the clear enunciation of certain words (i.e., 'you have the right to remain silent . . . '), their damning evidence might not have been challenged. Contracts too may be regarded as binding or not, depending on whether they were written down in specified ways. In each instance, legal relationships are determined by extrinsic, empirically verifiable symbols.

Secondly, law-making and law finding may reflect a strictly **logically rational type** of formally rational law if they begin from premises that are not religious, political, ethical, or ideological, or require formalized empirical declarations. Such legal systems are more commonly associated with civil codes (i.e., civil rather than common law) and statute-based forms of law. They proceed from abstract, generally formulated statutes (concepts), and are associated with the development of specialist legal bureaucracies, as well as judges and lawyers with specialized training.[16]

R. v. Collins reflects both kinds of formal rationality. On the one hand, we have already noted the empirically verifiable procedures required of officers. On the other, the case decides on the facts before it in a thoroughly logical fashion. The judgment explicitly argues that the issue before the court is not whether the original trial was just in ethical terms; rather, the key issue is whether or not s. 24(2) of the *Charter* was violated in a particular set of circumstances. The ratio begins with that section as its major premise, along with findings of previous cases relating to this section. The specific facts of this case are framed around whether admitting the forcefully obtained evidence would bring the administration of justice into disrepute (minor premise). This is followed by the conclusion that, in the court's logically considered view, a new trial should be ordered because the use of this evidence does, in this instance, tarnish the reputation of the administration of justice, and so contravenes s. 24(2). Through this syllogism, both elements of Weber's (1954: 301ff.) formally rational type of legal thought appear to be very much alive in Canadian law.

According to Weber, this rationalization of the law is peculiar to Western culture, where modern states with professional administrations and specialist bureaucrats operate through the law of a 'state'. Against Marx, however, he argues that many factors—not only a capitalist mode of production—contribute to the rise of formally rational types of law found in much of Europe. How so? Interestingly, Weber refers directly to Canada to argue that common law approaches, which tend toward substantively rational types, often trump civil law (and its formally rational law) in capitalist contexts: ' . . . wherever the two kinds of administration of justice and of legal training have had the opportunity to compete with one another, as for instance in Canada, the common-law way has come out on top and has overcome the continental alternative rather quickly' (1994: 224). He continues, 'We may thus conclude that capitalism has not been a decisive factor in the promotion of that form of rationalisation of the law which has been peculiar to the continental West ever since the rise of Romanist studies in the medieval universities' (1994: 224).

Instead, many other factors have contributed to its rise on the European continent. For example, 'The alliance of monarchical and bourgeois interests was . . . one of the major factors which led towards formal legal rationalisation (1954: 267).' No doubt, this alliance was neither calculated, nor intentionally co-operative; nevertheless it encouraged the spread of bureaucratic administrations that became foundations for rational law. Weber views that spread as providing unprecedented individual 'freedoms', but law's 'rigorously formalistic' character is also stifling, producing 'peculiar antinomies' (1994: 226). Such antinomies are canvassed in Weber's extended analysis of changing forms of contractual relations.

'Purposive Contracts' and New 'Juristic Personalities'

Weber's detailed analysis of the 'freedom of contract' and the 'juristic personality' outlines the various rights and freedoms of contract law from its early status to modern purposive types (1954: 98–191). Weber is here specifically concerned with the creation of new *rights* through modern contract law, and ponders the freedoms associated with a new 'freedom of contract'. Basically, for him, these freedoms do not yield unfettered liberty; at best, it is a freedom to choose one's own chains as defined by specific types of law. Modern, purposive contracts have enabled freedoms useful for market economies that champion a 'decentralisation of law-making processes' (1954: 189). Let us merely isolate selected elements of his complex discussion.

In terms that deliberately extend beyond modern precepts, Weber regards a contract as 'a voluntary agreement constituting the legal foundation of claims and obligations' (1954: 105). Understood thus, contracts exist in all societies, but 'the farther back we go in legal history, the less significant becomes contract as a device of acquisition . . . ' (1954: 105). Even so, he outlines key 'qualitative' differences in the ways that contracts operated in kin-based versus modern societies. For him, modern contract law emerges as markets and new forms of exchange develop outside the pre-modern household. Before modernity, legal rights were largely established within the context of inherited family position. The modern individual, by contrast, chooses (or not) to enter into contracts with other individuals, thereby unleashing clearly specified legal rights and duties.

Status contracts existed in limited areas (family transactions, inheritance) of societies based on clan and kinship, where the household made up the basic economic unit, and barter the basis of exchange. Transactions with other members were contingent upon one's standing in that household. When a legal person entered into a status contract, he or she underwent a complete (universal) change; i.e., changes in fraternal positions quite literally meant that 'the person would "become" something different in quality (or status) from the quality he possessed before' (Weber 1954: 106). Fraternal status contracts typically involved transactions to enable one clan member to become another member's child, father, mother, slave, and so on. In this sense, status contracts were involved in establishing specific relationships of 'fraternization'—the basic sphere of operation was the household. Collective responsibility, rather than individual liability, was key, and the whole community—via the elders—'enforced' contracts (mainly through ostracism or boycott). These status contracts were put into effect by appealing to magical or supernatural forces.

With the development of markets, commercial trading, and an emerging money economy, kinship relationships beyond the household were qualitatively transformed, as was the basic structure of contract. Fulfilling the new demands for predictability and stability occasioned by the growth of transactions in markets, **purposive contracts** emerged with a new **juristic personality** that became an abstract bearer of rights—one might here refer to the individual granted a new freedom to enter into specified contractual relations with others. With liability and responsibility now located in the 'individual', purposive contracts relied on specialized state justice systems for enforcement. Unlike status contracts, purposive contracts do not involve an all-inclusive change for contracting persons, or require fraternal obligations from contracting persons. They were instead driven by abstract, market-orientated exchanges (without reference to familial or blood oaths between members of a household), and actively sought to eradicate magic from law.

Here, Weber again evokes, through rational purposive contracts, his recurring theme: the rationalization of law is part of a more general rationalization of modern society. The new, abstract juridical subject is born; each subject appears equally before the law and is granted new freedoms and responsibilities. Does this mean that freedom overall in society has increased and, by contrast, coercion has decreased? Weber again is ambivalent: 'the increasing significance of freedom of contract' may suggest a 'relative reduction' of coercion, but this is only of direct benefit to 'those who are economically in the position to make use of the empowerments . . . ' (1954: 190). Rationally free contracts may have opened new horizons for 'individuals', but they closed off substantively orientated quests for social justice.

Social Action, Law, and Justice

Unlike Durkheim, and to a lesser extent Marx, Weber does not formulate an absolute conception of society as the basis of law and justice. Rather, as we have seen, his less totalizing vision of social action, comprising subjective meanings and objective behaviour, always emerges out of given relational contexts with others. Society is predicated on behaviour that, one way or another, takes meaningful account of others. These social relations comprise the basis of any social formation—there is no Durkheimian abstract society, nor a fixed economic reference point for the emergence of any given social order. Instead, it is the complex relations between people and, especially, power relations in various forms (e.g., legal, disciplinary, bureaucratic, legitimate domination, economic, political) that shape and order social forms. In that sense, any social form should not be considered as absolute, but a moving relational complex that arises from, and helps to define, a given historical moment.

This is why Weber understands law to be a specific type of social action in which behaviours are orientated by and towards meanings of 'law'. More precisely, he tells us that law is a power that orders and requires obedience; what differentiates it from other orders is the presence of a specialized staff who are trained and work specifically to enforce compliance with that order. From this relational conception of law, Weber clearly extends his analyses beyond, say, Llewellyn's call to analyze 'law as a craft'. He clearly considers any behaviour that is shaped by its understanding (meaning) of law as appropriately located within the sociology of law. In many ways, Weber's approach to law recalibrates discussions of the relationships between law and society, but he clearly situates law as a 'social action', and so as founded upon the society within which such actions are meaningful. Yet, he understands all this to be located in history and to generate contextual forms of socialization, power, authority, and domination—all of which frame the law.

But what of justice? Given Weber's commitment to a value-free sociology, one might argue that justice—as an ethical value—must remain outside of a sociology of law's remit. However, two qualifications are required. First, as we have seen, Weber argues that values do determine what sort of questions a sociologist wishes to ask, and justice may indeed propel what thereafter must be a fact-based analysis. Second, Weber's fact-based analyses can be directed at values like justice by exploring how it is used as a concept in given legal settings. As Kronman (1983: 95) points out, Weber's various analyses of substantive law describe different forms of law-making that aim 'either to promote distributive justice or to realise a particular conception of the good'. By contrast, his analysis of legal formalism describes patterns of law-making that aspire to create a legal system that operates like a 'technically rational machine', maximizing freedom to individuals and predictive stability. The point is not that substantive law relies exclusively on ethical values and legal formalism not. Rather what distinguishes the two systems is a basic difference in 'normative premises': 'the first seeking to realise some conception of the good scheme of distributive justice and the second a "relative maximum" of individual freedom' (Kronman, 1983: 95). The ambivalence we have detected throughout many of Weber's discussions of modernity may stem from his fascination with legal formalism, *contra* his commitment to substantive law.

Concluding Reflections

Weber's sociology, and its emphasis on ideal types of specific social actions, offers a far-reaching analysis of the way in which modern society has developed. In broad terms, he charts the development of a growing tendency towards instrumentally rational types of social action, where actors increasingly understand the meaning of their behaviours orientated towards others as a means to an end. As such actions expand, so the rationalization of society takes specific forms, including the growth of instrumentally rational administrative institutions (bureaucracy), types of legitimate political authority, as well as economic and legal structures. As we have seen, he defines law as a kind of order differentiated from other orders by the presence of a staff of people (a bureaucracy in our society) who are expressly there to compel compliance to the order. With that definition in mind, he distinguishes between various types of law on the basis of its formality and rationality, with modern law increasingly tending towards being formally rational in either empirical or logical ways. This overall scheme allows him to provide an understated, but original, account of contract (and other forms of) law that is framed through a particular sociological approach.

Discussion Questions

1. What is lost and what is gained when the enchantment of pre-modern forms of social action is supplanted by modern instrumentally rational action?

2. What do you think Weber meant by claiming that we are trapped in an 'iron cage' of reason that is of our own making?

3. Is modern Canadian law formally rational?

4. How would you understand Canada's use of restorative justice from a Weberian perspective?

5. Do ideal types of social action offer an appropriate way to study today's legal systems?

Suggested Readings

Freund, J. (1968). *The Sociology of Max Weber*. New York: Pantheon Books.

Kennedy, D. (2004). 'The Disenchantment of Logically Formal Legal Rationality, or Max Weber's Sociology in the Genealogy of the Contemporary Mode of Western Legal Thought'. *Hastings Law Journal*, 55, 1031–76.

Kronman, A.T. (1983). *Max Weber*. London: E. Arnold.

Runciman, W.G. (1972). *A Critique of Max Weber's Philosophy of Social Science*. Cambridge: Cambridge University Press.

Relevant Websites

http://plato.stanford.edu/entries/weber/
www.sociosite.net/topics/weber.php
www.faculty.rsu.edu/~felwell/Theorists/Weber/Whome.htm
www.marxists.org/reference/archive/weber/index.htm
www.busting-bureaucracy.com/excerpts/weber.htm

8 Critical Confrontations: Law, Race, Gender, and Class

Questions to Consider

- ⊛ In what ways does law perpetuate social inequities based on race, class, and gender?
- ⊛ Can law become a force for significant social change?
- ⊛ Does feminist jurisprudence offer a way to challenge the sexist biases of liberal law?
- ⊛ Can a legal system that has helped to entrench forms of racism effectively challenge those forms?

The year 1968 is sometimes described as a turning point for the 1960s countercultural milieu, with massive street protests in France and Mexico, as well as the rapid formation of various civil rights and peace movements in the US challenging discriminations within civil society (gender, race, sexual orientation), cultural elitism, political policy, and economic inequalities (class, race, gender). A **critical legal studies** movement arose out of that anti-establishment ethos, and specifically targeted the manner in which law replicated and contributed to established social patterns. Echoing legal realism's discontent with the legal status quo,[1] critical legal studies gained traction at a conference that in the spring of 1977 presented this formative statement:

> The central focus of the critical legal approach is to explore the manner in which legal doctrine and legal education and the practices of legal institutions work to buttress and support a pervasive system of oppressive, inegalitarian relations. Critical theory works to develop a radical alternative, and to explore and debate the role of law in the creation of social, economic and political relations that will advance human emancipation (in Fitzpatrick and Hunt 1987a: 1–2).

The ascendancy of critical legal studies inspired crucial debates that echoed internationally,[2] and the movement initially developed through several symposia.[3] Its critical impetus aligned with civil rights struggles and political movements seeking to redress class, race, and gender inequalities, and was linked to an emerging feminist jurisprudence and critical race theory (Kairys 1990). In general, critical legal approaches highlighted the conjunction of 'law' and 'society', examining how these concepts mutually sustained one another and focusing attention on the socio-political processes that generate particular forms of law. This chapter cannot comprehensively reflect the vibrant complexity of their contributions to legal thinking, but will only discuss selected critical themes. For heuristic purposes, one might usefully turn to the following sentencing hearing as an illustrative case for the discussion.

R. v. Kahpeaysewat

In *R. v. Kahpeaysewat*, [2006] SJ No. 587, Justice Huculak of the Saskatchewan Provincial Court argued for a conditional sentence in a 'domestic violence' case that ended tragically with the death of a man and a woman's conviction for manslaughter. A 'sentencing circle', comprising members of the Aboriginal community in which the events occurred, helped frame the judgment. While babysitting at her brother's apartment, the accused had been drinking when a man she had 'dated on and off' for three years appeared. Physical abuse contoured the couple's relationship, which, the judge notes, 'included hits, slaps, hair pulling and [in the words of the accused] "forcing himself on me". He made it clear a number of times that she was his property and said, "you are mine I'll take it [sex] anyway"' (27).

On the fateful evening, the victim had repeatedly 'attempted to engage in intimate physical contact despite her demands to be left alone' (3). He continued 'with this course of advances' and even physically restrained the accused, but she escaped and threw objects to encourage his departure. When this proved to be unsuccessful, she 'grabbed a knife that was sitting on the kitchen counter. She swung at [the victim] three times, with the second strike inflicting a mortal wound on the victim' (3). She then called for help.

The accused reported to police feeling 'frustrated and angry', having repeatedly 'told him to leave, get out, leave me alone, he just wouldn't listen' (4). She considered him to be a 'pervert' because of 'the way he wanted sex all the time, got sick of him too that way, constantly bugging me in that way' (13). In seeking an appropriate sentence, the judge noted the background of the accused as a 44-year-old 'Aboriginal female' with 'just short of' a Grade 11 education, with seven children (one 'apprehended by Social Services') and two grandchildren. The judgment paints a picture of an 'unstable' family life in which the accused was 'sexually, physically and emotionally abused throughout her life and recalls experiencing racism as a child' (20). Her 'tumultuous relationship with the victim was marked by heavy bouts of drinking', and her 'primary problem relates to her use of alcohol', which resulted in Social Services taking her children (22). She considered the relationship with the victim 'scary', as he used 'mind games' to frighten and control her. An expert witness declared, 'I am of the opinion that she was a battered woman', noting that 'she reported symptoms consistent with post-traumatic stress disorder, precipitated by the victim's behaviour during the relationship' (28). The victim too was described as the product of a 'very dysfunctional family', and by age twelve was raised in group homes. He too 'suffered physical and sexual abuse', and was 'exposed to solvents as a child' (31).

Justice Huculak quotes from *R. v. Gladue*, [1999] 1 SCR 688, accepting that special sentencing consideration should be given to Aboriginal offenders because of certain 'background factors' that 'figure prominently in the causation of crime by Aboriginal offenders':

> Years of dislocation and economic development have translated, for many aboriginal peoples, into low incomes, high unemployment, lack of opportunities and options, lack or irrelevance of education, substance abuse, loneliness, and community fragmentation. These and other factors contribute to a higher incidence of crime and incarceration (54).

Thus, when 'deciding whether the aboriginal offender should be incarcerated', judges should assess whether, 'the goals of restorative justice' should outweigh 'traditional objects of sentencing', including 'denunciation and deterrence' (54). In our case, Justice Huculak argues that 'socio-economic factors' and the 'tragic upbringing' of the accused must be taken into account: 'the murder of her child, racism, victimization, abuse, addictions, family dislocation, poverty, fragmentation, lack of education and employment, family dysfunction, and her shattered life all contributed in a major way to her criminal record' (59).

Consequently, she deems a conditional sentence to be appropriate for 'this individual' and concludes thus: 'The tragedy reminds us of the need to intervene early in cases of domestic violence and provide support and resources to the victim, as well as the perpetrator. The socio-economic and environmental backdrop to domestic violence must also be addressed which is beyond the scope of this court' (84). On that almost resigned note, let us turn more specifically to how critical legal studies might approach this tragic case.

Critical Legal Studies

Like legal realism, critical legal studies generated a sort of 'movement in law', characterized less by a unified approach than a common rejection of the formalities and effects of the legal establishment. But unlike legal realism, critical legal studies expressly cultivated radical, left-leaning ideas that criticized the law, and considered law's potential for radical social change. It openly obliged committed scholarship and rejected the possibility of value neutrality in the study of law (Trubek 1984). As Fitzpatrick and Hunt mused at the time,

> Critical legal studies seeks to provide an environment in which radical and committed scholarship can thrive in diversity with no aspiration to lay down a 'correct' theory or method. The element of cohesion is provided, in the first instance,

by a shared rejection of the dominant tradition of Anglo-American legal scholarship, the expository orthodoxy or, more crudely, the 'black-letter law' tradition (1987a: 1).

In this sense, they echoed the realists' skepticism of formalism, but argued further that mainstream legal thought simply perpetuates the inequalities of society by mystifying and softening existing hierarchies (Mensch 1990). So, *Kahpeaysewat* may reference class, race, and gender inequalities, but the decision itself does little to redress these. The explicit aim of critical legal studies was to shatter such myths and expose the inequalities. It wanted to show how mainstream perpetuates social hierarchies, even if unintentionally, and to **raise consciousness** (i.e., change people's attitudes) to initiate the elimination of these inequalities. The overall objective was to change law from within, and to use that altered system to change society. In contrast to legal realism, though, social science is not simply used in the service of an a priori law; rather, critical legal scholars sought a 'true science of law as a social phenomenon' (Tushnet 1991: 1533).

The left-leaning persuasions of the advocates of critical legal studies led many back to Marx. Most, however, as Gabel and Harris (1983) note, rejected the simple economic determinism of orthodox Marxism, arguing that consequential change could indeed be achieved through law, and that Marx and Engels's work on **alienation** could be developed beyond the economy: 'The nature of alienation is best described as the inability of people to achieve the genuine power and freedom that can only come from the sustained experience of authentic and egalitarian social connection' (Gabel and Harris 1983: 371).

Here, alienation was understood as a product of societies in which **hierarchy** is 'the dominant form of social organisation' (1983: 371) and where powerlessness perpetuates repression. The events of *Kahpeaysewat* might be viewed as the outcome of capitalist alienation, and the decision (even if sympathetic) as reproducing 'class, race and sex hierarchies' passed 'from generation to generation' (1983: 371). With its associated ideologies (and mindsets), alienation in law supports capitalist inequities (Kennedy 1997: 5, 18–20)—hence the call to eliminate it 'by demonstrating the falseness or incoherence of our dominant legal concepts' in order to 'change through an imaginative reconstruction of our social reality' (Trubek 1984: 610).

The conditional sentence imposed by *R. v. Kahpeaysewat* suggests the ambiguity of law as ideology. On the one hand, imposing a conditional sentence on an individual, however compassionate, does little substantively to challenge the alienating social hierarchies silhouetted behind the tragic events. On the other, the decision clearly recognizes the effects of class, gender, and race inequities, suggesting at least a potential to counter dominant ideologies and to engage a politics of law. Several critics draw on Gramsci (2001),

Althusser (2005), and Poulantzas (2000) to argue that politicizing law could form part of counter-hegemonic strategies that challenge dominant legal ideologies and the hierarchies they support (see Kairys 1990). The nuances of such discussions aside, Gramsci (2001) helps critical attempts to highlight how law secures the '**consent of the governed**' through coercion but also through subtle discursive practices, rituals, rules, and so on; both aim to shape the ideologies of subjects. When these work in concert, supporting one another, it is difficult for people to think outside of dominant ideologies. Gramsci uses the term **ideological hegemony** to describe this situation, and **counter-hegemony** as descriptor of attempts to challenge it. Regardless of whether it is described as consciousness-raising, counter-hegemony, or, more broadly, critique, critical legal studies tries to expose how legal ideologies perpetuate unequal social hierarchies:

> Our objective is to show the way that the legal system works at many different levels to shape popular consciousness toward accepting the political legitimacy of the status quo, and to outline the ways that lawyers can effectively resist these efforts in building a movement for fundamental social change . . . the very public and political character of the legal arena gives lawyers, acting together with clients and fellow legal workers, an important opportunity to reshape the way that people understand the existing social order and their place within it (Gabel and Harris 1983: 370).

Thus, the movement challenges existing legal practices in various ways. For example, Kennedy (1990) accentuates how legal training reproduces capitalist hierarchies and inequalities (see also Kennedy and Carrington 2004). As a law student, he (1971) focused attention on the 'politics of legal training', contentiously depicting law schools as acrid microcosms of wider inequities, re-enacted by instructors' relations ('overwhelmingly white, male, and middle class'; 1982: 605) with each other (e.g., fuelled by ambition, instrumental competition, prejudice) and students (e.g., modelling how they ought to act, think, and feel, backed by consequential evaluation). As well, law schools tend to alienate students from one another: 'Very few people can combine rivalry for grades, law review, clerkships, good summer jobs, with helping another member of their study group so effectively that he might actually pose a danger to them. You learn camaraderie and distrust at the same time' (1982: 606).

He also describes how women and people of colour confront blatant, or systemic, sexism and racism in law schools, often reflected in the cases they study. In *Kahpeaysewat*, for example, Kennedy (e.g., 1987) might point to the stereotypical formulations of Aboriginal people and alcohol, family dysfunction, etc., or to the superficial formulation of Aboriginal criminality. Even if meant to work in favour of a particular individual, such assertions reinforce presumptions and ideologies that fuel existing hierarchies.

Furthermore, a liberal paradigm held by most instructors plays out in curricula that present legal rules, practices, and legal reasoning as neutral phenomena. However, such claims are ideological ruses; they claim to be 'objective', 'neutral' statements of being when in so doing they actually take a stance in favour of the status quo (Kennedy 1983, 1985). As such, dominant liberal legal theories need to be exposed as 'nonsense': 'But all this is nonsense with a tilt; it is biased and motivated rather than random error. What it says is that it is natural, efficient, and fair for law firms, the bar as a whole, and the society the bar services to be organized in their actual patterns of hierarchy and domination' (1982: 591). He therefore proposes a new, utopian law school curriculum—one not dictated by liberal professional bar associations, but which would enable the law school to become 'a counter-hegemonic enclave' (1982: 614).

Liberal ideologies of law champion values like equality before an independent rule of law, judicial independence, individual freedom, and human rights (see Kennedy 1997). However, Gabel and Harris (1983: 372) insist that liberal law mystifies and perpetuates social injustices in various ways. First, it channels social conflict into individualizing public settings that claim legitimacy through specified rituals and authoritarian symbols; as in *Kahpeaysewat*, the matter is isolated as a 'case' and heard before a judge in a courtroom whose architecture evokes historical traditions and symbols of justice, elevating physically the judge from all others. Gabel and Harris describe 'this **spectacle of symbols**' as 'both frightening and perversely exciting. It signifies to people that those in power deserve to be there by virtue of their very majesty and vast learning' (1983: 372). As well, the tragic events of that fateful evening are reduced to an individual case, where the accused presents singly before the judge to stand trial as a responsible individual. In this way, culpability is individualized, and even if the judge recognizes the 'socio-economic and environmental backdrop to domestic violence', the **individualizing structure of the court** leads her to conclude that precipitating factors are 'beyond the scope of this court' (84). As such, the law deals with basic social problems as individual maladies, allowing social inequities to remain intact.

Secondly, the basic precept of law is to accept 'society' as it is—with all its inequities, injustices, and hierarchies—and then to portray itself as an impartial, and equally accessible, institution. As noted by Marx (and Weber), such 'formal equality' perpetuates the underlying inequities—as seen in *Kahpeaysewat*—by refusing to address them. For critical legal studies, as an ideology, law legitimizes unjust social structures by framing its role in abstracted, neutral ways. The judge in *Kahpeaysewat* might justify her decision on the strength of past cases, on the philosophy of punishment (whether the sentence should be based on restorative or retributive justice), and so on; however, the decision does little to spur transformative actions to attack the inequities acknowledged to be at the foundation of the tragic events (Kennedy 1973). Hutchinson and Monahan propose another view:

Law is not so much a rational enterprise as a vast exercise in rationalization. Legal doctrine can be manipulated to justify an almost infinite spectrum of possible outcomes. . . . Legal doctrine is nothing more than a sophisticated vocabulary and repertoire of manipulative techniques for categorizing, describing, organizing, and comparing; it is not a methodology for reaching substantive outcomes (Hutchinson and Monahan 1984: 206).

Several critical legal theorists also challenge the idea that law protects formal individual rights and freedoms in capitalist societies. While most recognize the value of calling upon legal rights to restrict arbitrary authority, many critics ponder whether law in capitalist societies could ever enforce these effectively (Kennedy 2002). Most consider rights to be contingent elements of political struggle—they do not guarantee social equity, the prevention of hunger or sickness, and so on. Gabel and Kennedy (1984: 33) thus see rights arguments as potentially useful in political struggles, but do not view them as ends in themselves. Moreover, so long as rights are framed in individual terms, the underlying structural injustices remain untouched: 'If we conceive of injustice as the intentional violation of the victim's rights by a defined individual, we lose sight of the structural injustices caused by racism, sexism and class oppression' (Boyle 1992: xli). *Kahpeaysewat*'s failure to address the societal structures that foreground the domestic violence of this case results in it treating the events as an isolated malady—such individualized reasoning, even when framed sympathetically, effectively perpetuates those structures.

What Is to Be Done?

. . . if the real enemy is us—*all* of us, the structures we carry around in our heads, the limits on our imagination—where can we even begin? (Gordon 1990: 424).

Critical legal theorists offer various ideas on what could be done to change fundamentally the way law operates in capitalist societies. The aim was to radically restructure law from within, to debunk its self-interested myths, and to start to use emerging forms of law to alter wider social hierarchies. Kennedy's work on legal education, for instance, calls for a radical upheaval within the Academy, changing the 'old guard' of teachers, radically revising curricula in favour of social justice, encouraging collegiality among students, and revising the structures of hierarchy within the law school, the bar, and beyond. In addition, Kennedy (1987) outlines how practising lawyers could subvert the hierarchies of corporate lawyering, resist its seductive lures, and treat clients equally and respectfully. He seeks to demystify the symbolic hierarchies of the state and its legal processes. In general, critical legal studies aims to reframe conflict and to engage a politics of law that actively transforms the socio-economic and political foundations of all conflict and harm (Gabel and Harris 1983: 376). As such, lawyers are urged to adopt not a 'rights-centred' approach to law, but a 'power-centred' one whose goal is to overthrow the ideologies of liberal legalism that perpetuate the structural hierarchies of accompanying capitalist social formations. Here the use of a radically transformed law could be enlisted to achieve bolder social changes.

In succinct terms, Hutchinson and Monahan frame the political aims of the movement thus:

> The distinctive feature of the CLS movement, therefore, is its desire to shatter the limiting conceptions of the possibilities of human association and of social transformation embodied in liberal legal thought. The CLSers' enterprise is to complete the modern rebellion against the view that social arrangements are natural or inevitable. They want to expose society as the vulgar and contingent product of interrupted fighting. Their central strategy is to suggest that social order exists only because, at some arbitrary point, the struggle between individuals was halted and truce lines were drawn up. These truce lines define the structure of a society's politics and production (1984: 216).

If the class struggle is one such 'truce line', gender and race reflect two others. The intersection of these complicates the entire discussion further, opening further questions about how these interact, and whether one remains, as for Marx, fundamental. For many feminist scholars, law's role in maintaining women 'in an inferior status' (Taub and Schneider 1990: 151) is crucial, while others see racism as contouring both gender (Crenshaw 1990) and class (Burns 1990).

Feminist Jurisprudence: Law's Patriarchy

> Thus humanity is male and man defines women not in herself but as relative to him; she is not regarded as an autonomous being . . . she is defined and differentiated with reference to man and not he to her; she is incidental. . . . He is Subject, He is the Absolute—she is the Other (de Beauvoir, 1983: 16).

Confirming de Beauvoir's claim, the history of jurisprudence is replete with theories by men, sharing an androcentric focus, and embracing methods that either sustain patriarchal power relations, or are unable to expose them. Feminist voices, though often subjugated, have nevertheless spoken up to expose the experiences of woman, and to vindicate the meanings often subjugated as other (see Sydie 1994). In particular, various feminist 'waves' have over the past century exposed the political, economic, social, cultural, and legal elements of male domination, and have actively exposed, resisted, and transformed many aspects of **patriarchy**—power structures that enforce the dominance of men over women (Davies 2008; Barnett 1998; Smart 1995: 162–85). The rise of **feminist jurisprudence** is commonly allied with wider liberal, socialist, radical, and more recent postmodern feminisms (see Davies 2008; Barnett 1998; Jaggar 1983), but could also be described as challenging key elements of law (Lacey 1998: 1–18). The present discussion is silhouetted against that diversely complex body of thinking, but focuses on selected aspects of feminist jurisprudence's attempt to expose law's patriarchy.[4]

Despite consequential differences, most feminist legal scholars emphasize the continuities between women's experience, formal theory, and everyday practice. Women experience patriarchy through overlapping attempts to understand, evaluate, and practically react to its structures. Thus legal positivism's (and Weber's) distinction between fact and value is rescinded—using **malecentric** methods to declare supposedly 'neutral' facts masks the patriarchal values embedded in legal theory (Scales 1986). Equally, however, natural law theories do not expose the patriarchal values embedded in Western culture and law. In efforts to change this, feminist jurisprudence emerged as a politically engaged endeavour designed to expose and anul the oppressions of patriarchal power in legal arenas. Broadly, it shares an agenda that aims, as Davies puts it, to achieve a tolerant 'social and political environment in which women and men of all ethnicities, class backgrounds, sexualities, and abilities are equally valued and empowered' (2008: 220).

How might one conceive of patriarchal relations and their effects within the context of law, understanding perhaps the 'gendering strategies' of the 'power of law' that subjugates women (Smart 1989)? By way of a brief introduction, I shall refer to *Kahpeaysewat* to discuss selected but influential ways in which feminist jurisprudence responds to this question.

Through its liberal formulations, feminist jurisprudence starts from the assumption of a universal standard of humanity—rational, autonomous individuals who equally confront the law, and who possess certain irrevocable rights. However, because of the perverting effects of patriarchy, with its sexist stereotypical prejudices, the promise of an equal, neutral law for all individuals is impossible. For **liberal feminists**, law tends to reference women as a group, rather than individuals, and so treats them differently from men (Fineman and Thomadsen, 1991). In the context of *Kahpeaysewat*, such theorists would certainly laud the judge for developing an individualized sentence that strives for equality and fairness (*contra* critical legal studies), but they are likely to be concerned by the seeming importance placed on the role of the accused as a mother whose children were removed from her (Fineman and Karpin 1995). If the accused were a man, would this issue have affected the decision? This approach seeks to expose how legal rights are not always equally granted to individuals. It tends to see 'sex' as a relatively stable biological given, but views 'gender' as a contingent socio-political and cultural matter that can be transformed. Liberal feminists thus champion legal reforms to ensure that all individuals, regardless of gender, are treated equally.

A **radical feminist** approach to the question of women and law focuses specifically on the nature of patriarchy, exposing (rather than trying to overcome) fundamental differences between men and women. Early radical writers like Firestone (1971) argued that men, by virtue of their biological makeup, are aggressive, controlling, and predator-like beings; they are marked by their differences from, not similarities with, women. A more socially orientated formulation is found in Catherine MacKinnon, whose work has profoundly influenced feminist jurisprudence. She (1987) blatantly rejects the equality versus difference arguments between liberals and early radical thinkers as futile, seeking a general theory of women's oppression. Against Marx, she argues that society's most basic oppression is patriarchy, and that the basis of women's domination lies in constructions of sex (male and female) and **sexuality** (sexual preferences; 1989, 1987). For her, the complex issue of sexuality and its role in reproducing society (not class or work) is the defining characteristic of our identities as human beings. However, that defining characteristic—sexuality—has been appropriated, warped, manipulated, and deformed by male interests and patriarchal power formations. Reworking elements of Marx, she (1983) argues that women have been alienated from that which is essential to being female (sexuality). The pervasiveness of male power alienates women from their essence, nurturing a false consciousness that leaves very little room for authentic self-understandings—there is 'no interior ground and few if any aspects of life free of male power' (1983: 638). In consequence, women's consciousness has been largely shaped by male power; their thoughts and actions most often serve male interests, as do prevalent, 'normal' images of sexuality and sexual identity.

MacKinnon's assessment of law is therefore direct: 'I propose that the state is male in the feminist sense. The law sees and treats women the way men see and treat women' (1983: 644). So, when law claims to be neutral, it most perniciously expresses gendered interests; when the state is 'most ruthlessly neutral, it will be most male; when it is most sex blind, it will be most blind to the sex of the standard being applied' (1983: 658). In other words, there is no neutral terrain in socio-political relations between men and women—they are all gendered, and this is especially evident in the context of law. In many ways, she sees a totalitarian gendered state in which law serves to exploit women and their sex/sexuality (hence her analyses of pornography). So effective and total is this exploitation that women have come to speak as the very subjects that patriarchy has constituted. In this sense, women's real nature is silenced; they have become a lack, a 'presence of absence'. And the key to the exploitation is the manner in which men, through patriarchal relations basic to all social relationships, control reproduction and sexuality.

Were MacKinnon to analyze *Kahpeaysewat*, she might highlight the abusive relationship between accused and victim as a reflection of more general patriarchal power relations. For example, 'Sexual violation symbolizes and actualizes women's subordinate social status to men. It is both an indication and a practice of inequality between the sexes, specifically of the low status of women relative to men. Availability for aggressive intimate intrusion and use at will for pleasure by another defines who one is socially taken to be and constitutes an index of social worth' (1991b: 1302).

The victim's reported demands for, and expectations of, sex without regard for the rejections of the accused illustrate the patriarchal control over sexuality MacKinnon alleges. More controversially amongst other feminists (e.g., Smart 1989: 76ff.), she takes this position further; to be a woman really means to be 'the end of the sexual pleasure of one more powerful'. This 'degraded status' identifies 'the female position': 'Sexual aggression by men against women is normalized. In traditional gender roles, male sexuality embodies the role of aggressor, female sexuality the role of victim, and some degree of force is romanticized as acceptable' (1991b: 1302). Therefore, for MacKinnon, *Kahpeaysewat* is not anomalous—it is yet another expression of ubiquitous patriarchal relations; the tragic reactions of the accused may be viewed as a form of recognizing and resisting a case of patriarchal exploitation seeking to control sex and sexuality at a local level.

MacKinnon might also argue that the judge does not entirely avoid the snares of patriarchy. For example, the judge's attempts to frame a neutral and abstract judgment actually affirm patriarchy by not emphasizing and challenging the victim's violent, forceful, and manipulative control of the accused person's sexuality, and by failing to recognize the intimate knowledge the accused possesses of the events. Furthermore, by not naming, exposing, and redressing the patriarchal structures that have produced both accused and victim, the judgment does little to overthrow those structures. While the individualized judgment captures the accused as a 'battered woman', allowing for some mitigation of sentence, it does little to redress the sexual inequalities that underlie the circumstances of this case. But more than this, MacKinnon might say, 'Much sex inequality is successfully accomplished in society without express legal enforcement and legitimation. Yet the law is deeply implicated in it. Law actively engages in sex inequality by apparently prohibiting abuses it largely permits, like rape, and by hiding the deprivations it imposes beneath ostensibly gender-neutral terms, like abortion' (1991b: 1300). In *Kahpeaysewat*, therefore, to repeat MacKinnon's claim above: 'The law sees and treats women the way men see and treat women' (1983: 644).

For MacKinnon, radical feminism faces a difficult task of exposing a deep-seated alienation and false consciousness born out of patriarchal power relations. However, it has to do so from within a context where there is very little left of what it is to be a woman in a 'pre-cultural' state; consequently, raising consciousness becomes a difficult prospect.[5] Even so, consciousness-raising must tap into woman's basic experience, and she calls for a sort of praxis-based theory that produces action from woman's experiences.[6] She argues that law is one of the various political contexts where patriarchy might be exposed and contested. For her, ' . . . we who work with law need to be about the business of articulating the theory of women's practice—women's resistance, visions, consciousness, injuries, notions of community, experience of inequality. . . . That is, I want to investigate how the realities of women's experience of sex inequality in the world have shaped some contours of sex discrimination in the law' (1991b: 14). In the context of *Kahpeaysewat*, this would require both lawyers and judges to be much more forthright in exposing the effects of patriarchy, in validating the experiences of women, and in directly challenging law's perpetuation of the sexually exploitative bases of women's oppression.

As influential as MacKinnon's work is, several feminists have challenged key aspects of her approach (e.g., Davies 2008, Butler 1999). Within the context of law, Carol Smart (1989) has contested her **essentialized** conception, which sees all women as necessarily sharing a common essence, and also the idea that patriarchy is so far-reaching and determining that it is difficult for anybody to evade. She calls for feminists to think outside of such strictures, and to think 'outside the confining concept of the natural/sexed woman' in order to 'deconstruct law's truth rather than unwittingly colluding with it' (1995: 87). Contributors to Naffine and Owens (1997) offer various analyses of the manner in which 'legal subjects' (e.g., the legal person) are 'sexed' in diverse legal contexts through various legal procedures. One might here consider the ways that accused and victim are conceptualized as sexed subjects in *Kahpeaysewat*. Butler's (1999) work also challenges approaches to sex and gender conceived in essential forms, envisaging **gender as a performance**; that is, gender, 'requires a performance that is repeated. This repetition is at once a reenactment and the reexperiencing of a set of meanings already socially established' (2004: 140). Embedded in this is her sense that fixing women's identity, as MacKinnon seems to require, would deny the never-fixed repetitions that create subject identities in the first place. As Butler puts it, the 'temporal paradox of the subject is such that, of necessity, we must lose the perspective of the subject already formed in order to account for our own becoming. "Becoming" is no simple or continuous affair, but an uneasy practice of repetition and its risks, compelled yet incomplete, wavering on the horizon of social being' (1997b: 30).

In this formulation, to which Part III will return, gender does not coalesce around a particular set of forms, but rather is continuously re-enacted around historically established meanings. The significance of placing the subject—man or woman—in history challenges the quest to find the 'essential' woman, and has prompted a 'post-identity politics of law' (see Danielsen and Engle 1995: xiii).

From another vantage, Smart agrees with MacKinnon's sense that law often silences alternative discourses for women; however, she rejects the faith that MacKinnon appears to have in law's transformative capabilities. By contrast, Smart sees law as 'far less powerful in transforming society to meet the various needs of all women' (1989: 81). As such, for Smart, law cannot be a vehicle for consequential social change—other struggles are more likely to achieve this. Why should that be? Smart's basic argument is as follows: 'In accepting law's terms in order to challenge law, feminism always concedes too much . . . by this I mean that it is important to think of non-legal strategies and to discourage resort to law as if it holds the key to unlock women's oppression' (1989: 5).

Thus, Smart has significant reservations about the very idea of a feminist jurisprudence because, 'In criticising law for being male it cannot escape the related criticism of promoting a (classless, white) female point of view as the solution. Neither can it escape idealising the law as a solution to women's oppression' (1995: 185). She refers to Foucault's conception of power—discussed in the next chapter—and its intricate relationships with knowledge to note how legal knowledge and practice disqualify other forms of knowledge, especially those that challenge its basic precepts (such as feminism). By privileging particular legal discourses, and legal rights, law disqualifies the experiences of women, disqualifies feminist knowledge, and assumes naturalistic formulations of gender and biological determinism (e.g., in *Kahpeaysewat* the expert testimony defines the accused as reflecting 'battered woman syndrome'). Although Smart emphasizes law as a form and system of knowledge, rather than rules, she calls for attempts to think about women outside of legal knowledge. Valverde (2006, 2003) develops this idea further, and challenges law's aspiration to universalize a system of knowledge. In such approaches one detects a rather more ambivalent engagement with law, rejecting calls to secure legal reform or validate rights, and pursuing a more broadly based political agenda to secure justice for women (see Brown and Halley 2002).

Agreeing with Smart's sense that feminist jurisprudence promotes 'a (classless, white) female point of view as the solution', Watson expressly challenges MacKinnon's appropriation of 'woman', arguing that her frame of reference centres on privileged white women, and excludes others. She speaks instead of a more fundamental Aboriginal law already known by women (1998: 36). For her, Western conceptions of womanhood, law, and patriarchy adopted by feminist analysis do not adequately address the plight of Aboriginal people, nor do they come close to understanding the depth of issues implied by *Kahpeaysewat* (see also Moreton-Robinson 2000). Razack (1991) too argues that feminist jurisprudence has tended to cloak 'women's experiences' in collective, scientific garb that effectively undermines the real experiences of minority women, allowing courts to privilege notions like the 'battered woman syndrome' over the articulations of the accused regarding her experience.

Similarly, various formulations of queer theory and activism challenge the implied essentialism that defines—in exclusive terms—experiences of womanhood as singular, often eclipsing the diversity of other voices (Davies 2008: 266ff.). From such precepts, Matsuda (1989) detects an emerging **outsider jurisprudence**, a 'jurisprudence for people of color', which seeks to revise history by trying to understand how race, and not only gender, is central to the subject of law. She also detects a new methodology that 're-jects presentist, androcentric, Eurocentric, and false-universalist descriptions of social phenomena' in efforts to describe law uniquely (1989: 2324). This emerging 'jurisprudence of outsiders' uses 'the experience of subordination to offer a phenomenology of race and law. The victims' experience reminds us that the harm of racist hate messages is a real harm, to real people. When the legal system offers no redress for that real harm, it perpetuates racism' (1989: 2380). This approach takes seriously that, 'We are a legalized culture. If law is where racism is, then law is where we must confront it' (1989: 2341). With this express call for an outsider jurisprudence, we can delay no further. How, in brief, has critical race theory emerged in jurisprudence, and influenced formulations of law and society?

Critical Race Theory

In efforts to revitalize what was perceived to be a stalled movement of civil rights struggles of the 1960s, **critical race theory** emerged to confront race and racism in legal contexts within the US and beyond (Delgado and Stefancic 2001: 4). It had various links with critical legal studies, but some scholars found limited support there and even report its tendency to alienate minorities (Delgado 1995). While endorsing critical legal studies' overall critique of law as a neutral set of rules, and its view of law as a political activity that subjugates and excludes, early critical race theorists challenged its unrefined tendency to 'trash' elements of the legal system for no apparent reason. They saw this sort of 'deconstruction' as failing to formulate how better societies could be reconstructed; in some cases the challenged element, if removed, would leave people of colour with even fewer options, eliminating potentially useful weapons in the struggle to overcome racial oppression (Delgado 1995).

Although a diverse constellation of approaches and ideas, critical race theory has tended to present: ' . . . racism not as isolated instances of conscious bigoted decision making or prejudiced practice, but as larger, systemic, structural, and cultural, as deeply psychological and socially ingrained' (Matsuda et al. 1993: 5).

Delgado and Stefancic (2001: 6–9) and Matsuda et al. (1993) identify several key themes as hallmarks of the field, addressed by many theorists. For instance, most agree that racism is intractably endemic to Western life—it is not unusual but omniscient. Thus it is not surprising that law is never colour-blind, neutral, or objective, and is key to struggles that generate, manipulate, and use various conceptions of race for different political ends. As such, critical race theory emphasizes the need to develop sophisticated historical analyses of law to render explicit its long-standing role in perpetuating racism. Critical race theory may, in many cases, use deconstructive methods to expose such racism, but it also explicitly claims to offer reconstructions and the prospect of a differently ordered society without racial, or indeed other, forms of oppression. In addition, critical race theory takes the experiences and the experiential knowledge of people of colour as the foundation of its knowledge—a posture that it seeks to embed in all law and society analyses. But it is important to note that while race as a construct is developed in history, and so is never fixed, its consequences are profound and tenaciously enduring (see Davies 2008: 326ff.). Race is a category of thinking invented, manipulated, exploited, and sometimes discarded when no longer required (Andersen 2005). And law is often involved in such presentations of race. Necessarily, this implies an interdisciplinary approach that works through methodologies to capture and enunciate diverse experiential knowledge; from here critical race theory engages with law as an instrument to expunge oppression from society, recognizing law's pervasive attachments to various historical forms of racism.

Such critical race theory themes have much to offer for cases like *Kahpeaysewat* (see Aylward 1999). Some liberal theorists might take the decision, with its overtures towards Aboriginal conditions, as indicative of Canada's racial and cultural tolerance, perhaps its multicultural ethos. However, as Aylward notes (1999: 42ff.), this is a dangerous myth and overlooks **racial subjections** that: sideline Aboriginal voices (except when quoted in snippets by experts or in police reports); take the sentencing circles' decisions as advisory rather than mandatory; privilege abstracted judicial rules, rather than Aboriginal frameworks of law (e.g., Napoleon and Overtall 2007, Andersen 2005); elevate specialist knowledge (psychology, criminology, judicial process, etc.) over Aboriginal experiential knowledge; acknowledge limited racism in passing as a factor in describing the accused person's background; perpetuate stereotypes (alcohol, family dysfunction are imperially imputed to Aboriginal criminality); and so on. Even a thoughtful and sympathetic decision (such as *Kahpeaysewat* surely is) does not escape the ubiquitous racialized structures that contour both Canadian law and society (Hogeveen 2010). Hence, critical race theorists like Aylward tackle myths that create racism, and seek to deconstruct 'legal rules and reconstruction of principles and policies from a critical race perspective' (1999: 49). Specifically, she calls on practitioners to 'ask "race" questions in all areas of legal practice . . . and to identify the oppressions which can be overcome through law . . . we should not ask why "race" is an issue, but rather why "race" is *not* an issue' (1999: 191).

But through what methodology might critical race theory approach law not as an inherent good, but as a 'tool of necessity' in struggles to rescind oppression? Here one senses again the unease that some critical race theorists have in engaging the law. Simply put, there are paradoxes in using an institution that often perpetuates racism to fight racism (Matsuda et al. 1989). At the same time, most recognize that we are historically situated beings who must make use of whatever is available; it is thus crucial to be aware of the potential contradictions and to develop effective *political* engagements with law (Andersen 2005). The strategic point here is not simply to spurn law, as is sometimes seen to be the case with certain 'postmodern' approaches; it is to use it as a weapon for social change. And to do that, clarity of thought and experience is key—this is why critical race theory has developed around **narrative**, storytelling methodologies designed to expose the subtle processes, effects, and mechanics of racism, and to use these as the basis of strategies to overcome racism. Patricia Williams (1991, 1988) and Derrick Bell (2004, 2000) are perhaps exemplary in this regard, and, though they are merely referenced here, one would be remiss not to urge a reading of their insightful narratives. Here one finds an outstanding example of **law and literature** approaches, graphically showing how lived experiences expose the complexities of race and law. Such storytelling names—in concepts, voices, and registers not often heard— the ways by which a subject's conceptions of self and others emerges out of structural intersections between socially generated and historically specific categories of race, class, gender, sexual orientation, and ethnicity. It is perhaps for this reason that Delgado and Stefancic (2001: 55) refer to **intersectional individuals**, people with diverse experiences and perspectives, recognizing the value of literature and lived cultures in a search to overcome exclusionary oppressions, and to respectfully value all facets of human life.

Concluding Reflections

With this general outline of critical race theory, feminist jurisprudence, and critical legal studies, we have glimpsed a shift away from strict jurisprudence or sociology to questions of, and engagements with, law and society as ways to confront justice, exclusion, and oppression. Despite repeated references to law and society, one senses a growing recognition that both are historically located relational practices with integral ties. They are not absolute, totalizing entities that exist a priori; instead, both are contingent processes that can be transformed through effective political struggle and social movement. In other words, with the approaches of this chapter, the law-society couplet is increasingly fused, erasing distinctions between the two concepts and embracing their dynamic, contingent expressions. The transient dynamism yields historical concepts of law and society as mutually constituted entities, reciprocally reflecting the inequities and hierarchies of the day. Consequently, in such theories, neither law nor society can be posited as fixed identities, leaving socio-legal studies with a somewhat destabilized point of reference. The various frameworks to be canvassed in the final part of this book take this dynamic instability as a given, working with nominal conceptions of 'law' and 'society' as predicates of underlying political processes without fixed, inherently stable, or essential forms of being. The explosive effects of that shift may have surfaced in the field, but the outcomes are still very much undecided. This leads us to the final part of the book, which explores various approaches that do not try to understand society through law, or law through society, but explicitly focus on the perpetual *becoming* of both law and society.

Discussion Questions

1. How can law challenge the hierarchies and alienation of modern society when it is central to securing that sort of society?

2. Is consciousness-raising an effective way to challenge the ideological hegemony of liberal ideas that contour most Canadian legal structures?

3. Do law schools perpetuate inequities of race, class, and gender?

4. What examples can you think of where law has brought about positive changes for women? What does this say about Smart's critique of feminist jurisprudence?

5. Are the seemingly basic categories of sex (male and female) and gender (men and women) merely social creations born out of specific histories?

6. What role does law play in perpetuating social hierarchies based on race? How might this be changed?

Suggested Readings

Delgado, R., & Stefancic, J. (2001). *Critical Race Theory: An Introduction*. New York: New York University Press.

Hutchinson, A.C. (ed.) (1989). *Critical Legal Studies*. Totowa: Rowman & Littlefield.

Kairys, D. (ed.) (1990). *The Politics of Law: A Progressive Critique*. New York: Pantheon Books.

Smart, C. (1995). *Law, Crime and Sexuality: Essays in Feminism*. London: Sage Publications.

Tushnet, M. (1991). 'Critical Legal Studies: A Political History'. *Yale Law Journal*, 100, 1515–44.

Relevant Websites

http://topics.law.cornell.edu/wex/Critical_legal_theory
http://cyber.law.harvard.edu/bridge/CriticalTheory/critical2.htm
http://plato.stanford.edu/entries/feminism-law/

http://duncankennedy.net/home.html
www.utm.edu/research/iep/j/jurisfem.htm
www.pages.drexel.edu/~jp49/

PART III

Promising Justice: The *Becoming* of Law and Society

9 | Michel Foucault: The Power of Law and Society

Questions to Consider

- Do power relations create historical concepts of society, law, justice, knowledge, state, and even individual subjects?
- Is power simply a constraining, repressive force, or can it be seen as a creative and productive set of relations?
- Is a sovereign-law model of power, based on spectacular shows of force, now less significant than modern discipline and powers that 'manage' populations?
- What happens to law and state in contexts where sovereign models of power are surpassed by other, more locally exercised, powers?

I start from the theoretical and methodological decision that consists in saying: Let's suppose that universals do not exist. And then I put the question to history and historians: How can you write history if you do not accept *a priori* the existence of things like the state, society, the sovereign, and subjects? (Foucault 2009: 3).

In the above quotation, Foucault borrows heavily from what Nietzsche referred to as a focus on **becoming** rather than **being**: 'one must admit nothing that has being—because then Becoming would lose its value and actually appear meaningless and superfluous. Consequently one must ask how the illusion of being could have arisen . . . ; likewise: how all value judgements that rest on the hypothesis that there are beings are disvalued' (Nietzsche 1967: 708).

Although not often explicitly referenced, this theme provides a point of departure for most of the approaches in Parts I and II. The shift is subtle though consequential: no longer do these approaches assume the *being* of something (e.g., law, society) as a focal point. Instead, they are united by their attempts to theorize the *becoming*, emergence, and consequences of particular forms of law and society.

Nietzsche's emphasis on power as the shaper of this becoming is echoed by the work of Michel Foucault (1926–84), the focus of the present chapter. *Discipline and Punish*, for example, opens by detailing the gruesome fate of Robert-François Damiens, whose unsuccessful assassination attempt on Louis XV led him on 2 March 1757 to a public execution. By describing this event, Foucault highlights how power is always exercised, and rendered explicable, within a given context, and how it shapes historical forms of existence (i.e., is centrally involved in their 'becoming'). Spectators at this excruciating ritual might have witnessed the red hot pincers tearing away at the regicide's flesh, hot oils poured into his wounds, sulphur eating away his hand, a quartered and broken body—kissing a crucifix and asking for God's pardon—unceremoniously dumped onto searing flames.

In a slightly less vicious fashion, Mary London (née Osborne) and George Nemiers too met their end at a public spectacle on 17 August 1801 in Niagara-on-the-Lake, Upper Canada (Fraser 1992: 316–19). Mary was the first woman to be executed in the settlement after being convicted of murdering her husband, Bartholomew London, one of the early settlers in the region. Both originally from Pennsylvania, the older London married the younger Mary, a 28-year-old widow. Not long after, a George Nemiers, with whom Mary was previously acquainted, joined them as a farm hand. They become lovers, and quarrels surfaced, one ending with Nemiers fracturing Bartholomew's skull with a shoe-hammer. The lovers eventually murdered the older man by poisoning his whisky. After their trial, with witnesses and the expert testimony of a doctor (who declared poison as the cause of death), a petit jury returned a guilty verdict; the judge pronounced that on the morning of 17 August 1801, both Osborne and Nemiers were to be publicly hanged, 'until they be dead, dead, and afterwards the bodies to be dissected' by 'medical men' (Fraser 1992: 317). The actual execution attracted a large crowd of spectators who saw the bridled pair walk to appointed spots on the scaffold, and, with nooses around their necks, trap doors launched them into 'eternity'. Sylvester Tiffany, the founding editor of the *Niagara Herald*, reflected on the event, not with horror, but by pointing to its moral message: 'Visible in the whole of this business, [is] the hand of Providence pursuing with vengeance offenders even in this life; for in it we see punished adultery, disregard of marriage vows, and murder: and to those who indulge themselves in the two former, it may be a lesson of instruction, that from them to the last is but a step' (in Fraser 1992: 318–19).

Tiffany's statement is revealing, for it suggests the taken-for-granted quality of public executions at that time. However, echoing Foucault (1995), one could also take note of the simultaneously emerging use of prisons as punishment. Scarcely 34 years later, in 1835, a hugely expensive penitentiary was erected in Kingston, based on principles of 'security, economy and reformation'. As an instrument for corrective punishment, 'the arrangement of cells was ingeniously devised to facilitate surveillance of the prisoners prone on their beds' (Hennessy 1999: 14–15). Reminiscent of Weber's bureaucracies, the duties of each agent of the prison (wardens, keepers, physicians, chaplain, etc.) were specified and governed by regulation, discipline, and regimentation. The convicts were to be 'constantly employed at hard labour', 'must not exchange a word with one another under any pretence whatsoever nor communicate with one another nor with anyone else by writing', 'are not to gaze at visitors', and 'must not carelessly or wilfully injure their work', and so on (Hennessy 1999: 21).

Rather than describing the shift from public spectacles to reform-minded prisons as introducing humane, or enlightened, forms of punishment, Foucault understands the change as signalling the rise of new 'political technologies', and the emergence of a new type of power (discipline) in modern society. For him, spectacular punishments (like public executions) surfaced in medieval contexts, where scattered and smaller populations could—given the political resources of the day—only be subjected to sovereign power in limited bursts; the public spectacle provided an important way to demonstrate the sovereign's strength. But with burgeoning, more concentrated populations in cities, and the emergence of capitalist industrialism, spectacular punishments lost their efficacy (even at times enabling disturbances and riots). In such an ethos, Foucault argues, technologies appeared (e.g., the 'disciplinary' techniques of the penitentiary) that worked by carefully shaping individual subjects and collective bodies (societies), or by managing broad 'populations'. With this case in mind, let us first examine the overall approach before focusing on his sense of law, society, and justice.

A Nietzschean Debt

Commonly, jurisprudential and socio-legal analysts tend to view Foucault as a **postmodern** theorist, as someone who writes outside the tropes usually associated with the modern, or modernity (e.g., Litowitz 1997; Wacks 2006, 2005). I shall not emulate that tendency here, for, as Foucault notes, 'rather than seeking to distinguish the "modern era" from the "pre-modern" or "postmodern", I think it would be more useful to try to find out how the attitude of modernity, ever since its formation, has found itself struggling with attitudes of "countermodernity"' (Foucault 1997: 309–10). Nietzsche's 'madman', who stands before a gathering and 'pierces them with his eyes', illustrates an important modern outlook: '"Where is God?" he cried; "I'll tell you! *We have killed him*—you and I! We are all accused murderers . . . how can we console ourselves, the murderers of all murderers? . . . there was never a greater deed"' (2001: 119–20).

The point is this: where once mythical symbols, religion, and the sacred provided a customary world view, the 'death of God' institutes a new cosmos without transcendental foundations for authority, or meaning. If Nietzsche's madman wanders through churches singing '*requiem aeternam deo*' (grant God eternal rest), Foucault analyzes a society without religious foundation that 'permits profanation without object, a profanation that is empty and turned inward upon itself and whose instruments are brought to bear on nothing but each other' (1977: 30).

This creates a distinctively **modern attitude** that, on the one hand, seeks order and constraint; on the other, it simultaneously pursues ongoing **rupture** and **transgression**. The limit-break, constraint-rupture couplets reflect an ethos without overarching, transcendent certainties, caught between a fascination with its present limits and the unthought, forever leaning out towards impossible, unimaginable, futures. Nothing remains stable: the subject, the object, or indeed the putatively universal patterns of representation that colonize current 'grids of intelligibility'. Everything is located within history, an insight that has escaped conventional history with its quest for ahistorical truth, and its tendency to reduce complex phenomena (e.g., the First World War) to a search for **origins** (e.g., the assassination of the archduke in Sarajevo). By contrast, Nietzsche's **genealogical approach**—like a family tree—becomes more complex, ramified, and detailed as it pursues a phenomenon's multiple 'lines of descent', and the 'emergence' of power relations—the 'lowly beginnings'—that create it (Foucault 1977: 139ff.). Nietzsche's genealogy thus differs from even the most critical of histories of his day, overturning at least three assumptions: 'the veneration of monuments becomes parody'; 'the respect for ancient continuities becomes systematic dissociation'; and, instead of using 'truths' held by subjects living in a present to judge the past, he championed 'the destruction of the subject who seeks knowledge' and who is driven by a never-ending 'will to power' and knowledge (1977: 164).

Working with such Nietzschean ideas, Foucault—as we shall see—emphasizes the role of power and knowledge. Yet he provides neither a theory *nor* methodology of power, opting instead for what he calls an '**analytics**' that charts how power is exercised in local contexts (1978: 82); the point is not to 'represent' power in the abstract, but to name and confront existing power relations. He does not pursue a 'history of the past in terms of the present', but seeks a detailed 'history of the present' (1995: 31). In short, his genealogical analysis maps the lines of descent and emergence of **power-knowledge** relations that have constructed our present limits, and he does so as a 'preface' to their transgression (1977: 29). Let us examine this seemingly cryptic approach in more detail.

Power-Knowledge Insurrections

Foucault focuses on how power, knowledge, and subjects intermingle to create social forms, law, given truths, and so on. As such, for him, there is no truth outside of the social contexts that power creates. So, against those who claim to provide universal truths, he says:

> We should admit rather that power produces knowledge . . . that power and knowledge directly imply one another; that there is no power relation without the correlative constitution of a field of knowledge, nor any knowledge that does not

presuppose and constitute at the same time power relations . . . the subject who knows, the objects to be known and the modalities of knowledge must be regarded as so many effects of these fundamental implications of power-knowledge and their historical transformations (1995: 27–8).

Truth, the subjects authorized to espouse it, and the objects of such espousals are all fashioned by '**regimes of truth**' and associated **power-knowledge relations**. As such, individuals do not exist as primordial, a priori entities: 'individuals are the vehicles of power, not its points of application . . . the individual is not to be conceived as a sort of elementary nucleus, a primitive atom' (1980: 98). The individual, then, is one of the 'prime effects' of power, as well as 'the element of its articulation'; that is, 'the individual which power has constituted is at the same time its vehicle' (1980: 98). If this challenges liberal concepts of individuality, Foucault also contests Marxist notions of ideology on the grounds that an ideology is always contrasted with something 'supposed to count as truth' (1980: 118). Since Foucault—echoing Nietzschean uncertainty—regards truth as always 'a thing of this world', the notion of ideology loses traction. Societies develop 'regimes of truth', a politics that differentiates between true and false statements, and authorizes which 'techniques and procedures' and people may enunciate the truth (1980: 131).

Nowadays, scientific methods and scientists are often accorded a privileged ability to declare truth, just as elders and oracular rituals might have once served a similar function. But what of Foucault's own claims? On this matter, he is clear: his own claims to truth emerge from and circulate in current 'regimes of truth'. However, he explicitly engages that truth regime to 'problematize' the limits of, and possibly transgress, dominant political formations. Just as knowledge may support a given power structure, so too can an '**insurrection of subjugated knowledges**' (1980: 81), or knowledge that has been disqualified by an existing hierarchy of truth, rise up against it. His work may even be regarded as akin to 'fiction', that can only function as 'truth' in different power-knowledge formations (2007a). And precisely when it achieves that status, no matter how partial, the moment has arrived to rejuvenate a modern **limit attitude,** and to seek ways to open out to new ways of considering and doing things (see 1997: 303ff.).

In short, Foucault champions a genealogical form of **critique**[1] whose aim is not to deduce what can be known from our current historical truths, or the limits beyond which we cannot go; rather, 'it will separate out, from the contingency that has made us what we are, the possibility of no longer being, doing, or thinking what we are, do, or think'. (1997: 316). Its mantra is not so much how to be, but 'how not to be governed thus' (1997; see also Pavlich 2000). Such critique does not attempt to universalize (or make absolute) current historical ways of being as necessary or natural; nor does it judge being against purportedly ahistorical criteria enunciated by a given context. His more politically orientated problem concerns the possibility of 'constituting a new politics of truth' by changing 'the political, economic, institutional regime of the production of truth' (1980: 133). Of course, he does not mean a willy-nilly rejection of every limit; rather he seeks to expose those limits that, in our historical contingency, can be defined as oppressive, unjust, unfair—a challenge mostly mounted from disqualified, local knowledges.

However, what exactly does Foucault mean by the concept of power? Perhaps we might respond by referring to Nietzsche's (1967) well-known concept of a **will to power**, a 'creative drive' of all living organisms. For Nietzsche, this will to power

> can manifest itself only against resistances; therefore it seeks that which resists it—this is the primeval tendency of the protoplasm when it extends its pseudopodia and feels about. Appropriation and assimilation are above all a desire to overwhelm, performing, shaping and reshaping, until at length that which has been overwhelmed has entirely gone over into the power domain of the aggressor and increased with the same (1967: 619).

It is a paradoxical 'instinct for freedom' that produces historically conditioned patterns of existence; however, for our purposes, it includes the ways in which human beings are constituted as modern political and legal subjects (Pavlich 2010, 2009b). Nietzsche influenced Foucault's approach to power, but Foucault framed his formulation along these lines: 'Power is not a substance. Neither is it a mysterious property whose origin must be delved into. Power is only a certain type of relations between individuals. . . . There is no power without potential refusal and revolt' (Foucault 2000: 324).

This conception of power contrasts with conventional views of power as all-constraining, as possessed by powerful agents, and exercised in a restraining, asymmetrical fashion, from the top down. Against many of the theorists previously discussed, and particularly Hobbes and Marx, Foucault (1978: 94) rejects the idea that power can be conceived as *necessarily* the property of a dominant class, state, sovereign, or even individual person. Rather, he views power **nominally**; that is, as a name analysts might give to all the techniques (micro and macro), tactics, and instruments that contour and shape relations between historically fashioned subjects—the actions directed to structuring the action of another subject. For him, the key question is therefore not 'what is power?' or 'where does it come from?' Rather, he focuses on questions like 'how (i.e., by what means) is this power exercised in context?' and 'what are the effects of such an exercise of power?' (2000: 336–8). Thus, power cannot be abstracted from historical context; it is a specific sort of relation premised on the 'possibility of action on the actions of others that is coextensive with every social relationship' (2000: 345). In other words, he focused on the instruments by which power is contextually exercised—rather than some abstracted essence of power. If anything, it appears through unique sorts of relation not directed at others, but on actions: 'an action upon an action on possible or actual future or present actions' (2000: 340). By shaping action, power produces ways of becoming and being— it is not simply a mechanism of constraint.

Furthermore, 'the other' whose actions are acted upon must always be 'recognized and maintained' for power relationships to survive. So while, say, a relationship of violence tries to break down or destroy possibilities for action, power—like Nietzsche's organism—requires **resistance**. Freedom, refusal, and recalcitrance are thus intrinsic to power relationships, which may be characterized as a 'mutual incitement and struggle; less of a face-to-face confrontation that paralyzes both sides than a permanent provocation' (2000: 342). If a subject's capacity for resistance is removed, as with Bartholomew London's poisoning, there is no power relation—violence perhaps, but not power. To be sure, power relations would have contoured all the actions and decisions that led Mary and Nemiers to murder, but—for Foucault—at the moment the older London's ability to resist was removed, power ceased. In this sense, power relationships require a permanent capacity for subjects to act: 'where there is power, there is resistance, and yet, or rather consequently, this resistance is never in a position of exteriority in relation to power . . . ' (1978: 95). The very existence of power relationships, therefore, depends on multiple points of resistance. As well, power relations are imminent in—and shape—other relations (economic, social, knowledge, sexuality, and so on).

Consequently, power should not be seen, as is often the case in political theory, solely in terms of the sovereign state: 'I don't want to say that the State isn't important; what I want to say is that relations of power, and hence the analysis that must be made of them, necessarily extend beyond the limits of the State' (1980: 122). So, even if power is coterminous with many other relations in society, one needs to understand it beyond presently dominant institutional and discursive frameworks. With these orientating remarks, let us turn specifically to Foucault's conception of law and society.

Reading Foucault on Law

Wickham notes that 'when describing Foucault's treatment of law, we largely find ourselves raking through the fallen leaves of his work and picking up a hint here and a suggestion there. . . . Foucault simply did not say enough directly about law and its role to allow more than this. At very least it is a fertile ground for argument' (2002: 265). To be sure, as Golder and Fitzpatrick's (2009) succinct canvassing of this fertile ground indicates, there is much value in returning to Foucault's various statements of law and their implications for jurisprudence/socio-legal studies. Let us, therefore, even if briefly, allude to Foucault's sense of law, especially as it appears in relation to his work on discipline, and later biopower and governmentality.

Law and Discipline

> In Western societies since the Middle Ages, the exercise of power has always been formulated in terms of law. . . . In political thought and analysis, we have not cut off the head of the King (1978: 87–9).

Foucault's classic *Discipline and Punish* analyzes the 'birth of the prison' in France as an instance of a 'new' **disciplinary mechanism of power** in modern societies. He considers discipline—in polemically strong terms—to be 'absolutely incompatible with relations of sovereignty' (1995: 35), and an 'exact, point-for-point opposite of the mechanics of power that the theory of sovereignty described or tried to transcribe' (1995: 36). If medieval law was often codified in rigid statutes, it was also authorized by a central sovereign authority and exercised over abstract legal persons, and transgressions were punished in spectacular ways (e.g., to reinforce the sovereign's strength). By contrast, a new modern **disciplinary power** operated very differently. Functioning through variable and changing (statistical) norms rather than laws, discipline spreads itself across a social network in a highly ramified, decentralized fashion (schools, prisons, hospitals, factories, etc.) and is most efficient when its operations are invisible (e.g., subjects consider themselves to be choosing freely when the range of choices are narrowly circumscribed in advance). Furthermore, discipline targets, and thereby fabricates, living (i.e., not abstract), normal 'individuals' who also become the vehicles of its exercise; any 'abnormal' forms of individuality are targeted for correction, or rehabilitation, through subtle, indirect, and judgmental micro-practices.

Foucault (1995: 170–94) suggests that the medical examination in a doctor's rooms provides an exemplar for these disciplinary techniques. As one steps into such rooms, a facet of one's body is presented for the doctor's scrutiny, in turn informed by one or other disciplinary knowledge (medicine, anatomy, etc.). Such disciplines specify how to examine, and what diagnosis might be appropriate in particular circumstances. The doctor decides whether what is presented should be considered normal or not, and this assessment is used to prescribe a treatment (or not), all of which is recorded in detailed patient notes. In Foucault's view, this medical situation highlights several key 'instruments' of discipline that are found more generally: **hierarchical observation** (a 'docile' body is rendered 'visible' to the gaze of disciplinary apparatuses); **normalizing judgment** (directed to a mass of behaviours that 'the laws had left empty' in which court-like, but now normalizing, judgments aim to create standardized individuals (1995: 178)); and **the examination** (a composite of the previous two instruments that uses science to help shape and create normal individuals).

To elaborate further, Foucault refers to Bentham's **panopticon** as an exemplary technique of discipline. Bentham's blueprint for an efficient, rationalized penitentiary is well known, and has inspired the design of many prisons, including the Kingston penitentiary previously noted. The basic idea behind the panoptic architectural plans is this: a central tower overlooks radiating, backlit cells; the lighting allows guards in the tower to see prisoners in the cells at all times, but the guards are invisible to the prisoners. Here, Foucault argues, 'Bentham laid down the principle that power should be visible and unverifiable . . . the inmate must never know whether he is being looked at in any moment; but he must be sure that he may always be so'. Its major effect was, 'to induce in the inmate a state of consciousness and permanent visibility that assures the automatic functioning of power' (1995: 201). This principle of power, for him, is evident in earlier plague regulations developed by the army and prison regimes, and has become a dominating element of the '**carceral**' (prison-like) forms of modern society. In short, discipline has escaped the prison walls and is now a generalized feature of most aspects of modern existence. Its apparently **perpetual gaze** nurtures constant self-surveillance among subjects, who become complicit in the production of themselves as 'normal individuals', enjoying the pleasures and pains of judgment. All of these—pleasure, pain, individuals, disciplinary surveillance, the science of penology, normality, etc.—are products of this new power.

Now where does law fit into all of this? Golder and Fitzpatrick (2009) nicely capture the debate that Foucault's early sense of law and discipline has generated. In brief, the basic critique is that Foucault 'failed to appreciate the importance of the law in modernity and indeed expelled it from his analyses of contemporary power relations' (Golder and Fitzpatrick 2009: 12). However, three versions of this critique have surfaced. First, Hunt and Wickham (1994)[2] argue that Foucault prematurely 'expels' law from his analyses. They applaud his attempt to understand power beyond 'law and sovereignty' (see Pavlich 2010), because it allows us to identify new political technologies, e.g., discipline (1995, 2004), biopower (2004, 2009), and governmentality (2007a, 2007b, 2000).[3] While Hobbes's theory sufficiently reflects the power relations of his day, it missed the full spectrum of unfolding *modern* power relations. Therefore, Foucault calls on us to 'abandon the juridical model of sovereignty' (2003: 265) when studying modern power relations, and 'to study power outside the model of the *Leviathan*, outside the field delineated by juridical sovereignty and the institution of the state' (2004: 34).

Here, Hunt and Wickham (1994) detect a problem: Foucault unnecessarily de-emphasizes law's place in modern regulation. They argue that his expulsion of law from this analysis is seriously flawed because it fails to recognize the rising—not diminishing—importance of law for modernity. Hunt elsewhere emphasizes the point: 'Law has become a primary agency of the advance of new modalities of power and provides one of the distinctive methods of operation of the new technologies of power' (1992: 37). Both he and Wickham (2002: 265) also challenge Foucault's sense of law and sovereignty as a constraining and 'mainly negative power' against the productive capacities of discipline. Consequently, they want to 'retrieve' law in Foucault's work, and to recover its profound, and continuing, relevance to contemporary life. Both also see great potential for such a retrieval in Foucault's later treatment of governmentality and law (Wickham 2002; Hunt 1992).

Rose and Valverde (1998), Valverde (2003), and Smart (1989, 1995) develop a second version of this critique. They extend Foucault's intriguing idea that law (and sovereignty) has survived massive upheavals from medieval to modern society only because of the expansion of disciplinary power. The creation of normalized, disciplined individuals, for example, provided the 'order' that enabled a liberalized 'law' to persist. Not, therefore, persuaded by the view that Foucault 'expelled' law from his analyses, this version of the basic critique implies that he paid insufficient attention to the ways in which new political technologies (discipline) enabled medieval law and sovereign models of power to survive, and the profound ways in which this has transformed previous forms of law (e.g., our case above already shows the way that medical disciplines were used to establish the truth about London's poisoning). These approaches reflect on important tensions and contradictions that emerge from the law-discipline alignment.

A third version of the critique is more fully discussed by Golder and Fitzpatrick (2009), but, in brief, Ewald (1988, 1986) recovers from Foucault a way to understand law as it is practised in a welfare state, what he terms a socialized law, or 'social law'. This is, for him, both a 'process of transforming the law' and 'the development of a new type of law' where law increasingly functions normatively (Ewald 1986: 41). Effectively, modern law and society both operate as normalizing powers, erasing clear distinctions between them. In all these critiques, one gleans attempts to elaborate upon Foucault's image of law in changing modern societies.

Law, Biopower, and Governmentality

In his later works, however, Foucault does provide the rudiments of a rather different image of law. Complementing his earlier work, Foucault now analyzes another sort of power—**governmentality**—that appears before discipline and has a longer history. For him, it arose because, ' . . . far too many things were escaping the old mechanism of the power of sovereignty, both at the top and at the bottom, both at the level of detail and at the mass level' (2004: 249). Discipline took care of details and the individual body, but an older rationality of governance (governmentality) was enlisted to create modern forms of liberal rule, focused more on shaping and managing general objects, like 'society' and 'population'. Operating through such knowledge as statistics and actuarial science, governmentality nurtured new powers, including one that was specifically directed to shaping life processes; he refers to this as

biopolitics, or **biopower,** a power that seeks to manage the *life* (conceived through biological and statistical [actuarial] knowledge) of human masses. It directs broad swaths of life, especially 'the biological existence of the population'—not an individual body, but the body of a population (2004: 249). This biopower is concerned with improving a population's health, decreasing its mortality and obesity rates, increasing its longevity, etc.

In this way, biopolitics is an instrument of a wider governmentality by which modern liberal subjects are increasingly called upon to govern themselves outside of direct, formal institutions (2009). Foucault (2000; 2007b) notes that governmentality was certainly not new—this form of power was referred to in Greek thought, and in Mesopotamian and Semitic texts (2007b: 127, 136). It also appeared in Roman and early Christian contexts, where images of a shepherd (pastor, oblate) caring for a flock suggested how to govern appropriately. This pastoral image of power was, with the Reformation, adapted and changed to suit secular contexts, and became an important inspiration for new discourses on good governance, such as 'police science' and 'reason of state'. This paved the way for liberal formulations of governmentality that expressly focused on limiting state governance, and opening up allied spaces (civil society) in which subjects would govern themselves, using new techniques of self-formation (2007a). No doubt, the specifics of this discussion are beyond this chapter; suffice to note that Foucault's (2004) analysis of governmentality (and biopower) highlights new arenas of governance focused on enabling indirect regulation—not by direct control, but by nurturing new ways to govern through the 'conduct of conduct' in which subjects increasingly regulate their own being in contexts deployed by governmental formations. Therefore, he describes governmentality as a form of power 'that has the population as its target, political economy as its major form of knowledge, and apparatus of security as its essential technical instrument' (2007b: 108).

With echoes of Weber, he argues that medieval forms of sovereignty were gradually, in the fifteenth and sixteenth centuries, **governmentalized** in concert with the emerging modern 'administrative state' (2007b: 109), and this was precisely 'what has allowed the state to survive'. But Foucault is clear: 'We should not see things as the replacement of a society of sovereignty by a society of discipline, and then of a society of discipline by a society, say, of government. In fact we have a triangle: sovereignty, discipline, and governmental management, which has population as its main target and apparatuses of security as its essential mechanism' (2007b: 107–8). There is no expulsion of law and sovereignty here, but a recognition of three intersecting instances of power.

From this, Golder and Fitzpatrick offer a novel interpretation of law from Foucault's work. Specifically, they note that Foucault, on the one hand, conceptualized modern law as constraining and limit-preserving, directed 'negatively to control and circumscribe' (2009: 79). On the other, they detect its perpetual tendency to open up limits, to respond to otherness beyond existing limitation. Instead of seeking to integrate or 'correct' these seemingly disparate moments of Foucault's law, they see it as a productive tension:

> Law, if it is to rule effectively and secure the requisite certainty and predictability in the world beyond, must constantly relate to the ever-changing nature of society, the economy, and so forth. There is a constituent requirement for law to respond to the infinity of relation which can impinge upon its determinate position. And yet, whilst the law cannot simply ossify in the determinacy of its position, neither can it dissipate itself in a pure, unalloyed responsiveness to the other and to the changing world 'outside' it. (2009: 80).

In other words, law is both determining in existing limits, and responsive to wider precepts that relentlessly disrupt the limits within which it currently settles (just as Foucault understands modernity in terms of 'closure' and 'rupture', as discussed above). So, for Golder and Fitzpatrick, Foucault's conception of the law never settles into the rigidities of existing limits, nor does it disappear into in an amorphous ether of responsiveness. It settles in this 'bipartite' unity, i.e., it never merely secures a 'determinate order' but must also always remain 'amenable to the ceaseless unmaking of any given order, to the very disordering of the present' (2009: 81). In this sense, they argue that Foucault's law is both 'presently containable and yet ultimately uncontainable', and has an 'insistent capacity to be otherwise than what it is' (2009: 86).

The Becoming of Law, Society, and Justice

Whichever of these Foucaultian-inspired appropriations of law one pursues, a basic insight remains: Foucault emphasizes law's 'becoming' over its 'being'. Since there is no definitive 'law' that exists outside of history, to ask the question, 'What is the nature of law?' is to misunderstand how power-knowledge in specific contexts yields truths that generate specific types of 'law'. In this sense, for our purposes, it is not law that is expelled, but the idea that law exists *sui generis*; it appears as a 'historical ontology' that 'becomes' through complex power-knowledge relations that produce juridical and legal forms. Thus, '*Law enforcement* is the set of instruments employed to give social and political reality to the act of prohibition in which the formulation of the law consists' (Foucault 2009: 254).

More generally, law refers nominally to the 'instruments' deployed at a given moment in time, and that have wider collective effects. It is not an arbiter of, but a player in, power and conflict. Considered thus, we can see why Foucault (2000: 1–89) examines 'judicial practices' in an intriguing series of lectures entitled *Truth and Juridical Forms*. Analyzing juridical forms over time, he notes how 'wrongs and responsibilities are settled between men, the mode by which, in the history of the West, society conceived and defined the way men could be judged in terms of wrongs committed, the way in which compensation for some actions and punishment for others were imposed on specific individuals' (2000: 4).

Looking at the changing 'regimes of truth' by which judicial practices, over several millennia, understand and sanction truth statements, Foucault conceives of law as always becoming. For example, he refers to Homer's *Iliad* as an early instance of how judicial processes find the 'truth'. A dispute arises between Antilochus and Menelaus as contestants in a chariot race; an official who ensures compliance to the rules of the race witnesses it. Menelaus loses but accuses Antilochus of a foul. The latter denies it, and, instead of turning to the witness, Menelaus challenges his opponent to 'swear by Zeus'. By refusing to do so, Antilochus forfeits the race. In this judicial practice, 'an investigation, a witness, an enquiry, or an inquisition' does not procure truth; rather truth is pursued by calling for an oath and a test—both techniques recur, especially in the law of the later Middle Ages (2000: 18). Even if some centuries later, Sophocles' *Oedipus* suggests the continuing relevance of oaths and tests to determine judicial truth, it also indicates that a new, inquiry-based judicial procedure has by then emerged. Such inquiry is less prophetic and more retrospectively orientated, and resounds with consequential effects in later judicial forms, each time it is contextually adapted and changed. The inquiry as a mechanism of truth discovery becomes especially influential as fifteenth- to eighteenth-century philosophers and 'scientists' appropriate its basic precepts, becoming 'a rather characteristic form of truth in our societies' (2000: 4). Foucault also describes the rise, in the nineteenth century, of the *examination* as a form of juridical truth production, and alludes to its association with an emerging disciplinary power. No matter the details: this evocative analysis reflects his sense of law as an ongoing historical accomplishment, of something that *becomes* as a result of shifting power-knowledge relations in given contexts.

Likewise, society is, for him, a product of underlying power-knowledge relations:

> . . . power relations are rooted deep in the social nexus, not a supplementary structure over and above 'society' whose radical effacement one can perhaps dream of. To live in society is, in any event, to live in such a way that some can act on the actions of others. A society without power relations can only be an abstraction . . . the 'agonism' between power relations and the intransitivity of freedom is . . . the political task that is inherent in all social existence (2000: 343).

In this sense, the local taunting and reaction, the 'permanent provocation' through which a subject acts to shape another's conduct ('agonism'), ultimately shapes collective formations (2000: 342). Although, at times,

Foucault ambiguously refers to collective formations as society, his later work on governmentality is more specific: the term 'society' is a unique product that emerges out of eighteenth- and nineteenth-century liberal rationalities of governance. In particular, liberalism is the first discourse to declare that 'one always governs too much' (2009: 319). In efforts to restrict governance, whether of sovereigns or judges, to regulate only when absolutely necessary, liberalism generated a new concept and arena for analysis; in short, it developed a 'new problematic' centred on the concept of 'society' as a means to ascertain whether a specific governmental intervention is necessary (2009: 319). As such, for Foucault, liberal thinking starts, not from the state, but 'from society, which exists in a complex relation of exteriority and interiority *vis-a-vis* the state. It is society—as both condition and final end—that makes it possible to no longer ask: how can one govern as much as possible at the least possible cost? Instead the question becomes: why must one govern?' (2009: 319).

In order to facilitate this kind of discourse, liberal thinking proposed a concept of society to serve as a buttress between the economy on the one hand, and the 'democratic' state on the other. In liberal governmental rationales, 'society' refers to a domain outside of the state within which subjects are thought to govern themselves. As he puts it,

> What was discovered at that time—and this was one of the great discoveries of political thought at the end of the 18th century—was the idea of *society*. That is to say, that government not only has to deal with the territory, with the domain, and with its subjects, but that it also had to deal with a complex and independent reality that has its own laws and mechanisms of disturbance. This new reality is society. From the moment that one is to manipulate society, one cannot consider it completely penetrable by police. One must take into account what it is (1989: 261).

As with modern law, Foucault here understands 'society' as historically embedded in a liberal governmentality. Society and law are thus products of a time; just as they have been made, they are—by virtue of modernity's continuous clash between constraint and rupture, determination and responsiveness—likely to be unmade. Society, if anything, is always becoming, a rising tide that flows with the influence of classical liberal thinking and that will ebb with the emergence of other power-knowledge formations.

Although Foucault has less to say about justice, he is clear that we cannot rely on fixed ideals of justice to guide social change. Morality and ethics are always contingent matters (1997). So, 'It seems to me that the idea of justice in itself is an idea which in effect has been invented and put to work in different types of societies as an instrument of a certain political and economic power or as a weapon against that power' (in Chomsky and Foucault 2006: 54).

With that in mind, he rather elliptically calls upon us 'to emphasize justice in terms of social struggle' (Chomsky and Foucault: 50). As I understand this, his point is not that a just society can be specified in advance, but rather that the comforts of our present limits are shaken ('problematized') by radically unforeseen events that inspire us to re-conceive our political horizons. Out of such unforeseeable events come creative realignments of our 'grids of intelligibility', and it is such openings that rupture the contained closures of our time, and nod receptively towards other ways of becoming. Located in history, and shaped through power-knowledge relations, law, society, and justice are consequential— though fleeting—moments in the process of becoming: their constraints (limits) are inextricably linked to their (responsive) ruptures. The historical objects are transient, the process enduring.

Concluding Reflections

Interestingly, Weber and Foucault were influenced by Nietzsche's work, and that is perhaps why both focus on concepts of power (and, indeed, discipline), and emphasize its role in creating law and society. However, as we have seen, Foucault's analysis is unique in that it rejects the usual idea of power as a means of repressing and coercing subjects to act in particular ways. Rather, he offers a far broader, nominal account of power as a relation that produces the kinds of thinking, acting, and communicating we mostly take for granted in our everyday lives. The subtle operation of power always directly implies knowledge, and vice versa. On this basis, Foucault's work troubles much thinking about power in modern societies (e.g., Hobbes's views of a central sovereign who exercises a suppressive power, through law, over subjects). He argues instead that the sovereign model of power is a throwback to medieval political formations, and one that both survives and is altered by other models of power such as discipline and governmentality (biopower). His analysis implicitly frames law in a different light, and suggests that at least its way of operating in modern contexts is quite different from its previous incarnations. This chapter has outlined several possible ways to conceive of law and society in Foucault's work, but the overarching theme is simply this: law and society are not essential beings, but are rather always historical outcomes of underlying power relations. And by charting changing power formations, Foucault's approach invites us to conceptualize the law and society terrain through an analysis of the ways in which 'objects' appear in history: they do not exist a priori, but rather become!

Discussion Questions

1. Is freedom intrinsic to, rather than suppressed by, power?

2. Do you agree with Foucault that power relations can only be exercised with resistance? Does this mean that relationships of violence do not involve power?

3. Does Foucault's analysis of power help or hinder feminist attempts to resist patriarchy?

4. If power relations that are everywhere create subjects and their freedom, what is the point of resisting? Is it futile to revolt?

5. What is the power of modern law?

6. Can you think of examples that allow us to understand how modern law has been disciplined (normalized) and governmentalized?

Suggested Readings

Golder, B., & Fitzpatrick, P. (2009). *Foucault's Law*. London: Routledge.

Hunt, A., & Wickham, G. (1994). *Foucault and Law: Towards a Sociology of Law as Governance*. London: Pluto Press.

Pavlich, G.C. (2000). *Critique and Radical Discourses on Crime*. Aldershot: Ashgate.

Relevant Websites

http://plato.stanford.edu/entries/foucault/
www.michel-foucault.com/
http://foucault.info/

10 Contested Sovereignties, Violence, and Law

Questions to Consider

- ⊛ In the wake of challenges to the state's claims to sovereignty, has law's role in preserving order changed?
- ⊛ Is law necessarily a violent way of preserving order, or does its real function lie in ensuring that justice is served?
- ⊛ Following Foucault, are we today confronting governmentalized forms of law?
- ⊛ What are the long-term effects of 'states of exception', where laws are passed to limit the ordinary jurisdiction of law?
- ⊛ What do post-colonial political formations tell us about the politics of law and sovereignty?

Legal interpretation takes place in a field of pain and death. This is true in several senses. Legal interpretive acts signal and occasion the imposition of violence upon others: a judge articulates her understanding of a text, and as a result, somebody loses his freedom, his property, his children, even his life. Interpretations in law also constitute justifications for violence which has already occurred or which is about to occur (Cover 1986: 1601).

Late on 15 October 1970, Canada's federal government took the exceptional step of proclaiming the *War Measures Act*, deploying the army in Quebec and restricting various civil rights elemental to conventional ideas of the rule of law. As is well known, such a drastic measure was in direct response to ongoing activities of the Front de libération du Québec (FLQ), a national liberation movement that emerged in 1963 with the aim of achieving Quebec independence (Tetley 2007; Saywell 1971). With both socialist and revolutionary aspirations, a cell of the group kidnapped James Cross (the British trade commissioner) on 5 October 1970. Shortly thereafter, the FLQ presented various demands to the Quebec government. The federal and provincial governments refused to negotiate, and another FLQ cell abducted Pierre Laporte (a minister in the Quebec government) five days later. The Canadian army was deployed in Quebec, and key political figures deemed the 'law' unable to meet the crisis, calling for 'emergency powers'. With the proclamation of the *War Measures Act* through the *Public Order Regulations, 1970*, 'conclusive evidence' was thereby asserted 'that insurrection, real or apprehended, exists or has existed for any period of time therein stated'.[1] The legislation declared the following:

> And whereas there is in contemporary Canadian society an element or group known as *Le Front de Libération du Québec* who advocate and resort to the use of force and the commission of criminal offences, including murder, threats of murder and kidnapping, as a means of or as an aid in accomplishing a governmental change within Canada and whose activities have given rise to a state of apprehended insurrection within the province of Quebec . . .

This law effectively declared an exceptional state of affairs that suspended elements of the ordinary rule of law in context, and allowed the state to quell the 'insurrection' by extraordinary means. In the event, many citizens were arrested or detained in a resulting roundup, and, tragically, Laporte was murdered. Cross was released alive in early December, and his kidnappers were exiled to Cuba.

Many of the events in question have been hotly debated, with diverse political interpretations offered for motivations, actions, and their socio-political effects (Daniels 1973). However, for our purposes in this chapter, at least two things are significant: Canadian state sovereignty and law were explicitly challenged; and the rule of law was suspended through an exceptional sovereign act that curtailed ordinary rights (e.g., the detention of people without charge or bail) and that, in effect, sought to suppress the FLQ's rival claim to legality. If Foucault's emphasis on the power of law, society, and justice highlights the forces that constitute diverse historical appearances, others examine the legal arenas that have arisen around a sovereign's attempt to enforce its law as universal and inviolable, but at the same time to exclude (as in the above example) itself from that law.

The approaches of the present chapter refuse static images of law and society as fixed ontological forms; the gesture enables various readings of the changing contours through which law and society become, four of which are discussed below. First, some analysts, such as Benjamin and Cover, focus on the underlying violence that enables institutions of law; from this, one might consider the October Crisis in light of the constituting violence that simultaneously creates, and yet conceals, law. Secondly, others, such as Agamben, emphasize how so-called exceptional states of emergency have in recent political times become the norm. Dubbing these 'states of exception', Agamben detects a political logic that requires sovereigns to except themselves from their own laws; this is fundamental, not exceptional, to sovereignty politics. Locating instances where states suspend the rule of law as a matter of course (e.g., security certificates, detention without trial, Guantanamo Bay), he considers the politics of sovereignty as producing depraved lives, paradigmatically related to the 'bare lives' lived in (refugee, concentration, etc.) 'camps'. Third, Butler's allied analysis detects in exceptional measures, and the law's complicity in its own suspension, a resurgence of sovereignty politics that unexpectedly (compare to Foucault) gives new meaning to a 'governmental state'. Finally, recognizing law as plural, contested, and historically situated processes (rather than an object) allows one to comprehend the hybrid persistence of colonial legal forms in post-colonial settings. All such approaches, limited though ensuing synopsis might be, highlight debates that are possible once the law, society, and justice are understood to be processes located in history. Let us examine each approach in turn.

Law's Violence

Under which circumstances can processes of state law serve as a legitimate dispenser of violence? How does law's violence relate to wider norms? Do judges have to be forces for state violence? What other, more justice-inclined, roles might they play? These are the sorts of questions that are implicit in Cover and Benjamin's analyses of law. For instance, Cover[2] argues that, 'We inhabit a *nomos*—a normative universe. We constantly create and maintain a world of right and wrong, of lawful and unlawful, of valid and void (1983: 4).'

In modern contexts, where the open-endedness of that **normative universe** is properly acknowledged (i.e., is subject to rational discussion), the law might play a role in debating key aspects of this *nomos*. Were it to do so, law could also offer a 'potential restraint on arbitrary power and violence' (1983: 68). However, law currently fails to engage in rational discussion about norms, but is instead focused on preserving a given order at all costs. As a result, 'Judges are people of violence. Because of the violence they command, judges characteristically do not create law, but kill it' (1983: 53).

Activist, 'revolutionary lawyers' could again return to issues concerning the justice of a given law, or legal process, and so challenge the current lack of attention paid to justifying state violence (1983: 60). Cover thus reminds us of the ethical horizons of current claims of 'law'.[3] However, there are few incentives for lawyers to do so, which further enables the state to eliminate any ethical ideals from the law. As a result, jurists tend to fall prey to a positivist trap that separates law from ethics and views law as instrumentally (not ethically) related to violence.[4] In this context, no justification for using violence is offered beyond the state's instrumental need to legitimate and perpetuate its own rule. But, Cover insists, if law must use violence, as is sometimes the case, it should do so for legitimate and well-reasoned ethical ends; the best prospect for redemptive aspirations to non-violent relations between people may, he argues, lie with small-scale, informal communities that recognize the importance of justifying normative interpretations through ethical argument beyond state violence.

Without engaging Cornell's (1988: 1627) challenge to Cover's perhaps unduly pessimistic assessment, we might use these brief remarks as an opening to Benjamin's (1996) related essay, *Critique of Violence*. In this notoriously dense text, Benjamin (1996: 236–8) offers a critique directed to uncovering the conditions that make specific relations between law, justice, and violence possible. The text is structured around two themes. First, he examines violence as a 'means' to securing a particular sort of law, noting two sorts of violence; namely, **law-constituting** and **law-preserving** violence. In the shorter second part, he considers violence as a divine (just) end without law; here he distinguishes between 'mythic' and 'divine' violence. What on earth does this all mean?

Turning to the first theme, Benjamin challenges jurisprudential distinctions between natural and positivist conceptions of law, noting their shared attachment to **mean-ends** calculations: natural law justifies legal violence through the ends it serves; legal positivism focuses on the means, regardless of moral end. Unlike Cover, however, Benjamin calls for us to explore justice outside of this means-ends structure, thereby conceptualizing law-justice-violence relations without recourse to dominant positivist/natural law approaches. But he also agrees with Cover that modern law no longer explicitly pursues normative ideals of collective justice. As Azoulay nicely puts it, 'Law forgets or represses the morality enfolded within it. But in order to forget the morality, it engages in violence, and in order to seize power and become ruler it must forget this violence too' (2005: 1018).

For example, Benjamin argues that legal punishment does not actually do what it usually claims to do—deter criminals, offer revenge, rehabilitate offenders, etc. Rather, it serves a more basic purpose. Its violence may be forgotten (or hidden) behind walls, but this does not take away its original function—to violently constitute a new legal system and then to preserve that system once established. For example, the violence of punishment serves as a terrifying law-constituting (law-making) violence that licences a given legal system (e.g., think of capital punishment, maximum security prisons, etc.). It must be displayed (spectacle) when necessary, but should also be concealed in the everyday running of law (hence it is placed behind walls).

There are also other examples where law-constituting violence appears ambiguously at the limits of law. Here Benjamin references the 'great criminal', the workers' strike, military law, and police enforcement as examples that sit on the threshold of law and lawlessness. The *War Measures Act* in Quebec provides another such example in which the boundary between preserving the law and constituting new law is blurred. He takes all such examples as evidence of a dialectical relation between law-creating and law-preserving violence that lies at the heart of modern law. But we should not forget that law-making violence is the prior one: any force used to entrench a specific law always rests on the shoulders of a prior violence through which that law was originally created. If we agree with this seemingly plausible statement, then we face a recursive condition where legal violence exists solely to uphold the law—law has a monopoly of legitimate violence, the purpose of which is to uphold the law (i.e., through 'law-preserving violence'). From this discussion, Benjamin appears to say that—contrary to the best efforts of legal theory/jurisprudence—law is entirely arbitrary. The violence that constitutes any legal system simply cannot be justified. Like fate, it simply is: 'For if violence, violence crowned by fate, is the origin of law, then it might readily be supposed that where the highest violence, that over life and death, occurs in the legal system, the origins of law jut manifestly and fearsomely into existence' (1996: 242).

In the shorter and more enigmatic second part of the text, Benjamin discusses—in outline at least—a **redemptive politics** grounded in ethics (rather than law) and that relies on violence only in pursuit of unsullied justice. He distinguishes this violence from the images of justice that preoccupy modern law. If law is born to arbitrary fate, it is never universal, and can only emerge through violent acts that repeatedly convey it as a superior force. The founding sacrifice that establishes a legal system is thus repeated through continuous acts of punishment. He calls such fateful, violent sacrifices **mythic violence**—its foundations lie in age-old myths (e.g., Niobe). Jurisprudence is also based on mythic violence, and its means-ends analysis of law justifies the gratuitous violence of a degenerate law: a law that operates purely to shelter a sovereign power, and works through processes of guilt and vengeance. In Benjamin's (1996: 248–9) terms, such law needs to be replaced by a **divine violence** that always serves justice and replaces its mythic counterpart. He equates law with power for its own sake, and divine violence with justice: 'Lawmaking is powermaking, assumption of power, and to that extent an immediate manifestation of violence. Justice is the principle of all divine endmaking, power the principle of all mythic lawmaking' (1996: 248). For him, law's mythic violence is the exact opposite of divine violence: 'Mythic violence makes law, creates boundaries, threatens and operates through guilt and violence; divine violence destroys law, boundaries and strikes directly in the name of expiation' (1996: 249). To this mysterious division he adds one more definitively so: 'Mythic violence is bloody power over mere life for its own sake; divine violence is pure power over all life for the sake of the living. The first demands sacrifice; the second accepts it' (1996: 250).

However one elects to interpret such statements, it seems that, for Benjamin (echoed by Cover), the violence of modern law has lost sight of its association with justice; it is now centred on power and self-preservation, operating negatively through guilt and retribution. However, he does not merely want to reform jurisprudence, or develop a different conception of the relationship between law, power, and violence; instead, he sees no way that modern law can redeem itself, or recover notions of justice beyond the 'means-ends structure' entrenched by jurisprudence. He understands that some conflicts can be resolved without violence, but argues for a new sort of justice-based violence when it is needed to resolve disputes. For him, this divine violence completely opposes the way that violence is used to uphold law; it would destroy law's mythic violence and its associated focus on guilt, vengeance, and so on. Divine violence is not associated with the law, or the gods of myth; it comes to exist outside of the law, always destroying the conditions of conflict in specific contexts, without the universal pretences of law (1996: 252). In this, one hears his call to return to justice, but in a way that deliberately rejects natural law's sense of justice.

The theoretical contours of such work have inspired several important debates with implications for law and society. These—*inter alia*—emphasize: the sacrificial dimensions of law (Sarat et al. 2007; van der Walt 2005); the meaning of violence in relation to law and justice (Sarat, 2001; Cover et al. 1992); the politics of capital punishment (Sarat 1999); and an attendant call to understand law not as a realist (or social) but as a cultural phenomenon (Sarat and Simon 2003), thus highlighting the links between the study of literature and law.[5] They have also spawned discussions on the political form of modern sovereign-law models of power—examples of which are contained in both Agamben's and Butler's work.

Agamben: Law's Vacuous Force in Exceptional States

To understand Agamben's approach to law requires at least some sense of his broader project. In *Homo Sacer*, he reads Foucault as mistakenly distinguishing biopower from sovereignty when they are, for Agamben, integral to one another (Agamben 1998: 3–7). However dubious the merits of his reading of Foucault may be (Pavlich 2010; also see Norris 2005), he draws on Benjamin to argue that modern liberal sovereignty politics has emaciated—not enhanced—freedom, democracy, and critique. For him, the so-called exceptional states of emergency reflected by such events as the October Crisis represent an increasingly normal way that contemporary states operate (Agamben 2005). These **states of exception** embrace a new sort of **'biopolitical' sovereignty** that blurs Aristotelian distinctions between *zoe* and *bios*, between 'natural life' and 'political life', what is determined and what is not. Consequently, politics increasingly defers to 'biological necessity' (e.g., the claim that genes determine criminals) and shuts down discussions of political autonomy (Pavlich 2009b). For Agamben, while there are new elements to modern formulations, the basic paradigm of Western sovereignty politics is to distinguish between natural or biological life and politics in a unique way: it includes natural life in politics as something that is excluded. This 'included exclusion' idea animates much of his analysis (1998); the express intent, following Benjamin, is to pursue **'forms of life'** beyond the limits of life forms that are created by this totalitarian 'biopolitical sovereignty'.

From Carl Schmitt's famous adage, 'sovereign is he who decides on the exception', Agamben deduces a paradoxical **logic of sovereignty**[6]: a sovereign entity (e.g., the state) emerges by declaring a universal and inviolable law, but at the same time it excepts itself from that law (e.g., the October Crisis). Echoing Benjamin, he takes modern law to be the product of arbitrary law-making violence—not a consensual (Hobbesian) social contract (Mills 2008: 60ff.).

Stated differently, Agamben argues that the founding juridico-political rela-tion is one that 'bans' (prohibits, bars; 1998: 111).[7] This **ban** is a unique sort of relation that has no positive content, and performs a basic function: it links 'terms' that exclude one another. For instance, the *Public Order Regulations, 1970,* declare an 'insurrection' and so include this as something that it—law—is not. The ban is thus a way of relating through exclusion, of holding things together that are only related by excluding one another. The sovereign relates to law, and law to life, in exactly this way (1998: 29). In other words, mod-ern law does not protect—as is oft asserted in liberal formulations—human life; instead, it abandons life by including it 'in itself by suspending it' (1998: 28). Moreover, in Western politics, this ban allows the sovereign to exercise unfettered power over the thing it excludes—namely 'bare life': 'what the ban holds together is precisely bare life and sovereign power' (1998: 111). This is the basis of a unique 'biopolitical sovereignty' that—against Hobbes—does not prevent a state of nature and bring peace to a commonwealth. Instead, with every sovereign ban, bare life is abandoned to a brutal state of nature, a biopolitical domain from which law excepts itself (1998: 6).

In other words, these biopolitical forms of sovereignty actually generate **bare life** in a 'state of nature', rather than bringing this condition to an end. For instance, the unlimited power of the sovereign exemplifies the terrifying state of nature (the war of 'all against all'), just as bare life excluded from politics is rendered, like a sovereign, outside of law/politics. He argues that the **camp** (refugee camps, concentration camps) provides a kind of model by which to understand this degraded life form that is excluded from the opera-tion of law, and where a sovereign ban is exercised over such bare life without the protections of law. The life generated by 'biopolitical sovereignty' thus involves 'an unconditional subjection to a power of death' (1998: 90), and this (not natural life) has become the source of its politics.

Working out of this logic of abandonment, Agamben describes political environments that have sovereigns creating **bandits,** or subjects deposited (banned) in a netherworld that is neither 'animal' nor 'man', included nor excluded—they live within the law but as outlaws, as neither 'man nor beast'. These subjects are both banned and abandoned by law as excluded entities; they are named by law as outlaws, and treated accordingly. Consequently, Agamben (2005; 1998: 36–8) characterizes politics in the West as totalitar-ian, in which exceptional measures have become normal, so that 'states of exception' are more or less models for their governance (2005: 1–31). In such contexts, needless to say, law suspends itself as a matter of course. As a result, the restraints the rule of law can place on unfettered sovereign commands are relinquished by law's complicity with this new politics. From this, Agamben concludes that the operation (force) of law and the state of nature (law and life) are now all but indistinguishable.[8] Moreover, in such contexts, 'law' and the 'force of law' are separated—in some cases the 'law' (statute, rule, norm) may exist on the books but it is not enforced; in others, 'acts that do not have the value of law acquire its "force"' (Agamben 2005: 38).

In other words, law now operates as a force, but without the key elements that one usually associates with the rule of law. It is stripped of its normative (justice-based) content and simply exercises force, becoming a 'force of law without content' (2005: 39). It has—as Cover and Benjamin have argued—become divorced from its normative content. As such, the law cannot be called upon to restrain sovereign power; it simply enforces vacant 'included exclusions' and increasingly suspends itself from checking capricious, sovereign decrees (as with security certificates, detention without trial, etc.). In the process, subjects are abandoned by law as 'outlaws', and fall prey to a kind of law that often operates by suspending itself. Thus, law emphasizes process, guilt, vengeance, and enforcement without normative or ethical content (e.g., justice). It allows the sovereign to preserve 'his natural right to do anything to anyone' (1998: 106), and, as this 'right' spreads, so 'the realm of bare life—which was originally situated at the margins of the political order—gradually begins to coincide with the political realm, and exclusion and inclusion, outside and inside, *bios* and *zoe*, right and fact, enter into a zone of irreducible indistinction' (1998: 9). This terrifying totalitarian regime founds itself on this excluded inclusion of 'bare life'.

To resist such an authoritarian ethos, Agamben seeks a new politics outside the empty, but spectacular, terrain of contemporary power, exposing the 'secret' grounding of sovereignty and bare life. His aim is to 'bring the political out of its concealment and, at the same time, return thought to its practical calling' (1998: 5). Here (drawing on Benjamin), he holds out the prospect of a revolutionary state of limbo that develops new 'forms of life' not incorporated by sovereignty politics, or law, and that reveals ways to be without reference to modern law, state, community, guilt, retribution, and bare life (see Mills 2008: 69). In other words, he seems to be calling for new political and legal arenas not centred on either sovereignty or law, or at least where the latter are suspended. Butler works with elements of Agamben's theory to develop a rather different, more Foucaultian, approach to contemporary patterns of sovereignty, thereby exploring an intriguing line of enquiry made possible by the suspension of essentialized conceptions of law and society.

Governmental Sovereigns

> Sovereignty's aim is to continue to exercise and augment its power to exercise itself; in the present circumstances, however, it can only achieve this aim by managing populations outside the law (Butler 2004: 98).

Let us recall Foucault's claim that governmentality, a more management-focused and risk-based way of governing subjects, has altered state sovereignty (a **governmentalized state**), allowing such sovereignty to survive under current conditions. Judith Butler (2004: 50–100) interprets Foucault's claims here not to mean that governmental powers 'devitalize' sovereignty and law, as might reasonably be suggested. Instead, she detects a 'resurgence' of sovereignty in governmental contexts that animates older forms of sovereignty, before there was a **separation of powers** between state and law. On this point, she agrees with Agamben's sense that there now exists 'a contemporary version of sovereignty, animated by an aggressive nostalgia that seeks to do away with the separation of powers . . .' (2004:61).

A lawless sovereign emerges as the law removes itself by suspending its operations: ' . . . we have to consider the act of suspending the law as a performative one which brings a contemporary configuration of sovereignty into being, or more precisely, reanimates as a spectral sovereignty within the field of governmentality' (2004: 61). In other words, the many performances through which law suspends itself (e.g., emergency decrees, security certificates, indefinite detention provisions) actually generate a new version of sovereignty that exists happily without law and operates through a governmental logic directed to managing life directly.

Echoing her earlier work on **sovereign performatives** (1997a), which notes that sovereignty is the product of repeated political performances and subjections (1997b), Butler describes this new sovereignty as no longer centralized within a state; it disperses itself across governmental management regimes. Located amidst governmental technologies and fields, this governmentalized sovereign power becomes an extra-legal one without clear time and space constraints. Such an 'extra-legal' power has existed before (e.g., monarchies), but now it has an indefinite quality; it effectively extends its powers without limit, into an open future. For her, Agamben's description of exceptional states is overblown—they are not literally states of emergency. Instead, through various and often subtle suspensions of the rule of law, a new version of 'unaccountable' sovereign power has emerged. It is focused on managing security with or without the law. Consequently, she describes a situation in which 'The future becomes a lawless future, not anarchical, but given over to the discretionary decisions of a set of designated sovereigns—a perfect paradox that shows how sovereigns emerge within governmentality—who are beholden to nothing and to no one except the performative power of their own decisions' (2004: 65). In this political landscape, there are many localized **petty sovereigns** who make discretionary (extra-legal) decisions and seldom appreciate their enormous impact. Many of their decisions are not subject to review or appeal.

But what about law? In this context, a very different meaning is ascribed to law. It is neither that which retrains a sovereign, nor is it primarily concerned with distinguishing 'between lawful state action and unlawful' (2004: 83). Now it has become an 'instrument' in the hands of a sovereign to be applied or suspended 'at will'. As such, a new sort of power has created the space for a 'resurgent sovereignty' to emerge, where sovereigns take the form of delegated managers, with law as one of their instruments. Legal officials, courts, tribunals, and even statutes are part of the sovereign's political arsenal; tools by which it can consolidate an amorphous 'national security', and the 'protection of principality' (2004: 95). If the law becomes a tactic, a technique, in this ethos, perversely, so too does the idea of sovereignty. The new governmentalized sovereign that emerges out of law's suspension itself becomes a management tactic. Butler argues:

> What we have before us now is the deployment of sovereignty as a tactic, a tactic that produces its own effectivity as its aim. Sovereignty becomes that instrument of power by which law is either used tactically or suspended, populations are monitored, detained, regulated, inspected, interrogated, rendered uniform in their actions, fully ritualised and exposed to control and regulation in their daily lives (2004: 97).

In a recursive gesture, sovereignty, law, and the 'social' that governmental forms of power constitute appear as tactics, as new arrangements of power. And by releasing the grip of law as a fixed point of reference, Butler opens up a critical space for understanding how performances of law generate new governmental regimes—a fertile field for further exploration. Such insights, interestingly, parallel post-colonial legal analyses, a selection of which are discussed below (see McLeod 2007).

Laws and Post-colonies

> . . . the postcolony is a period of embedding, a space of proliferation that is not solely disorder, chance, and madness, but emerges from a sort of violent gust, with its languages, its beauty and ugliness, its ways of summing up the world (Mbembe 2001: 242)

Legal anthropology has long recognized cultural constructions that constitute colonial and post-colonial images of law and order (Moore 2005). It has also recognized that in any context there are many different intersecting and often contested fields of law— hence the name **legal pluralism** signals an approach that recognizes different arenas claiming to be law can exist simultaneously in most contexts (Moore 1986; Fitzpatrick 1984). Legal pluralists usually challenge the typical privileging of formal over customary, informal, or Aboriginal law (Bell and Napoleon 2008; Tie 1999; Merry 1988), recognizing plural, fluid, and changing processes of law with porous borders that pervade contemporary legal environments (Merry 2006; Moore 1978). Their discussions have detailed clashes between legal claims in colonial and post-colonial contexts, and attempts (never successful) to construct imperial sovereigns as the sole legitimate source of legal authority (see Benton 2002).

In her review of the field, for example, Merry details the exclusionary gendered and racialized hierarchies that have contoured **colonial law** (i.e., law in the colonies of imperial powers). Fitzpatrick (1992) locates in these hierarchies a grand 'mythology' that founds modern law (see also Andersen 2005; Mbembe 2001: 24ff.). In all these approaches there is a sense that, as Merry notes, 'The law of contemporary societies was forged in the colonial era. . . . One legacy of this history is a racialized system of law, in which different legal systems are used for racially distinguished populations' (2004: 569).

Indeed, a chief legacy of colonial law was its 'pervasive pluralism' that played out in multiple local contexts, a plurality that (ambiguously) provided both 'a mode of control and a place of resistance' (2004: 576). For many, colonial legal practices were subsumed by post-colonial contexts and were complicated by a new, global imperialism, the rise of new patterns of sovereignty, and emergent resistances to law (Fitzpatrick and Tuitt 2004; Fitzpatrick 2001). There are also important questions about the dogged persistence of colonial categories of thought that have reappeared in the new contexts (Merry 2004; Sarat and Kearns 2001). Indeed, as Merry notes: 'The new international legal order is ideologically and politically the descendant of the colonial order of empire. The same economic and political inequalities of that era pervade the present, despite its apparently different legal organization' (2004: 583).

With this in mind, many have studied legality in post-colonial contexts throughout Africa, Asia, Europe, and Latin America, where colonial governance was formally replaced by new states, claiming independence from imperial powers. Here a fertile field has emerged around attempts that grapple with new political horizons (beyond simple ideas of one clear sovereign and one legal system) and how law *becomes* in such contexts. A burgeoning literature also explores the residual legacies of colonial law and the ensuing attempt to understand new, non-imperialist interpretations of law and sovereignty in contexts as diverse as South Africa (Worden 2007; Chanock 2001: 1985), Canada (Hogeveen 2010; Woolford 2009; Bell and Napoleon 2008; Woolford and Ratner 2008; Napoleon and Overstall 2007; Maaka and Andersen 2006; Razzack 2002), New Zealand (Pavlich 1998), Australia (Byrne 1993), Hawai'i (Merry 2000), and so on. In Canada, one can refer to significant attempts to conceptualize the law of First Nations (Napoleon and Overstall 2007) or to contest existing legal fields (Andersen 2005) without essentializing cultural identity or legality (Mawani 2002). Yet, such important frameworks continue to struggle with the hierarchicies, laws, racism, and persistence of colonial power (Tuitt 2004; Darian-Smith and Fitzpatrick 1999), even as new dynamics emerge.

The term '**post-colonial**' has also become a kind of open placeholder for attempts to conceptualize, say, law without Eurocentric reasoning and knowledge regimes (Said 2003; Spivak 1990), to get beyond imperial 'truths' and the effects of denigrating rather than being responsible to otherness. Recall Fanon's words: 'When I search for Man in the technique and the style of Europe, I see only a succession of negations of man, and an avalanche of murders' (Fanon 1965: 252). The horrific 'starlight tours' of the Saskatchewan Police that left First Nations people at the edge of town in freezing temperatures, some to horrendous deaths, adds appallingly to that historical avalanche (Green 2006). The mindset that enables such actions is precisely what is to be studied and challenged. Others detail the histories and hybrid ways that law has become in post-colonies without returning to the hierarchies of law (Andersen 2005; Bhabha 2004; Mawani 2002).

Mbembe (2001), too, outlines different ways to address the lived experience of those subject to new powers in post-colonial contexts (e.g., the Cameroon), seeking new concepts to address the complexities of political life in Africa today. He draws on the likes of Foucault and Derrida to challenge the Western descriptions of Africa. Consequently, he speaks of the 'state of becoming', the way people 'exercise existence', and implores us to be cautious about fixing the term 'post-colony' temporally, but to see it as '*time that is appearing*' (2001: 15–16). It never is, but is also always becoming. Yet, as Comaroff and Comaroff (2006: vii) point out, despite their dynamism and diversity, 'post-colonies' in Western discourse are often portrayed as excessively 'violent and disorderly', characterized by chronic 'conflict, coercion, and chaos'. So fixed is this description that few even bother to theorize a more widespread unfolding of 'violence, sovereignty, illegality, modernity' in many contexts, or their paradoxical 'fetish of the rule of law'. This deficit suggests an opening to frame law and 'the postcolony' not as static beings, but constructs that are always on the move.

Mbembe's (2001) view of an emerging '**necropolitics**'—a politics contoured by death or the threat thereof—provides one such attempt to theorize post-colonial sovereignty politics and the changing ways in which it distributes 'life and death' (Hogeveen 2010; Rose 2009). As well, Comaroff and Comaroff (2006) draw on Benjamin, Agamben, Mbembe, and Foucault to ponder a rekindled fetishism of law in many post-colonial political contexts. Here, citizens are cast as legal subjects, turning politics into 'lawfare', encouraging a legal culture that has woven itself through most social relations, producing 'a horizontally woven tapestry of partial sovereignties' (2006: 35). The net effect is not only a culture of legality but also a peculiar legalization of politics in which litigation abounds (Hogeveen 2010). Echoing Agamben and Butler, they describe law as being enforced to suppress, less concerned with content than it is with suppression (e.g., contemporary Zimbabwe).

According to Comaroff and Comaroff, this fascination with law (and crime) has become a sort of cultural obsession, and has marked politics in contemporary South Africa. Referring to cultural performances (theatre, drama,

fiction) that mesmerize spectators with graphic details of crime and criminality, they detect an 'inversion' of Foucault's *Discipline and Punish* (2006:
293). The obsession with various aspects of criminality could be described
as a new spectacle of crime: far from discipline replacing law and sovereign
models of post-colonial power, there is a nostalgic fantasy for authoritative
state government. They take this to be a 'decidedly post-Foucauldian predicament, wherein disorder seems to exceed the capacity of the state to discipline
or punish. It is a predicament in which both those who would wield power
and their putative subjects find it necessary to resort to drama and fantasy to
conjure up visible means of governance' (2006: 292).

For them, that is, dramatic performances of crime and punishment are
not 'reflections, inflections, or refractions of a simple sociological reality'.
Instead, these are 'a vital part of the effort to produce social order and to
arrive at persuasive ways of representing it, thereby to construct a minimally coherent world-in-place' (2006: 292). Perhaps there is some of this too
in Mbembe's (2003) interpretation of Foucault's images of politics as war,
where the unfolding rationales of governance of an amorphous **post-colony**
have a militaristic logic that brings death and destruction to the forefront of
subject mentalities.

In all these ways, one might say that colonial law is very much in the
process of *becoming* other in those specific contexts where liberal, Western
conceptions of a rule of law, evidence, and process confront pervasive and
opposing local cultural frames. Perhaps one of the clearest examples can
be found in situations where local groups demand that legal process enable and legitimate discourses on witchcraft (see Geschiere 2006; Comaroff
and Comaroff 2004b). What happens to, say, liberal formulations of criminal
law when an accused demands to bring evidence to court that he killed a
neighbour because the latter had turned into a bat? The clash between local
belief and liberal law's so-called universal principles (e.g., individual culpability, free will, personal responsibility) is made particularly acute in such
cases (Davies 2008). Turning to a more common example, one might point
to contested quests for indigenous sovereignty claims (Monture 2007), or
sovereignty claims in Quebec (Couton 2007). The very assumption of one
sovereignty and one law applicable to all is challenged by all such examples,
indicating—at least—the continued plurality of claims to law in post-colonial
contexts. In this light, one can then understand why Napoleon and Overstall
would argue, 'We contend that legal principles and obligations of aboriginal
law are reflected in the actual work, structures, and life of present day aboriginal peoples and communities. Furthermore, in every society, legal norms
and law are constantly changing. It is critical, therefore, that research strategies be designed to prevent creating static or reified constructs of aboriginal
legal orders and law' (2007: 1).

Concluding Reflections

In their various ways, the approaches discussed in this chapter challenge the myth of a clearly demarcated, centralized sovereign commanding law over obedient and peaceful subjects. This myth is becoming something quite different, a difference unleashed in part by the turn away from fixed images of law and society, and diverse appeals to justice. As indicated in this chapter, too, the ensuing arena of analysis opens onto some broad thematic matters regarding the contemporary politics of justice, law, and society: the violence of the law should not be assumed, but explicitly framed by questions of justice; the emergence of a totalitarian sovereignty politics that reduces law and legal subjects to 'bare life' and nature should be understood and overcome; the changing nature of sovereignty with its governmentalized management processes and tactics, including law, should be understood in the plural ways in which life, populations, and post-colonies rule; and the highly stratified ways that law and society become in post-colonial contexts all point to the importance of focusing on dynamic and unfolding claims to law, society, and justice. But how is one to address that dynamism, to find a *logos* of *juris* or *socius* that opens to the becoming of law and society in the name of justice without fixing or falling into the abyss that collapsed the Tower of Babel?

Discussion Questions

1. Has law become nothing more than a violent way to enforce a sovereign's command, a 'force without content'?

2. What are the political implications when law declares exceptions to the usual protections it offers to unrestrained sovereign power? Has this become normal?

3. In what ways could law serve justice, or can justice only be served outside of law and state? What does this mean for the study of law?

4. If law and society are no longer easy to 'fix' as objects of study in post-colonial contexts, what should socio-legal approaches study?

5. Is it ever possible to achieve 'justice without law'?

Suggested Readings

Barbour, C., & Pavlich, G. (eds.). (2010). *After Sovereignty: On the Question of Political Beginnings*. New York: Routledge-Cavendish.

Merry, S.E. (2004). 'Colonial and Postcolonial', in A. Sarat (ed.), *The Blackwell Companion to Law and Society*. Malden: Blackwell, 569–88.

Mills, C. (2008). *The Philosophy of Agamben*. Kingston: McGill-Queen's University Press.

Relevant Websites

www.wbenjamin.org/walterbenjamin.html
www.iep.utm.edu/agamben/
www.egs.edu/faculty/giorgioagamben.html
www.egs.edu/faculty/butler.html
www.eurozine.com/articles/2008-01-09-mbembe-en.html
http://slought.org/content/11431/
http://plato.stanford.edu/entries/femapproach-analy-cont/

11 Just Events: Law and Society

Questions to Consider

- ✳ How are we to address the events by which law and society *become* in the name of justice?
- ✳ Is language (in a broad sense) the basis of all being?
- ✳ What does deconstruction have to do with law, justice, and society?
- ✳ Understood as a process, is there a logic to the becoming of justice, law, and society?

Becoming is not a merely *apparent state*; perhaps the world of beings is mere appearance (Nietzsche 1967: 377).

The appearance of law and society as distinct beings in jurisprudence and sociology has been eroded by tendencies discussed in previous chapters. Alongside critical theories of law, Foucault's Nietzschean-inspired analysis had expressly cast these beings as historical artifacts. His approach influenced several theorists discussed in the previous chapter, and the rather different formulations of law, violence, sovereignty, as well as a moving sense of the post-colony. Of course, the sweep is broad, but does suggest that conventional understandings and objects of jurisprudence, legal theory, socio-legal studies, and the sociology of law—law, society, justice—are no longer considered by many to be the discrete identities previously envisaged (Bauman 1997, 1992; Lyotard 1984). Consequently, no longer is the law and society field marked by the pursuit of eternal, essential understandings of its objects. Instead, a more fluid appropriation of these concepts as always on the way—becoming—calls for markedly different ways to address the concepts of justice, law, and society.

This chapter refers to three analysts in an effort to carve out a way to address this idea of becoming in context. It starts with a key essay by Jacques Derrida that goes beyond a **metaphysics of presence**, or a philosophical approach that assumes being to have an essence that can be captured through appropriate (logic-based) methods. If Derrida uses another approach to address law and justice, Fitzpatrick develops the idea of two inextricable components to law—its determined capacity to decide in a given instance that is made possible by its responsiveness to whatever is beyond that particular instance. In many ways, both consider the law as an event that forever unfolds as a promise of something much larger than the here and now decision that is made. Finally, a brief look at Nancy (2000) affords a glimpse of what it might be to 'associate' without fixed concepts of society. Overall the discussion prefaces the final chapter's speculations about what such developments might mean for the future of the law and society field staked out by jurisprudence, the sociology of law, and socio-legal studies.

In the Name of Justice . . .

The following case is an intriguing one. Here, in a rare instance, the court explicitly considers how to understand justice, and the idea of law in relation thereto. In it, Justice Boyle of the BC County Court dismissed a criminal charge against a defendant in *R. v. Smalbrugge*, [1984] BCJ No. 133. The accused was a food service officer in a federal prison at Mission, and allegedly smuggled money to an inmate on two occasions, ostensibly to help the inmate pay for a hairdressing course. He accepted 40 dollars after the second transaction, and was subsequently charged under ss. 109(a)(i) and (iv) of the *Criminal Code* for contravening this provision: 'Everyone who, being a peace officer, corruptly accepts for himself any money with intent to interfere with the administration of Justice, is guilty of an indictable offence' (9). As Justice Boyle argues, this immediately requires some clarification of the meaning of 'justice' in context. To that end, he refers to an Ontario County Court case, *R. v. Whalen* (1974), 17 CCC (2d) 217, in which the following appears (13): 'Justice after all is not confined to the Courts of Law, parliament or the legislatures. It is not to be found constrained within legalistic frameworks of formal police investigation, arrest and charge.'

In this statement, the terms 'justice', 'Courts of Law', and the 'legalistic frameworks' of police enforcement are distinguished. That is, justice is distinguished from law; justice is more than law, even in the limited context of this section of the Code. Elucidating further, Justice Boyle asks:

> So what does Justice mean here? The Criminal Code and our common law and, in certain cases, equity are concerned with rendering to each person, to the law and to the public their due in the name of Justice. This includes assigning to each convicted offender the proper punishment for his crime, but it does not include the punishment itself, unless in the infliction of that punishment there arises a violation either by the punished or by those executing the punishment. In such a case Justice may be called upon for redress (18).

Again, the concept of justice proves elusive, despite the direct question. Now justice is deferred—as a tautology—to the idea of getting one's 'due in the name of justice', or the notions of redress, or punishment for crime. As such, in seeking to define justice, the judge repeatedly defers to other terms (e.g., due, redress); and if we ask what these terms mean, they too will be deferred to other terms. In recognizing the problem, the judge appears to return to the 'mysticism' of common law:

> There is a danger in attempting to define Justice because, like a butterfly, once caught it may die. It is a concept fixed in our traditions, and not only can too close definition weaken it, but also, attaching to it meanings that are not fixed in our past, can trivialize it. For instance, the now popular phrase 'Justice system'; that phrase would turn the protection of rights into a committee project (19).

Thus, justice, 'like a butterfly', may die if 'caught', gathered into one absolute definition: the 'concept' is fixed in 'our traditions' that defy 'close definition', implying an open-endedness to law and justice that extends beyond today's legal language (e.g., as with the phrase, 'the justice system'). Here, the judge distinguishes present processes of law from a more eternal 'justice' that we receive from past, and project out to future, generations. This case provides an instructive opening into Jacques Derrida's deconstructive interpretation of law and justice, to which we now turn.

Deconstruction, Justice, and Law

Jacques Derrida's oeuvre is vast, and so beyond the scope of our more specific focus on his approach to law (Goodrich 2008). However, here I will touch on two strands of his work. One allows us to understand how meaning is constituted by its relation to other terms—these other (absent) terms paradoxically structure meanings in the present. The second concerns his conception of the relations between law, justice, and deconstruction as discussed in an essay 'Force of Law: The "Mystical Foundation of Authority"'. The second is often taken to reference Derrida's turn to politics, but it also makes clear that his work on language and writing was distinctly 'political' rather than exclusively 'linguistic' (see Beardsworth 1996).

Meaning, 'Differance', and Deconstruction

It may be customary to view Justice Boyle's inability to define justice concisely, and without question, as somewhat of a failure. However, for Derrida (1995, 1981, 1976), this is not so because we can never settle definitions absolutely. **Language** simply does not work in that fashion. Rather, for Derrida, language always operates by deferring signs to one another in a dynamic way to produce provisional, context-specific meanings. The implication of this insight is profound: for example, what we might commonly assume to exist as a being that is absolutely 'present' is, in fact, produced by historically sanctioned repetitions of language use. That is, an entity appears as meaningful, or becomes present, through a range of conventionally accepted ways of using language (usually specific in grammatical rules). So, if we formulate justice, law, and society as essential beings, this is not because of their essential nature—it is, rather, a product of the ways those terms are authorized (by a language's grammar) to relate to other terms.[1]

Thus, in *Smalbrugge*, the judge defines justice as, say, an obligation framed 'in the name of justice', or considered punishment, or 'traditions'. We might define justice differently, as might another judge in another case. Worse, the issue cannot be resolved by turning to a dictionary that would, in turn, defer to such terms as 'the maintenance of legal, social, or moral principles by the exercise of authority or power' (Oxford English Dictionary 2002: 1373). Other dictionaries might add to the list. The point, in short, is that language works not by closing off discussion, but forever deferring terms to others. The impact of this insight should not be underestimated: quite literally it means that what we call 'language' is not a static implement that independent subjects (us) learn and intentionally use. Rather, the open, active, and constantly shifting patterns of deferral of one term to another are never closed—they are always dynamically on the way. As such, the words around which a given view of law surfaces and the rules that define its meaning are always in flux. As well, jurisprudential attempts to close off the being of law, or sociology's emphasis on society, are the products of language use in specific contexts.

Derrida (1976) has famously explored this **play of differences** and coined the neologism **differance** (in French, connoting both 'to differ' and 'to defer') to suggest how the process of deferring to other terms actually creates meaning, being, and presence. The unstable, open-ended and paradoxical quality to language is unavoidable. Furthermore, his famous statement, '*There is nothing outside the text*' (1976: 158), points to the idea that pre-existing subjects do not intentionally fashion meaning through word choices that correspond to, or reflect, objects 'out there'. Rather, out of the process of learning, participating, and being proficient in a given language's grammar, both subjects and objects appear. Moreover, when we, as given language speakers, follow authorized ways of using signs (e.g., 'a full sentence should have a subject, a verb, and an object'), and refer one word to another in 'accepted' ways, we participate in performances, or events, that allow beings (subjects, objects, etc.) to materialize. But the meaning of such entities is never fixed—they always defer to other terms and so are always of the future. This realization defies any attempts to find absolute, fixed, or closed definitions. If this permits us to understand Justice Boyle's relentless deferrals, it also allows us to approach the *becoming* of concepts like justice, law, and society as historical achievements authorized by (e.g., socio-legal, jurisprudential) patterns that are influenced by, but also go beyond, the grammar of language—the study of these patterns may be termed '**grammatology**'. Historically accepted patterns for how words (signs) are thought to relate to one another never arise from unshakable foundations; they are always products of contingent, if ultimately arbitrary, differentiations based on incalculable ruptures, paradoxes, and aporias. Thus, all language formations are inherently unstable. Moreover, disruptions to the way that a given language spawns meaning can have potentially vast consequences, not only for everyday meanings, but also for what and who is said to exist.

Clearly, then, if one were to disrupt accepted flows of language, the very things that it deems to exist as fixed beings would be disrupted (see Pavlich 2007a). Derrida's famous concept, **deconstruction**, is precisely a way to think about what is involved when ordinary flows of language are disrupted (and subsequent images of being reframed). Although notoriously difficult to summarize, one might say deconstruction has to do with opening up conventions and arrangements that constitute a given text as meaningful. Though not directly definable, deconstruction appears unpredictably and without warning in the silenced, supplemental, marginal, excluded, and degraded elements of texts. It is, therefore, neither a precise methodology, nor an absolutely definable term: 'Deconstruction is not a method or some tool that you apply to something from the outside. Deconstruction is something which happens and which happens inside' (1997: 9). If anything, then, it is an event that welcomes different ways by which the 'play of signs' and *differance* in a given context could generate new meaning; it involves poring over delegitimized elements of a text, making room for alternate sign patterns, new chains of deferral, and opening texts to what is impossible, incalculable from within their meaning horizons. It is also a way to be other, to produce new ways to become. Through such openings, deconstruction does not destroy (it is not destruction); rather, it involves reorganizing a given language use by realigning accepted oppositions, thereby creating space for unexpected linguistic possibilities, meanings, and patterns of being. Furthermore, like the language patterns through which it operates, deconstruction is never a finite being predetermined for once and for all. It is without end, and never rests; by relentlessly opening texts, deconstruction tries to prevent any language from casting its meanings as set, necessary, and beyond dispute. The totalitarian effect of closed languages has marked our past with countless atrocities, and will continue to do so if left unabated.

In other words, deconstruction emerges unpredictably by happening, if at all. That happening may well be desirable, pleasurable, and even playful, but is always a 'double gesture' that appears (sometimes) from attentive readings that pay heed to what is in excess of a text, to the absences that enable the text's words to mean something in context. Here, one senses Derrida's preference for opening 'beings' to a deferred 'other' that enables their being; his aim is not to gather and consolidate such beings into rigid identities, but to show their contingent and arbitrary appearances. However, he recognizes that complete closure or openness is synonymous with death, suggesting that living language operates **'heterogeneously'** (from 'hetero'—other, and 'genus'—a kind). That is, to communicate, we close off signs provisionally, but those closures are always contingent and subject to reversal (Derrida 1997: 13–15). Here we glimpse Derrida's emphasis on engaging language as always becoming, as always 'yet to come'. And this provides an entry into his discussion of justice and law.

Between Justice and Law

Derrida's (2002) essay on law opens with a distinction between law and justice that Montaigne and Pascal draw in their respective analyses of the 'mystical foundations of authority'. For Derrida, this idea prepares us for a closer reading of Benjamin's 'Critique of Violence' essay, and he echoes Benjamin's sense that law is ultimately arbitrary because 'the instituting, founding, and justifying moment of law' is a **performative force** (2002: 241). In other words, this force is attendant upon its actually being carried out in a given context. Moreover, that force appears as something mystical because 'there is here a silence walled up in the violent structure of the founding act; walled up because this silence is not exterior to language' (2002: 241–2). Whatever one makes of this curious statement, a key point is that the ground of law (the origin of its authority) rests entirely on itself—it is ultimately beyond justification, even if the event of its founding remains 'within' language as a closeted and undisclosed element. Derrida distinguishes here between **law**[2] and horizons of **justice**[3]. For him, the law involves a temporal, finite calculation that makes decisions in the here and now; but those decisions are always made within a sense of justice that is unlimited in its responsibility to others. As he puts it, 'Law is not justice. Law is the element of calculation, and it is just that there be law, but justice is incalculable, it demands that one calculate with the incalculable; and aporetic experiences are the experiences, as improbable as they are necessary, of justice, that is to say of moments in which the *decision* between just and unjust is never insured by a rule' (2002: 244).

The language may be odd, but here Derrida seems to be saying that, while historical processes of law have to make decisions (calculate) 'in the name of justice', justice is itself incalculable and never coterminous with the here and now; it cannot, therefore, be actualized on its own terms. To appear as a historical possibility, justice requires the determination of a given law, or 'a decision that cuts and divides'. It is through the language of a given decision that justice appears. As such, justice and law are mutually constitutive: law requires the 'excess' of justice to avoid being a totalitarian, tyrannical decree, and infinite justice requires law's reductive calculations to appear, to be rendered manifest at a given historical moment. But this means that every legal decision is an event that paradoxically involves indecisiveness: 'The undecidable remains caught, lodged, as a ghost at least, but an essential ghost, in every decision, in every event of decision' (2002: 253).

But here one must be clear—law does not guarantee justice any more than justice guarantees good law. Because justice is incalculable, one can never declare that 'I am just', or that 'this law/decision is intrinsically just' without thereby betraying the excessive, ecstatic, illimitable sense of justice Derrida proposes. This notion signals that one can never say any decision is absolutely just—one could say that it is legal, or that it conforms to rules, statutes, and 'conventions that authorise calculation' (2002: 252). No finite calculation of law can ever fully appropriate the infinite promise of justice. At the same time, even though law and justice are distinct, they are also mutually constitutive: 'It turns out that law claims to exercise itself in the name of justice and that justice demands for itself that it be established in the name of the law that must be put to work (. . . constituted and applied) by force, "enforced"' (2002: 251).

Derrida's formulation of justice as always beyond law makes sense of the judge's circular quest for justice in *Smalbrugge*. But it also resonates with his concept of deconstruction. Like justice, deconstruction appears as a limitless responsibility to otherness, to what is to come, what is radically unforeseeable, and so on. Moreover, he argues, 'To address oneself to the other in the language of the other' is a 'condition of all possible justice', even if this appears to us as impossible (2002: 245). It is, therefore, perhaps not surprising that he should declare, with emphasis, '*Deconstruction is justice*' (2002: 243).

That is, for Derrida, law—as a historically located and limited calculation—is always deconstructible, whereas justice is undeconstructible because its perpetual responsibility to others is without limit. Justice is, in this respect, indistinguishable ('inseparable') from deconstruction. Therefore, Derrida argues, 'Deconstruction takes place in the interval that separates the undeconstructibility of justice from the deconstructibility of law'; and justice, therefore, enables both law and deconstruction (2002: 243). Equally, 'Deconstruction always finds itself and moves itself between these two poles [of law and justice]' (2002: 243). In consequence, Derrida isolates three unavoidable paradoxes that enable law to become. Here a close reading is required.

First, there is an irreconcilable paradox that attends to the 'decision of the judge': to be just, a decision cannot simply follow a rule; it has to be more than this. It must 'confirm its value' by 'a reinstituting act of interpretation' and by offering a fresh decision that treats each case in unique terms (2002: 251). In other words, a judge is not simply a rule-deciding machine, as the realists keenly noted, and as most ensuing schools of jurisprudence endorse. At the same time, the judge has to appear to follow rules, even though the uniqueness of a given context requires a fresh application that—by definition—extends the rule. Any decision, therefore, is both 'regulated and without regulation', in the sense that each decision is guided by rules, but it must offer a 'unique interpretation' that cannot be absolutely guaranteed by any prior rule.

Secondly, as noted, an undecidable, illimitable, and incalculable justice haunts all limited, calculated, legal decisions. This paradox (limitation versus illimitability) suggests that any decision in the name of justice exceeds a legal decision. The contradiction here is between a legal decision made urgently in response to given events and its promise to yield a justice that never arrives (see Pavlich 1996).

Thirdly, although justice is never presentable, it urgently calls for calculation: 'a just decision is always required *immediately*, right away, as quickly as possible' (2002: 255). But judicial decisions entail the 'madness' of deciding that cannot be totally guaranteed, guided, or determined by rules. As judges perform the act of deciding, they make rulings that they claim are just—the very justice that is illimitable, incalculable, and infinitely open to the other, the future, the to come, that yet to arrive.

Derrida insists we must nevertheless decide and calculate:

> The excess of justice over law and calculation, this overflowing of the unpresentable over the determinable, cannot and should not serve as an alibi for staying out of juridico-political battles, within an institution or a state, between institutions or states. Abandoned to itself, the incalculable and giving [sic] idea of justice is always very close to the bad, even to the worst for it can always be reappropriated by the most perverse calculation . . . incalculable justice *commands* calculation (2002: 257).

In other words, even though fraught with paradox, we have to calculate justice and make decisions through law. However, we should always keep in mind that no calculation is ever completely just. This requires us always to keep open the possibility of changing how we decide, and what sorts of claims to justice we make.

At this point, Derrida moves into a tantalizingly close reading of Benjamin, but let us leave the text to note some implications of Derrida's work for the present book. Most centrally, his work suggests we can study concepts of law, society, and justice without assuming that they are fixed or have an essential nature to be discovered. The concepts could be approached as heterogeneous events that become, through calculations of an excess, an illimitable promise that remains forever responsible to what is absent (other) to current possibilities.[4] The becoming of law in the name of justice, therefore, appears only by virtue of its rendering, its finite decisions, in a determined context, and yet that rendering is only ever possible because of the excess that justice implies. Derrida's approach to law and justice suggests a way of approaching law and society, jurisprudence, and socio-legal studies, without assuming fixed objects of study. One could frame such fields through a responsibility to the absences that prop up any 'objects'. In recognizing this responsibility, openness, to what is currently impossible may yet be another form of the constraint-rupture that we have previously described in connection with Foucault. One prospect for such a field of study is to develop further what this might mean for the historical practices and ideas that claim the mantles of 'law' and 'society'.

Rethinking 'Law's Empire'

One way to approach the ideas of Peter Fitzpatrick, who we have previously encountered, is to recollect Constantine Cavafy's poem 'Waiting For The Barbarians', and the subsequent novel of the same title by J.M. Coetzee. In the poem, Cavafy begins thus:

> What are we waiting for, assembled in the forum?
> The barbarians are due here today.
> Why isn't anything happening in the senate?
> Why do the senators sit there without legislating?
> Because the barbarians are coming today.
> What laws can the senators make now?
> Once the barbarians are here, they'll do the legislating
> (Cavafy 1992: 18, lines 1–7).

Coetzee's novel offers a similarly allegorical narrative in which a magistrate at the outer reaches of an imagined empire (with intended reference to the apartheid regime in South Africa) initially champions the superiority of his language, visions of law, and governance, as well as the need to protect his empire from an amorphous barbarism that is taken to embrace the exact opposite thereof. In anticipating the arrival of the never-to-appear barbarian invasion, Coetzee's magistrate narrates and later experiences first-hand the extraordinary measures (horrific torture) the empire is prepared to deploy in the name of protecting itself from the trumped-up threat of barbarian insurrections. In learning to speak the language of the other ('barbarian'), the magistrate is able to articulate a decline unavailable to 'protectors' of the empire, wedded to the myths of superior civilization in whose name extraordinary measures are deployed. The empire defines itself largely through the exclusions it musters. Cavafy's poem ends by making the point this way:

> Why this sudden restlessness, this confusion?
> (How serious people's faces have become.)
> Why are the streets and squares emptying so rapidly,
> everyone going home so lost in thought?
> Because night has fallen and the barbarians have not come.
> And some who have just returned from the border say
> there are no barbarians any longer.

And now, what's going to happen to us without barbarians?
They were, those people, a kind of solution
(1992: 19, lines 27–35).

Resonating with some of the themes of these rich texts, Fitzpatrick's (1992) analysis of the relationship between law and modernity centres on Nietzsche's claim, 'God is dead' (see also Fitzpatrick 2007). In the wake of that death, moderns allegorically claim to have surpassed a transcendental, religious, and **deific** (divine or godlike) **world** filled with irrational, mythic, and sacred symbols. Theirs is a new world imagined to be rational, scientific, and secular, one in which people must face the awesome question of how to define and understand themselves without creating 'barbarians' who will shore up fixed images of law and society. In this situation, law is freed from the limitations of theological revelation and divine provenance; but this view also—as Fitzpatrick's (2001, 1992) analysis of Hart and Dworkin demonstrates—divests law of a relation to justice in a modern myth that posits science and progress as the basis of law. With resonances of Benjamin, Fitzpatrick contends that, far from modern law being devoid of myth, as liberal protagonists would allege, it is very much part of modernity's broader myths about superior progress through science and universal rational law.

Paradoxically, however, in modernity the very denial of myth becomes itself an important myth that sustains a sense of 'superior', imperialist ways of being against 'myth-ridden' others (1992: ix)—not unlike Cavafy's or Coetzee's barbarians. Legal theory and its liberal formulations of a universal rule of law, posited as a rational or scientific (rather than mythic) modern process, is very much part of modernity's myth sustained by the 'solution' offered by amorphous 'barbarians' of one kind or another. Carefully reading several jurisprudential writers in a non-linear fashion, Fitzpatrick (1992) draws on Foucault and Derrida to develop a way of approaching law that does not repeat the imperialism of law's liberal empire (note too the resonances with critical legal studies).

That trajectory leads him to an important account of modern law's foundations. It begins by noting contradictory demands at the heart of modern images of the rule of law. On the one hand, law claims to offer 'certainty, predictability, and order' through purportedly **closed, coherent**, and **complete** decisions (Fitzpatrick 2001: 71). On the other hand, law cannot be *closed* because it must always adapt to the uncertainties of new events. It must hold itself 'constantly responsive to all that is beyond what it may at any moment be' (2007: 71). And it is not *coherent*, for 'how could the law, in extending to what is continuously other to itself, avoid pervasive contradiction'? (2007: 71). As well, law cannot be *complete*, for it must relentlessly respond to the diverse circumstances that confront it. Law thus reflects opposing ambitions. As Fitzpatrick puts it, 'For law to rule, it has to be able to do anything, if not everything. It cannot, then, simply secure stability and predictability but also has to do the opposite; it has to ensure that law is ever responsive to change, otherwise law will eventually cease to rule the situation which has changed around it' (2001: 71). If this is so, then how on earth are we to understand law's foundations?

Fitzpatrick detects in the 'persistent squabbles' of jurisprudence the following paradox: law is simultaneously seen to be **determinate** (fixed, closed) and at the same time highly **responsive** to change. For example, we noted how the legal theories discussed in Part I conceive of law as an autonomous entity whose essential form can always be described, but it must also always be able to change. In Part II, sociological and critical legal theories posited the law as both determined by, and yet responsive to, society. Such 'squabbles' lead Fitzpatrick to this intriguing approach:

> Rather than seeking law in that which simply conforms to either side or both sides of the opposition, perhaps we could seek a law which 'is' in-between the opposed dimensions, which 'is' the experienced combination of them, and which has its being because each dimension is inexorable yet unable to be experienced by itself. And perhaps these dimensions are equivalent to the divide between law's autonomy and law's dependence (2001: 72–3).

So, for him, law is *both* determinate in that its judges close off and decide specific cases, and yet also responsive to as yet unknown, future others. It is worth repeating Golder and Fitzpatrick's way of explaining this point:

> Law, if it is to rule effectively and secure the requisite certainty and predictability in the world beyond, must constantly relate to the ever-changing nature of society, the economy, and so forth. There is a constituent requirement for law to respond to the infinity of relation which can impinge upon its determinate position. And yet, whilst the law cannot simply ossify in the determinacy of its position, neither can it dissipate itself in a pure, unalloyed responsiveness to the other and to the changing world 'outside' it (Golder and Fitzpatrick 2009: 80).

If the above quotation provides a framework for approaching law, Fitzpatrick's allied reading of Derrida allows him to explore how law 'becomes the combination of determination with what is beyond determination' (2001: 76). In particular, he argues that the law cannot only be a form of calculation that 'cuts into' and renders an amorphous justice present, because 'justice, responsiveness, responsibility' always also enable law to become—instead, law surfaces precisely in-between the determinate and indeterminate. In other words, for him, the foundation of law rests on a moving contradiction: it decides determinately while simultaneously reacting to an illimitable future being. For him, the 'tie' between responsiveness and determination brings 'existence to normative futurity' and surpasses any 'contained condition', making law 'the most independent yet the most dependent of things' (Fitzpatrick, 2005:

9). And here he detects law's makeup as something that always depends on what it currently is not, its 'incipient alterity': 'Law is continually orientated to, continually opening to, the possibility of its being otherwise. Law moves beyond the assertion of any singular, even predominant power and in some ultimate sense receives power in its, in law's, own terms, filtering an intrusive power and ultimately constituting its content' (2005: 9–10).

If there is a meaning to law, it is not some fixed referent because of the constituent requirement that it should always be more than what it may be in any one context. This contradictory foundation, and not some positive content, distinguishes law, or provides for its '**groundless grounds**'. It also provides a way of seeing law as relentlessly becoming in contexts of nationalism, imperialism, and globalism (Fitzpatrick 2001). But this 'law of laws' is not—as 'law and society' discourses often champion—simply a new way of saying that social formations shape law (2005: 8). Rather, Fitzpatrick regards the 'incipient alterity' that is law, the illimitability of its changing forms, as pointing towards the event of becoming 'social'. It entails 'an assembly' or 'a place of convergence and divergence, of association and dissociation' for the 'social bond', the 'being-in-common' (2005: 16).

Fitzpatrick is not here returning to the idea that 'law' determines 'social being', because law's ever-changing responsiveness can never be sufficiently 'monadic' to secure that. However, he is suggesting that the determination and responsiveness of law converges with the idea of 'society'. Indeed, society is also realized in and through the same determinate-responsiveness scheme that is the 'law of the laws'. In so doing, Fitzpatrick opens the law and society field to contemplate the logic of how 'law' and 'society' become through images of (legal and social) justice. We have touched on this logic in respect of law, but it may also be extended by referring to Nancy's (2000) often-overlooked concept of 'Being with'. This could provide a way to conceptualize the becoming of associative patterns without fixing notions of 'society' or 'community' (see Pavlich 2004, 2001b).

Associating without Society?

There is doubtless this irrepressible desire for 'community' to form but also for it to know its limit—and for its limit to be its opening. Once it thinks it has understood, taken in, interpreted, kept the text, then something of this latter, something in it that is altogether other, escapes or resists the community, it appeals for another community, it does not let itself be totally interiorised in the memory of a present community. The experience of mourning and promise that institutes that community but also forbids it from collecting itself, this experience stores in itself the reserve of another community that will sign, otherwise, completely new contracts (Derrida 1995: 355).

Derrida above refers to an **idea of community** that echoes his analysis of justice, and recognizes an 'irrepressible desire' for community. Elsewhere, he speaks of the promise of a 'bond between singularities' that exceeds a community: 'The promise of the bond forms neither a national, linguistic, or cultural community, nor does it anticipate a cosmopolitan constitution. It exceeds all cultures, all languages, it even exceeds the concept of humanity' (2002: 240–1).

One could refer to this bond as an enduring 'promise of association', distinct from historically specific calculations thereof (e.g., community, society).[5] The latter should be differentiated from the illimitable, incalculable, yet 'irrepressible desire' for nourishing ways to associate with others (Woolford and Ratner 2008; Pavlich 2005, 2001a). In trying to understand the bond that ties 'responsiveness' and 'determination' as an event that helps a given image of 'society' or 'community' to become, one might usefully interpret Nancy (1993 2000) as grappling with the promise of association beyond fixed notions of community or society (Woolford 2009).

If Fitzpatrick refers to the paradoxical becoming of law as an indication of sociality, Nancy argues that all being emerges erratically from moments of **'Being with'**—this concept refers to the 'finite' (i.e., non-universal, 'non-metaphysical') ways in which we co-exist, quite literally are simply 'thrown' together randomly into a world. That is, we are all thrown (or perhaps 'abandoned') into an indeterminate, arbitrary world with others, and out of this we are responsible for fashioning existence. But, unlike Sartre's well-known 'existence precedes essence' adage, Nancy argues that 'existence has no essence'. Nothing is fixed, and any notions of existence (the being of anything) appear only by virtue of our 'co-existence'. In other words, without human 'Being with', there is nothing; our co-existence (what he calls 'the with') produces historical forms of being: 'Being cannot be anything but being-with-one-another, circulating in the with and as the with of this singularly plural existence' (2000: 3). That is, 'The with is the most basic feature of Being, the mark of the singular plurality of the origin or origins within it' (2000: 62).

To some this may sound like gibberish, but he is here rejecting a whole tradition of social thought that claims to be able to tell us what a pure, progressive, and advanced society looks like. In other words, there is no fixed society, but only forms of 'Being with' that are without end, and that shape our singular and plural existences at any moment in time (1993).

Specifically, Nancy talks of the **singularly-plural** (or equally the **plurally-singular**) way in which we encounter our Being with, our being abandoned with others. Each instance of 'Being with' is a singular event, but it is one that occurs plurally amongst the abandoned: 'the singular is primarily *each* one and, therefore, also *with* and *among* all the others. The singular is a plural' (2000: 32). Any calculation of the 'we', 'they', 'us', 'them', etc., is possible only because human being is abandoned together; that abandonment is an illimitable, incalculable, inessential, potential, and generates the 'spacing' to enable such identifications as 'I', 'we', etc. The challenge to finite thinking is never to allow any given finitude (calculation) to be postulated as an absolute, infinite being. Any identities of one and many (e.g., individual-community, self-society), and any democratic freedoms contingent upon these, are conditional outcomes of given forms of 'Being with' in finite horizons; they are different incarnations of 'Being singular-plural'. Replacing nouns (society, the social) with active verbs (associating, Being with, becoming) indicates Nancy's sense of the relentless flow, and the responsibilities, of our Being with others.

Here, Nancy helps us to think about the **promise of association** (being with others) without absolutely fixed images of either 'individuals' or 'community'/'society' (Pavlich 2001a).[6] This is why he urges us not to try to 'discover' the essence of what it is to exist as society (2000: 37), or to imagine society can be grasped through the study of being (**ontology**). Instead, he asks us to think of the very study of being, ' . . . itself as a "sociality" or "association" more originary than all "society", more originary than "individuality" and every "essence of Being". Being is with' (2000: 38).

Neither individual nor society (community) provides a point of departure, for both co-appear in singular-plural instances of 'Being with'. Society co-appears in uniquely modern ways of Being with, as does the 'individual-society' nexus. That calculation, in Nancy's work, co-appears with singularly-plural instances of 'the with'; paradoxically, 'society' and 'individual' can be simultaneously singular, plural, singularly-plural (a collection of individuals or societies), or plurally-singular (e.g., many different versions of a 'society'). If nothing else, the paradox repudiates the distinction between one and many, contesting sociology's enduring focus—to declare essential, fixed images of the individual-society couplet.

In parentheses, we might also contrast Nancy's view with, say, Weber's call for a value-free sociology that studies society, a view that reverberates with positivist calls for scientific analyses of social facts. For Nancy, ethics is only ever possible in terrains that are not determined, whereas ontology is ordinarily associated with terrains that are fixed by a presumed determination. Marx and, later, critical theorists (and, to a lesser extent, Durkheim) sought to reconcile—while keeping distinct—a preferred image of society to guide supposedly progressive social change. All appear to distinguish between the being of society and the ethics that allows one to declare that one society is necessarily better than another. But Nancy insists that, 'There is no difference between the ethical and the ontological: the 'ethical' exposes what the 'ontological' disposes' (2000: 99).

In this strong formulation, all forms of being are indeterminate co-appearances that never settle as fixed, determined entities. If there is freedom in our arbitrary abandonment with others, there are also grave responsibilities associated with the ethics of given patterns of being on others, without any absolutely certain sense of what is right or just. All that we have is the relentless capacity to find new ways of Being with.

Reading Nancy on an admitted bias, one is able to recover from his work a similar approach to the perhaps 'unfounded foundations' of society that we have analyzed in both Derrida's 'justice-law' and Fitzpatrick's 'determinate-responsiveness' couplets. Now it is an illimitable promise of association that is contrasted with historical versions of that promise (appearing through, say, fixed notions of community and society). The scholars discussed above approach justice, law, and society as events of becoming. These events operate through contradictory and paradoxical logics that involve: calculation and incalculability; limitation and illimitability; possibility and impossibility; determination and indeterminacy; closure and openness; identity and otherness, and so on. At the heart of such contradictions lies the genesis of our transient laws, and a response to otherness; in both of these lies a further attempt to become in new ways and with a different sense of responsibility.

Concluding Reflections

Once intersecting terrains of jurisprudence, legal theory, the sociology of law, and socio-legal studies are no longer configured around fixed concepts of law and society (and justice), many alternative ways to engage the law and society field emerge. If the previous chapters have reviewed selected examples, the current one suggests various ways in which the concepts may be theorized and deconstructively approached as always on the way, as relentlessly becoming. As noted, Derrida's justice-law couplet was developed through Fitzpatrick's determination-responsiveness as the law of laws, and transposed to Nancy's promise of association that 'co-appears' with particular instances of 'Being with.' In various ways, these theories suggest frames of analysis outside of those discourses that have formed around absolute conceptions of, say, law or society. They are *after law and society* in two senses: they eclipse essentialized postulations of the concepts 'law' and 'society', but they continue to pursue, through discourses of becoming, the transient appearances of such ideas. This chapter offers the prospect of a redefined law and society field that does not seek to discover the essence of its assumed objects. Instead, it nurtures thinking that locates itself at the margins, and is continuously directed to the always changing ways that given contexts call upon law, society, and justice to run their affairs. There is an inherent instability to paradoxical performances of law and society that limit, or determine through concrete calculations of the now, while at the same time remaining open to the illimitable and incalculable indeterminacy. If this context abandons human beings to an awesome freedom, it also gestures towards the complexity of our ways of becoming. Realizations of this sort provide a very different way to approach how we might historically call upon notions of law and society to incarnate infinite promises of justice.

Discussion Questions

1. Is there, as Derrida provocatively argues, 'nothing outside the text'?

2. Are both subjects and objects generated by language? What does this mean for your 'being' as a person?

3. If meaning in language is always deferred, does this suggest that we can never define any thing (e.g., law, society) absolutely? What does this mean for socio-legal analysis?

4. If law is both determining and, at the same time, formed by something else, is it, at root, a contradictory enterprise? What are the implications of your response?

5. Can a passive and static noun like 'society' adequately encapsulate Nancy's active idea of 'Being-with'? What does this say about the law and society field?

Suggested Readings

Darian-Smith, E., & Fitzpatrick, P. (1999). *Laws of the Postcolonial*. Ann Arbor: University of Michigan Press.

Derrida, J. (1997). *Deconstruction in a Nutshell: A Conversation with Jacques Derrida*. Edited with a commentary by John D. Caputo. New York: Fordham University Press.

Goodrich, P., et al. (eds.) (2008). *Derrida and Legal Philosophy*. Basingstoke: Palgrave Macmillan.

Relevant Websites

http://cavafis.compupress.gr/kave_32.htm
http://plato.stanford.edu/entries/derrida/
www.cardozo.yu.edu/life/fall1998/derrida/
www.scribd.com/doc/6990110/Derrida-Interview-on-Holocaust-and-Forgiveness
www.believermag.com/issues/200510/?read=interview_fitzpatrick
www.egs.edu/faculty/nancy.html

Conclusion:
After Law and Society?

There are many lessons to be learned from Kafka's notoriously obscure parable 'Before the Law' (which also appears in a version spoken by a priest in his book *The Trial*). Famously, it begins:

> Before the law sits a gatekeeper. To this gatekeeper comes a man from the country who asks to gain entry into the law. But the gatekeeper says that he cannot grant him entry at the moment. The man thinks about it and then asks if he will be allowed to come in sometime later on. 'It is possible,' says the gatekeeper, 'but not now.' The gate to the law stands open, as always, and the gatekeeper walks to the side, so the man bends over in order to see through the gate into the inside. When the gatekeeper notices that, he laughs and says: 'If it tempts you so much, try going inside in spite of my prohibition. But take note. I am powerful. And I am only the most lowly gatekeeper. But from room to room stand gatekeepers, each more powerful than the other. I cannot endure even one glimpse of the third.' The man from the country has not expected such difficulties: the law should always be accessible for everyone, he thinks, but as he now looks more closely at the gatekeeper . . . he decides that it would be better to wait until he gets permission to go inside.[1]

The plot has the man repeatedly begging to enter for the remainder of his life, but he is ultimately denied entry. 'Everyone strives after the Law,' says the man at the end of his days, 'so how is it that in these many years no one except me has requested entry?' In a cheerless response, the doorkeeper, ' . . . sees that the man is already dying and, in order to reach his diminishing sense of hearing, he shouts at him, "Here no one else can gain entry, since this entrance was assigned only to you. I'm going now to close it."' (ibid.).

What on earth is one to make of this unusual tale? I openly acknowledge not having an assured response to this question. Perhaps, at one level of thought, Kafka addresses the idea that law cannot be grasped, objectified, and discovered. We may apprehend the rituals, the gatekeepers, and even encounter the many thresholds that lead to various institutional parts of a 'justice' system. Nevertheless, the law remains elusive, beyond our grasp, forever in excess of where we try to domesticate it, to make it something tangible (i.e., with doorways to enter). We may be drawn to law's resolute promise of justice, but it is beyond what appears before each one of us at its thresholds. Does this mean we all have a sense of law and justice that is never fully graspable, a recognition that becomes clear at the point of death? If so, then Kafka appears to be signalling that law (no more than concepts like 'society' or 'justice') is never available as a fixed, contained being. It is never discoverable, and yet we never give up on our pursuit of law, society, and justice. They are always in the process of 'becoming'.

Taking this insight as an entree to our concluding discussion, we might return to a question raised in the introduction, and discussed obliquely throughout Part III: what can we expect to happen in the law and society field once its putative objects ('law' and 'society') no longer appear as stable entities with essences awaiting discovery? What happens to the field, in short, 'after law and society'? As already noted, the last phrase is ambiguous, because the term 'after' refers both to 'in pursuit of', and 'following on from'. Furthermore, as we have seen, the law and society field reflects both meanings simultaneously. The creation of fixed images of law and society, and the fundamental critiques of such images, together have defined the contemporary shape of the field. That this field no longer conceives of itself as its predecessors did is certainly no critique of its accomplishments. On the contrary, it is indicative of a fertile field where ideas continue to be debated and grow out of the legacies bequeathed by scholars before. To be sure, the trenchant socio-legal critiques of the past few decades may have contested law and society as fixed concepts, but, far from annulling the field, they have spawned new ways to approach and make sense of these terms.

Reflecting across the various approaches discussed in the preceding chapters, this conclusion will briefly review some of the formative contributions before speculating on possible future avenues for the law and society field. Specifically, I will return to note how the theorists of Parts I and II focused on responding to a basic 'what is . . . ?' sort of question, before considering the rather different theoretical tack of Part III. While the approaches of the latter part did not simply discard concepts of law or society as unworthy of further discussion, they did challenge the fixed images proposed by jurisprudence and the sociology of law. Such vital critiques have left deep imprints on the field and are likely to shape where it might head.

A Jurisprudential Question: 'What is the Nature of Law?'

The first part of the book details how selected legal theorists within jurisprudence variously differentiated 'their' law from other kinds of laws, or conceptual objects. In the process of defining *this* law as an independent 'object', they implicitly or explicitly start with variations of a basic question: 'What is the nature of law?' Indeed, Raz's (2005) reflections on legal theory suggest that this question necessarily addresses the foundation of jurisprudential thought. He assumes that law does have a 'nature', and that this nature refers to 'those of the law's characteristics which are of the essence of law, which make law what it is. That is those properties without which law would not be law' (2005: 328). Unsurprisingly, then, his approach openly 'presupposes that law has—indeed must have—an unchanging nature' (2005: 328). In short, for him, despite contextual variations, legal theory's law has a stable, discrete, and enduring essence. This assumption is espoused by diverse jurisprudential approaches; new theories of law layer such espousals, imperceptibly fortifying the idea that law is absolute with a fixed essence.

Thus, as will be recalled from Part I, classical natural law approaches distinguished valid human law as having to reflect a universal justice embraced by an eternal moral authority (e.g., Plato, Aristotle, Cicero, Augustine, Aquinas, Grotius). Were an adage to summarize their contributions to the law and society field, it might possibly be the one Aquinas attributes to Augustine: *lex iniusta non est lex* ('an unjust law is no law'). More recent natural law theorists refined these ideas to argue that a law, to qualify as law, must embrace morally defensible processes (Fuller), or conform to basic moral principles arrived at through practical reasoning (Finnis). By contrast, legal positivist approaches emphasized the observable features of law 'posited' by human beings, calling for scientific legal methods to discover this law for what it is. Without denying that law has moral dimensions, they argued that the 'is', and not the 'ought', is directly relevant to scientific (as opposed to, say, moral) analysis. Early versions thereof (Austin, Bentham, Hobbes) identified law as a command of a sovereign, habitually obeyed by subjects, while more recent accounts (Hart, Kelsen) considered law as systems of rules, or norms, that order our actions.

Legal formalists (Langdell) envisaged law as no more than what was declared by judges via reasoning through formal doctrines, rules, and principles from past (usually Supreme Court) decisions. Against this 'law in the books'-type definition, sociological jurisprudence (Pound) and American realist approaches (Holmes, Llewellyn, Frank) studied 'law in action', and the pragmatic ways judges actually (in reality?) decide cases (see Hunt 1978: 11ff.). They agreed with formalists that the law is what judges decide in given contexts, but added that extra-legal factors—not just rules—structure their decisions. From this vantage, one can predict what law will be by examining the factors that shape judges' verdicts. Therefore, extra-legal (social, cultural, psychological) variables explain what the law, adjudicated by judges, is likely to be in given cases.

As disparate as these jurisprudential approaches and legal theories may be, they all assume that 'law' exists independently, as a moral or empirical phenomenon, with distinctive, essential qualities. Deflem describes these as 'internal perspectives of law'— they study 'law in its own terms, as part of the workings of law itself, in order to contribute to the internal consistency of law by offering intellectual grounding to as well as practical training in the law' (2008: 4). In other words, even if such approaches reference society and justice, their frameworks take for granted that law is a central, absolute—even if changing—being. Law, rather than, say, society, is the starting point. Social factors may indeed shape, or be shaped by, law; but the law always comprises their primary reference point.

The depth of this belief is again clear from Raz's view of the foundations of legal theory, in which he argues that, 'The concept of law is among the culture-transcending concepts. It is a concept which picks out an institution which exists even in societies which do not have such a concept' (Raz 2005: 340). This is a strong claim: Raz here argues that law exists even if a society's culture has only Spartan concepts of what it is, or indeed no concept thereof! Furthermore, this law exists as an absolute being: 'The law can and does exist in cultures which do not think of their legal institutions as legal, and a theory of law aims to give an account of the law wherever it is found, including in societies which do not possess a concept of law' (Raz 2005: 337). Notwithstanding the imperialism required to sustain such an assertion (it is not simply a matter of overcoming 'parochialism', as he suggests), one could take it as a frank reflection of the confidence with which jurisprudence assumes its 'object' (usually implicitly), and then frames its approaches to address that focal point. Here one might summon Milovanovic's caution that, 'Clearly the accepted definition of law—in essence—confines the scope of the analysis of law' (1988: 8). Thus, when law is taken to be a reflection of justice, the analytical (philosophical) theories of classical natural law become explicable; equally, if law is considered to exist, in fact, then empirical positivism or pragmatic realism are more likely.

Whichever definition is adopted, the basic point is this: the fields of jurisprudence and legal theory are overwhelmingly formulated around a seemingly open question: '*What is the nature of law?*'[2] I say seemingly open, for such a question is actually premised on a closed assumption that responders must accept in order to answer the question. It demands a subtle commitment to the idea of 'law' as a discrete, a priori being, inviting a response predicated on that assumed being. As such, it is not as open-ended as it may at first appear. Consider this apparently facetious response: 'Wait a minute! There is no such thing as law, so I can't answer your question if framed in this way—I could offer only a banal response like "nothing". But I shan't; I shall merely point out that your question forces me to accept that law exists, and that the only matter to resolve is what its essential characteristics might be. I reject this.' If nothing else, this retort exposes the faith required to sustain jurisprudential approaches to the law and society field. But that same gesture appears in sociological approaches that proffer 'society' as the primordial entity, positing 'law' as its predicate.

The 'Social' and its Laws

Part II of this book devotes itself to three influential sociologists—Durkheim, Marx, and Weber—who approached law as a social construct, amenable to distinctively sociological analyses pursuing social justice. Durkheim, for example, approached society as a thing, as something that exists in and of itself, *sui generis*. Law then emerged as an index of different kinds of society (e.g., pre-modern, modern). Marx's rather different formulation emphasized the 'mode of production' as the foundation of any society. All forms of law, and understandings of justice, are historically located and grounded in basic modes and social relations of production. Capitalist law appears, therefore, as a product of the interaction between economic and social precepts, and its conceptions of justice usually preserve ideological commitments to an exploitative system. He challenges this bourgeois legal justice, proffering social justice as a way to contour socialist societies that are still to arrive. What form law might take in these societies, or whether it will survive at all, are amongst the many issues that continue to be debated in Marx's name—they also anticipate parts of the discussion in Part III.

Another formulation of 'society' was discussed with Max Weber's version of 'hermeneutic' sociology, and elements of a sociology of law that he developed at the time of his death. Weber considered law to be a kind of social action whereby meaningful behaviour is centred on issuing a legitimate order that has a specially designated staff dedicated to enforcing compliance to it through sanctions. His typologies suggest how modern law is largely created out of rational forms of social action that increasingly define modern society. Law is a product of prior social action and the social forms that such action enables.

All of these sociological conceptions render law dependent upon underlying social concepts—this was to become the focal point for the sociology of law that was, by the 1970s and 1980s, well established in the broader law and society field.[3] In this ethos, one senses a remarkable commitment to an 'age of sociology' that could transform 'societies' and rescue 'law' from its jurisprudential constraints. Providing a particularly telling example of this tendency, Black offers this extraordinary prediction: 'Sociological knowledge will surely grow, creeping throughout the world with a faithfulness unknowable. We only know that the science of society changes society. Social action increasingly becomes a self-conscious application of sociology. Sociological power is harnessed, a new form of energy generated, its uses impossible to imagine. A sociological society' (1989: 103).

In retrospect, this is a remarkable preface to an equally notable view that, 'This must be a new stage of human evolution (1989: 103).' Even if such dubious assertions are not representative, they do indicate the zest with which some sociologists of law proffered sociological images of society as a better way to understand 'justice without law' (see Auerbach 1983). In stark contrast to those heady days, promising so much of the sociology of law, Deflem's recent and more subdued reflection hardly conceals a disappointment: 'Most noticeable is the lack of distinctness that is occasionally accorded to the sociological study of law, and other social scientists have begun to stake their respective claims in the study of law . . . the resulting situation is such that the sociology of law has, some exceptions notwithstanding, lost its distinct place in socio-legal studies as well as in sociology' (2008: 2). For all that, he seeks to reinvigorate a canonical sociological approach to law that recognizes, 'The most defining characteristic of the sociology of law is the specific manner in which it approaches law in disciplinary terms' (2008: 274). But such an appeal to sociology is unlikely to gain traction in an ethos where it is no longer clear how one might enunciate what a distinctive sociological approach is, to say nothing of assuming 'society' as a uniformly steady object of study.

Questioning 'What is . . .?' Questions

To reiterate, we have seen how both jurisprudence (legal theory) and the sociology of law developed approaches focused on the objects 'law' and 'society'. In each case, versions of the 'what is . . . ?' question frame contributions to the law and society field. And this returns us to a question that launched our discussion: without essentialized concepts of 'law' and 'society', what is to happen to the field of law and society? However, before we address this question, it is important to consider the grounds for suggesting that absolute visions of law and society have become difficult to sustain. In response, one could refer readers to Lyotard's (1984) decades-old report on knowledge that has spawned so much heated debate. He plausibly argued that the underlying foundations (the framing 'meta-narratives') of modernity's forms of knowledge have, in recent times, faced unprecedented assaults. As radically altering conditions irreparably crack these foundations, so the knowledge that depends on them is increasingly questioned (perhaps even viewed with 'incredulity' rather than as credible truth). Lyotard's point here is not that a particular knowledge claim about some or other fixed being (e.g., 'law' or 'society') is contested; rather, modernity's entire knowledge-producing ethos is in crisis. In the context of the present analysis, Lyotard might be referenced to argue that approaches revolving around the assumption that it is possible to identify (discover) fixed objects (like law and society) have become difficult to sustain in radically reordered truth regimes (see Pavlich 2000, 1996).

But even without accepting Lyotard's trenchant analysis, one could refer to specific debates within the law and society field. As noted, critical versions of jurisprudence and legal theory have endogenously challenged the very idea that law can be fixed in the way that Raz (see above) would like us to approach it (see Davies 2008). At the same time, several sociologists and social theorists have questioned the very existence of 'society' as espoused by the likes of Durkheim, especially in declining social welfare contexts and the rise of neoliberal thinking that no longer take the social for granted (see Pavlich 2001a, b). In the wake of such influential challenges, the certainty with which law and society were articulated as objects has assuredly been destabilized, rendering associated 'what is . . .?' questions without unequivocal referents. The law and society field has yet to fully assess the effects of such significant developments, but the reverberations are difficult to miss.

Specifically, within the context of jurisprudence and legal theory, classical common law theory had, from the outset, at least indicated the difficulty of establishing law as a fixed being, most succinctly through Hale's allegorical reference to the Argonauts' ship, or Titus's changing body.[4] How can something remain an absolute, essential being when it must continuously face radically new contexts, adapting—sometimes foundationally—to the passages of time and space? It may be possible to define law in a relatively generic fashion, but that cannot sustain the assertion of an absolute being necessary to discover the essences required by 'what is the nature of law?' type questions. It may even be that the idea of a universal and essential law as an object to be discovered by jurisprudence is doomed from the outset, a point recently underscored by critical thinking within jurisprudence (e.g., Douzinas and Gearey 2005), and reiterated by critical legal studies, feminist jurisprudence, and critical race theories that were reviewed in Chapter 8.

We saw how this broad critical legal studies movement challenged liberal images of law, insisting on the historical means by which it emerges through distinct socio-political processes. The point was made in various ways, but at base it emphasized that law cannot be objectified, reified, or hypostasized as an absolute being; it is instead always a contingent and dynamic 'problem' for those seeking justice. In Hunt's words, 'Critical scholars are motivated by a much broader political objective within which it is "the law" itself that is "the problem"; law is not conceived as being capable of resolving the problem that it apparently addresses. Rather law is seen as a significant constituent in the complex set of processes that reproduces the experience and reality of human subordination and domination' (1993: 180). Critical strands of feminist jurisprudence as well as critical race theories echoed this process-based formulation of the 'politics of law' that framed the experiences of those subject to oppressive, hierarchical, and alienating social forms.

As well, Veitch et al. (2007) note how the rise of new patterns of sovereignty politics in globalizing contexts nurtured paradigms that highlight 'the ways in which old certainties are being undermined, and which require us to "unthink" many of the core assumptions of the modernist conception of law' (2007: 205). Holding onto conceptions of law as an object, with essential characteristics to be discovered through science, or even metaphysics, is precisely one of those crumbling 'old certainties' that has yielded, and is yielding, to the emergence of new forms of sovereignty and judicial horizons in postcolonial and other contexts alike (see Barbour and Pavlich 2010). If nothing else, this should alert us to the devastating problems confronting those who would close off law as a singular object, a being *sui generis*.

Many commentators in sociology have reached a similar conclusion on the objectification of society, the social, social order, social need, social insurance, and so on (Pavlich 2001a: 1–5; Bauman 2002: 41ff., 1997, 1992). In general terms, with the changing fortunes of social welfare governance in advanced liberal (neoliberal and neoconservative) contexts, several theorists have noted the manner in which concepts like society are being redeployed. As O'Malley put it, speaking over a decade ago, 'During the last two decades the social has been increasingly challenged and extensively displaced by political rationalities of rule . . . that seek to govern through individuals, families and a multitude of quasi-contractual, quasi-voluntary connectivities such as the "community"' (1996: 27).

So comprehensive is this changing pattern of governance that some commentators have even declared, 'the social is dead'. Baudrillard (1983), for example, argues that the cultural mechanisms by which it may once have been possible to project an image (simulacra) of the social are obsolete; as a result, we cannot easily sustain the illusion of an amorphous society, or the 'social', as if it were an absolute being waiting to be discovered.

Rose (1999) offers another version of this challenge to fixed conceptions of society. For him, 'society' was once a legitimate way to conceive of collective experiences within (liberal) contexts where social welfare patterns of governance predominated: ' . . . the "social" does not refer to an inescapable fact about human beings—that they are social creatures—but to a way in which human intellectual, political and moral authorities, within a limited geographical territory, thought about and acted upon the collective experience for about a century' (1999: 101).

Like Sarat (2004a: 4ff.) and Bauman (2002), Rose argues further that this way of imagining collective experiences has been delegitimized in advanced global contexts where social welfare governance confronts significant challenges in neo-liberal contexts. As well, for Bauman, using the social as an orientating precept for sociology occurred at a time when a particular kind of 'modern science' was envisaged: 'One needed to know one's object because knowing one's object was tantamount to disarming it. Stealing the object's mystery was like stealing Jupiter's thunder. A known object would not put up any more resistance; or at the least one could anticipate such resistance as the object may put up, taking the necessary precautions to pre-empt its impact' (Bauman 2002: 1). But, he argues (1997), as the early forms of modernity transformed into current conditions (late modernity?), so the very ground sustaining both the object and methods of sociology have shifted. This is especially pronounced as new global political formations challenge the previously seamless connections between sovereignty, 'society', and 'nation state'. The complexities of his argument notwithstanding, Bauman notes how in such contexts ' . . . sociology, much like society, its long-time object . . . found itself in a double bind: *it lost its natural(ized) object together with its self-evident client*' (2002: 11).

So, in short, one need not accept the wholesale 'death' of 'the social' in order to recognize that the once easy assertion of society as an absolute object has lost its ground. Its significance as a trope through which to imagine collective being now appears less a solution than an emerging problem (Cotterrell 2008; Pavlich and Hird 2007; Fitzpatrick 2001; Pavlich 2001a).

In all these ways, critical tendencies within jurisprudence and sociology have effectively destabilized the certainty with which the objects, law and society, were once unquestioningly enunciated. Law and society are most certainly not dead, but a once dominant way of approaching these concepts is gravely wounded. This has produced a mounting disquiet in the field, with influential critiques confronting no particular definition of law or society, but rather the very possibility of establishing either 'law' or 'society' (or indeed justice) as objects *sui generis*—i.e., as essential and stable beings capable of serving as orientating points of reference for jurisprudence, legal theory, and the sociology of law to discover. The implications of this criticism are far-reaching: at stake is the very possibility of developing law and society around assumptions of a stable object.

Part III suggests how various approaches have offered alternative ways of conceptualizing and dealing with law and society. Significantly shaped by Foucault's reading of Nietzsche on the importance of focusing not on 'being', but 'becoming', these approaches did not seek to 'discover' the essence of 'law', 'society', or 'justice', but highlighted how these concepts are always on the way, always becoming. By arranging their discourse around such precepts, analysts could now engage the limits of any putative being. Whether considered a 'limit attitude', or a deconstructive grammatology, or something else, key theorists of contemporary and post-colonial law and society (i.e., Benjamin, Cover, Agamben, Butler, Mbembe, Comaroff and Comaroff, Derrida, Fitzpatrick, and Nancy) approached the field in another way: pursuing the contingent ways that images and practices in the name of law and society arise in specific contexts. These approaches did not try to 'gather' essential features of law and society as objects. They did not gaze upon closed concepts. Instead, they examined the ways by which seemingly closed concepts were solidified through specific contextual interventions, with the express aim of relentlessly pursuing more open promises of justice.

Three Speculations on a Transforming Field

All this returns to the question previously raised: What is to become of a law and society field that appears to have abandoned its original mandate to study stable conceptions of 'law' and 'society'? As I see it, at least three influential responses to this are already in place, and will likely serve as stepping stones to new field-defining areas. The first—the 'business as usual' approach—finds participants living out a nostalgic simulation, perhaps averting their eyes from crumbling foundations that once sustained their scholarly objects. The second tendency seeks to 'cross boundaries' between law and society, focusing on what fuses rather than distinguishes them. Finally, approaches that focus on how visions of law and society become in historical contexts have opened the way to new possibilities. All three tendencies are likely to spawn further socio-legal analyses. As conjecture, I openly concede the following to be a modest attempt to imagine possible futures that *could* grow out of the discursive drifts described above.

More particularly, the first ('business as usual') response finds areas of jurisprudence and the sociology of law (as suggested by Raz and Deflem above) seeking renewed empirical and analytic attempts to capture the essence of some facet of law, society, or the relations between these. In response to substantial challenges from critics, this tendency is likely to assume an increasingly defensive posture, perhaps describing its own efforts as the most scientific, or analytically rigorous, way of dealing with law or society. The net effect may be to expand the field by appropriating 'scientific methodologies' (quantitative, qualitative, ethnographic, etc.) and analytical methods in philosophy in renewed attempts to capture the essence of law and society. Within these circles, too, the tendency to reject out of hand critical challenges to the very ontology of these objects may persist, but more destructive would be a cliquish commitment to being-centredness. However, one could also envisage reflective forms of realism and the sociology of law seeking to engage contexts with new approaches to ontology. Here one might foresee attempts to link notions of being and event, to reconsider law and society as events of being in ways that, for example, Badiou (2009) has proposed. This would certainly enable new directions to emerge within jurisprudence and the sociology of law. Regardless, without embarking on interesting changes in direction, these scholars will likely wander nostalgically amidst the ruins of grand beliefs of yore, gathering up essential properties to ascribe to the self-asserted objects of their studies. Not without its attractions for adherents, I tend towards the view that this may in the longer term be a doomed prospect, a wistful attempt to recover what would appear to be irrecoverable from the transformations of contemporary contexts.

The second speculation centres on the fusion of law and society. There are already well-established socio-legal approaches that, for some decades, have deflected attention away from either law or society, focusing on the conjunction (the *and*) between these. As Sarat et al. argue, 'The identity of the scholarly field resides as much in the "and" of "law and society" as it does in the two terms that the "and" connects' (1998: 1). Pursuing with greater precision the realist formulation of law as a social process, this approach has valuably tried to understand the dynamism and mutuality of the concepts (Munger 1998). Nonet and Selznick make the point this way: 'The idea of law loses focus if it is identified with coercive power ("the gunman writ large") or dissolved into the broader notion of social control . . .' (2007: 10–11). Instead they too emphasize the *and* as pivotal for moving beyond either the formalism of conventional jurisprudence, or sociology's tendency to overshadow law by society. Undoubtedly, the framing supposition is not to preserve either 'law' or 'society' as absolute things; on the contrary, the relations between them are emphasized. Hunt's relational theory of law provides an example of this tendency: 'Its project is one that takes "law" as its object of enquiry but pursues it by means of the exploration of the interaction between legal relations and other forms of social relations rather than treating law as an autonomous field of inquiry linked only by external relations to the rest of society' (1993: 224).

More recently, Sarat (2004) and many contributors to that collection extend realist insights to take advantage of new opportunities. Specifically, Sarat argues, as the initial optimism and prestige of social science's law and society formulation wanes, so ' . . . the hold of legal realism on the law and society imagination has loosened, relaxing the pull of the normative, reformist impulse in much of law and society research as the dominant paradigm for work that seeks to chart the social life of law (Sarat 2004a: 4).' For him, the product of this loosening is likely to produce an 'era of freedom' with 'great energy, vitality, and . . . fragmentation of existing definitions and boundaries of law and society research' (2004a: 4). Amidst this fragmentation, Sarat and Simon (2003: 1ff.) propose a turn to 'culture', and a focus on the cultural dimensions of law, as a direct response to 'the death of the social'. Their overall claim is this:

> As the logics of governance in the late modern era turn from society to culture, legal scholarship itself should turn to culture to more fully embrace cultural analysis and cultural studies . . . we view cultural studies as a kind of epistemological corrective to the plethora of problems posed for postrealist legal studies by the crises of the social liberal state and its allied forms of knowledge (2003: 4).

Importantly, too, they note that, as socio-legal images of 'society' decline, and with a more amorphous cultural lens from which to analyze law, so questions of 'methodology' and approach become crucial. Whether one agrees with the suggested move to cultural studies or not, there is a growing body of research that has emerged out of declining epistemological frameworks— a move that has revived work in the semiotics of law (Milovanovic 2003), a well-established law and literature approach (e.g., Sanders 2007), and diverse cultural analyses of law (e.g., Sarat 2004a; Sarat and Simon 2003; Danielsen and Engle 1995). The fecund interdisciplinarity that has already been drawn to such conjunctions—the *and* of law and society—has gained considerable momentum. As this research strides into a greater appreciation of its relation to critical socio-legal thinking, and the possibilities of framing a positive program without descending into the easy comforts of unreflective empiricism, there are here far-reaching prospects for developing the field in challenging ways.

With areas of interest overlapping the previously discussed tendency, a third possibility for the future of the field is likely to proceed from the diverse approaches (Part III) that have eschewed the belief in fixed, identifiable beings like law and society, variously examining the ways that these happen as events in specific contexts. We have charted several contributions to this theme, and various developments could be anticipated as outgrowths of their approaches.

As noted, Foucault's work has inspired several important examinations of the changing forms of power—especially with respect to the fate of law and sovereignty models of power in contemporary contexts. His Nietzsche-inspired approach could also be used to reframe the very idea of critique in socio-legal research, given foundational changes to knowledge-producing contexts (Pavlich 2001a). As I see it, Foucault's approach is not critical in ways one might expect from conventional criticisms that normatively judge particular situations against putatively founded criteria, with the aim of achieving progress (Pavlich 2000). Instead, his work seems to call for approaches to critique that separate and open outwards, rather than those that cut, and judge, in efforts to define what kind of being should be considered absolute and necessary. Such new grammars of critique, therefore, do not try to discover what is essential to a presumed being. They are more attentive to opening up historical definitions of 'existence', preventing a particular historical definition from closing itself off as necessary and universally valid. This sort of critique is focused on how we become, rather than asserting what we supposedly (necessarily) are. Its aim is for us to remain receptive and open to unknowable futures, always making place for forms of being deemed impossible from within our limited, presented, horizons. Such openings are vital to preventing the sorts of totalitarian closures that have spilled so much blood in historical attempts to realize purportedly immutable images of what it is to exist as lawful, social, human beings. Avoiding such arbitrary closures provides significant scope for socio-legal scholarship to reach beyond the ruts that now constrain once vibrant grammars of critique within the field. And in pursuit thereof it is important to avoid the dangers of pledging unreflective allegiance to an amorphous, if unrefined, empirical science of fixed objects.

We have also seen how Foucault's scattered references to law have generated considerable socio-legal reflection, but there are at least three further ways in which it might be developed. First, his interesting statements on law as a way of embracing historically sanctioned, truth-testing relations to verify and judge past events has yet to attract sustained attention, but it would add an interesting element to future socio-legal analysis. The relation between such truth-seeking and the 'lore of accusation' by which strangers in the midst are declared might also be expanded further (Pavlich 2007b).

Secondly, as we have seen, Butler and Agamben develop Foucault's work to formulate new understandings of law and its relation to emerging socio-political formations. Considered as unfolding events, the very appearance of new forms of law, beyond liberal claims to a neutral rule of law, were described through Agamben's idea of a force without content, and Butler's formulations of law as a governmental tactic. Such formulations speak to a problematic unleashing of more or less unfettered sovereigns, with serious consequences for contemporary political and social arenas. Agamben's paradigmatic image of bare life in a 'camp' has already elicited considerable discussion, and is likely to continue to do so. But this line of inquiry could also be mobilized further in discussions about how such developments will affect specific kinds of law (criminal, property, contract, constitutional, administrative, and so on). It could also examine further the complexities of relations between emerging forms of law and emerging conceptions of 'life' and 'rights' (beyond natural law or national state-based rights), and could significantly alter the trajectories of both. No doubt, too, the idea of legal pluralism as it plays itself out in contexts of national, biopolitical sovereignty will continue to be an important theme. One thinks here of various claims to sovereignty (Quebec, First Nations) as well as local and historical claims to law in post-colonial (and other) contexts (e.g., Aboriginal legality, customary law). Indeed, the logical architecture of sovereignty, and its relation to law, politics, society, and life, offers fertile fields for future analysis (see, for example, Derrida 2009). Equally, there is the whole issue of global law, or attempts to frame new extra-national sovereign law (e.g., the International Criminal Court). In each case, the political role and effects of unfolding conceptualizations of law and society are poised for much further elaboration, especially in contexts where post-colonial patterns of governance bring issues to the fore that stretch, or defy, prevalent truths.

Thirdly, while discussions of the social in the context of neo-liberal or advanced liberal formations are well developed (see Rose 2009, 1999), an arena focusing on how the social could be assembled as an ongoing event has not been fully developed. This sort of approach could extend Nancy's somewhat abstracted formulations, and take a more tangible form such as Latour's (2005) call for a 'sociology of association' and his 'actor network theory'. The implications of this approach may yet have profound effects for the relation between the social as event, and the legal as historical assemblage. The conjunctions between such an analysis and collective oppressions arising from performances that generate contextual identities (e.g., race, gender, sex, class, sexual orientation) could continue to structure vital political agendas. This could also lead into discussions of new forms of law and society, highlighting how renewed social 'assemblages' might occasion new legal terrains (Butler 2004). This may also require the field to abandon entrenched distinctions between fact and value, or nature and culture (Latour 2005).

Another line of inquiry may be extracted from Benjamin and Cover's analyses of law as distinguishable by claims of law to the legitimate use of violence. They, along with Agamben and Butler, note that modern law has no real attachment to normative and moral content; it makes no significant attempt to justify its use of violence by consistently appealing to notions of justice (however framed). Cover nicely notes that this may well be a function of legal positivism's success, and its explicit call for lawyers not to account for the moral elements of law. Regardless, the view that law is constituted through a relation to violence has attracted considerable attention and is in the process of further elaboration in the US (Butler 2004; Rasch 2004; Sarat 2001) as well as postcolonial contexts (Comaroff and Comaroff 2006; Geschiere 2006; Mbembe 2003; Darian-Smith and Fitzpatrick 1999). In all of these perspectives, there lurks the prospect of new calls for law to serve justice rather than to simply be a 'fact' in a given social formation. If not simply a return to natural law, this call, if heeded, could challenge the established privilege of legal and sociological positivism and revitalize attempts to pursue the becoming of law and society through diverse promises of justice (legal and social).

Many of the previous potential ways of developing the law and society field may imply a broader theoretical edifice that ties, as did Derrida (2009), calculations of what law and sovereignty might become (and, we might add, what society might become) to a radically incalculable promise of justice. In effect, this implies the potential to theorize further the 'becoming of law and society through justice' idea in detail. Fitzpatrick's helpful 'law of laws' provides a key reference point for the contradictory, but nevertheless constitutive, tie that binds law's becoming to two requirements: the imperative to decide finitely and 'determinately' in a given case, and also to do so in ways that respond to the infinite otherness of radically unknown futures. That logic might equally be brought to bear on attempts to assemble the social in the name of justice, to recognize the imperatives of communality in a given instance that must also respond to a promise of association never represented by any given instance thereof. Here the call for new horizons of meaning and practice is explicit, and suggests that enunciations of law and society are always contingent, but they are also necessary and without end.

If such speculation signals fruitful avenues for new socio-legal analysis, it should also allay the unfounded qualms of now tired refrains and unproductive denigrations like 'legal theory and the sociology of law are simply ivory tower pursuits', 'all this post-structural and postmodern theory has led to nothing', and even 'law and society has had its day!' All three tendencies previously noted are likely to shape the boundaries of the field in new directions, revitalizing the field's offerings by recasting its objects dynamically. One might even say that the unfolding days of the socio-legal field, formed around diverse promises of justice, will never arrive. This recognition bestows renewed value to ongoing redefinitions of the broad and always-changing field of law and society scholarship. It also pays homage to past meaning horizons that inescapably contour even the most iconoclastic leaps into future openings.

Suggested Readings

Comaroff, J., & Comaroff, J.L. (eds.) (2006). *Law and Disorder in the Postcolony.* Chicago: University of Chicago Press.

Sarat, A., Constable, M., Engel, D., Hans, V., & Lawrence, S. (eds.) (1998). *Crossing Boundaries: Traditions and Transformations in Law and Society Research.* Evanston: Northwestern University Press and the American Bar Association..

Wickham, G., & Pavlich, G.C. (2001). *Rethinking Law, Society and Governance: Foucault's Bequest.* Oxford: Hart.

Notes ···

Introduction

1. That is, a system of governance with the Queen formally at its head, but with the *Constitution Act, 1982*, limiting and specifying the legitimate exercise of authority.

2. In an influential text that appeared several decades ago, the field was described as directed to various aspects of this underlying assumption: 'Within modern societies law has become the primary device for attempting to create and control social order. Law, for modern man, has become a metaphor for ordered social life.' (Campbell and Wiles 1979: ix).

3. Heuristically, and without claiming a rigid separation between these, I will use 'law and society' to refer to a broader and diverse field of scholarship directed to different images of law and society. Related to that, 'socio-legal studies' will refer to approaches that focus on the confluences of 'law' and 'society' rather than trying to assert clear separations between them, or holding on to rigid images of law's (or society's) true nature. Both 'law and society' and socio-legal studies have links with, but are less fundamentally attached to, sociology than is the sociology of law.

4. *Shorter Oxford English Dictionary*, 5th edition, 2002.

5. The term 'postmodernism' has been used in many different ways, but in the context of socio-legal studies, it mostly refers to a foundational critique of 'modern' claims to have created the most rational, universal, and advanced forms of law and society (see Pavlich 1996a, b). Postmodern thinking challenges modernity's sanguine assumptions, and particularly the view that sovereign government through law is necessarily better than other forms of governance, and that reason-based society is a definite improvement (advance) over 'primitive' societies.

6. This term is often used to refer to a group of French thinkers (most of whom reject the label!) who, in various ways, challenged the (structuralist) idea that the subject who signifies (gives meaning to) the world through language is the foundation of all that is 'signified' (i.e., crudely, meaning is generated by the signifier). By contrast, post-structuralists view meaning as created out of the interplay between signifier and what is signified (e.g., see Chapter 11 for a discussion of Derrida's analysis of meaning in language).

Chapter 1

1. See the 'simile of the cave' in Plato (1971, pt. 7, book 7, p178ff.). In this simile, Plato compares knowledge to a situation of people in a cave where sunlight enters through a gap. Those who are enslaved or otherwise bound to the cave see only shadows and images, believing (falsely) this to be true knowledge. However, it is only the philosopher king who, through a life of reasoning, is able to escape the cave, confronting the true source of the light and, by analogy, the essential forms of true knowledge.

2. On slavery Aristotle argues, 'It is clear, then, that some men are by nature free, and others slaves, and that for these latter slavery is both expedient and right (2004: 206).' On a related note, Davies (2008: 84ff.) discusses the misogynist commitments of his analysis,

highlighting the importance not only of reading Aristotle critically, but remaining alert to the inauspicious lineage of key jurisprudential foundations.

3. In particular, he notes that ' . . . a man is a just character when he acts justly of deliberative purpose, and he does act justly if he acts voluntarily' (2004: 95).

4. See Johnson et al. (2001: 16ff.)

5. The term 'ontology' refers here to the philosophical study of what it means to say that something exists, what the categories of being are, etc.—a kind of study expressly directed to the nature or logic of being.

6. It is worth noting that Cicero also evokes an organic analogy to argue that the integration of elements is crucial to the functioning of nature's whole: 'Just imagine if each of our limbs had its own consciousness and saw advantage for itself in appropriating the nearest limb's strength. Of course the whole body would inevitably collapse and die' (1971: 166).

7. See Finnis (1998: chap. 7) for more discussion on Aquinas's 'complete communities'.

8. Grotius's support for capitalism is perhaps not unrelated to his work for the Dutch East India Company. Regardless, this image of private property as an implicit good is exactly what Marx (see Chapter 6) will roundly contest.

Chapter 2

1. http://www.disa.ukzn.ac.za/index.php?option=com_displaydc&recordID=1 eg19490708.028.020.055, accessed 16 January 2009.

2. See also Dyzenhaus (1998) on this matter.

3. For example, Fuller argues that 'Substantive limitations on the power of government should be kept to a minimum and should generally be confined to those for which a need can be generally appreciated. In so far as possible, substantive aims should be achieved procedurally, on the principle that if men are compelled to act in the right way, they will generally do the right things' (Fuller 1957: 643).

4. As he puts it, 'Where the morality of aspirations starts at the top of human achievement, the morality of duty starts at the bottom. It lays down the basic rules without which an ordered society is impossible, or without which an ordered society directed toward certain goals must fail of its mark' (1969: 5–6).

5. In a rather turgid way he asserts that ' . . . it is my thesis that when we accept the full consequences that flow from a view which treats human action as goal-directed, the relation between fact and value assumes an aspect entirely different from that implied in the alleged "truism" that from *what is* nothing whatever follows as to *what ought to be*'.

6. See also his expanded, if convoluted, definition (1980: 276).

7. And in this regard, Cotterrell helpfully reminds us that Finnis's theory 'essentially offers a moral philosophy to give guidance as to what law's substance and purposes *should be*, rather than a normative legal theory to explain doctrinal components or characteristics of particular legal systems' (2003: 140).

8. This view is echoed by Finnis's sense that 'the ruler's use of authority is radically defective if he exploits these opportunities by making stipulations intended by him not for the common good but for his own or his friends' or party's or faction's advantage, or out of malice against some person or group' (1980: 352).

9. He tells us that this situation pertains 'wherever there is, over an appreciable span of time, a coordination of activity by a number of persons, in the form of interactions, and with a view to a shared objective' (1980: 153).

Chapter 3

1. See Hart (1957) and Fuller (1958).

2. The case is described in some detail by both Fuller (1958: 652–5) and Hart (1957: 619–20).

3. See Fuller (1958: 644–5).

4. See Davies (2008: 100ff.) for a helpful discussion of this point.

5. For instance, Wacks (2006), and see Hobbes's *De Cive*, chap. 3, note 6.

6. See Hobbes's *De Cive* at http://www.constitution.org/th/decive06.htm, accessed 5 February 2009. I will throughout the present book replicate emphases as they appear in original quotations, unless otherwise specified.

7. See Cotterrell (2003: chap. 3) for more discussion on their relationship.

8. As Hart put it, 'Law is not morality; do not let it supplant morality' (1957: 618).

9. This is perhaps not surprising given that Hart claims that the Concept of Law may be 'regarded as an essay in descriptive sociology' (1994: v).

10. It is perhaps important to note that Hart is not suggesting that the relationship between law and some very basic moral content is entirely arbitrary—he speaks of 'the minimum content of natural law' as providing some basic prescriptions (e.g., 'Thou shalt not kill') that are necessary for social survival and the preservation of conditions within which rules of the law can function (1994: 185–212).

11. See Hart (1994: chap. 7) for a discussion of these 'hard cases', and Johnson et al. (2001: 150–2) for a secondary description thereof.

12. Specifically, as Kelsen puts it, 'Hence the law is not, as Austin formulates it, a rule "enforced" by a specified authority, but rather a norm which provides a specific measure of coercion as sanction (1941: 2, 55).'

13. As he puts it, 'the reason for the validity of the norm is always a norm . . . the reason of validity of a norm leads back, not to reality, but to another norm . . .' (1961: 111).

14. We shall return to such law-making activities in Walter Benjamin's work (see chap. 10).

Chapter 4

1. The case points to the dangers of Holmes's decision (paragraph 9), and reaches an opposite conclusion: 'Sterilization should never be authorized for non-therapeutic purposes under the parens patriae jurisdiction. In the absence of the affected person's consent, it can never be safely determined that it is for the benefit of that person. The grave intrusion on a person's rights and the ensuing physical damage outweigh the highly questionable advantages that can result from it. The court, therefore, lacks jurisdiction in such a case.'

2. In an apparent reference to classical common law theorists, Holmes also argues that, 'When we study law we are not studying a mystery but a well-known profession' (1897: 991).

3. For Pound, an interest is simply 'a demand or desire which human beings, either individually or through groups of associations or relations, seek to satisfy' (1968: 66).

4. In parentheses, one might here note the resonance with more recent social control approaches (Black 1984).

5. This is one of the reasons that Pound has been called the 'torchbearer of progressive legal thought' (Willrich 1998: 67).

6. It is common to differentiate the 'American' legal realists from Scandinavian realism, which also focused on the 'day-to-day' processes and rituals of law (see Johnson et al. 2001).

Chapter 5

1. Durkheim's concept *conscience collective* refers to both the collective consciousness and conscience (moral view of right and wrong)—the connotations of both are implied in my use of the concept in this chapter.

2. As he puts it, 'Every society is a moral society' (1984: 173).

3. Interestingly, Durkheim argues that, 'What limits the legal power of the State is not the just claim of the individual, but that of the clan or the family, or at least what remains of it. This is not an anticipation of our modern morality, but an archaic survival' (1983: 117).

4. As both Hunt (1978: 86) and Milovanovic (2003: 36) note, this is very similar to Henry Sumner Maine's (2002 [1861]) argument that law progresses from 'status' to 'contract'.

5. He (1983: 229) singles out the institution of inheritance with particular vehemence, and notes its incompatibility with a meritocracy, the sort of society he champions. He also refers specifically to usury and labour laws as examples that try to counter unfair structural conditions behind will-based contracts.

6. As Hunt (1978: 88) observes, Durkheim's formulation resembles Pound's 'socialization of law' stage, discussed in Chapter 4.

7. That is, legal frameworks that enabled private entities (e.g., individuals) to own specified chattels.

Chapter 6

1. However, he explained the rise of socialism as part of a receding collective consciousness (see Giddens 1971: 199–204).

2. See Laxer (1989), Angus (1981), and Avakumovic (1978).

3. He references Canadian 'spy trials' to confirm that 'some Canadians became so indoctrinated with Communist ideology that they convinced themselves they should secretly befriend Russia even to the extent of doing irretrievable harm to their own country'.

4. See discussions by Hindess and Hirst (1975, 1977) and Giddens (1971: 24–34).

5. As he puts it, these 'productive forces' involve 'an historically created relation of individuals to nature and to one another, which is handed down to each generation from its predecessor' (1965: 51).

6. See, for example, Reiman (2004); Fine (1984); Collins (1982); Phillips (1980); Hirst (1979, 1972); Poulantzas (1978); Hindess and Hirst (1977, 1975); and Cain (1974).

7. See, for example, Reiman (2004); Pavlich (2000); Taylor et al. (1975, 1973); and Hirst (1972).

8. See, for example, Pashukanis (2002) and Bonger (1967).

9. See also Beirne and Quinney (1982); Collins (1982); Phillips (1980); and Hirst (1972).

10. From http://www.absoluteastronomy.com/topics/Anatole_France, accessed 18 May 2009.

11. For example, 'Communism is the positive supersession of private property as human self-estrangement, and hence the true appropriation of the human essence through and for man; it is the complete restoration of man to himself as a *social*—i.e., human—being, a restoration which has become conscious and which takes place within the entire wealth of previous periods of development . . . it is the genuine resolution of the conflict between man and nature, and between man and man, the true resolution of the conflict between existence and being, between objectification and self-affirmation, between freedom and necessity, between individual and species' (1844: 3rd manuscript).

Chapter 7

1. For example, Weber insists that, 'the structure of every legal order (not only the "state") has a direct influence on the distribution of power, whether economic or of any other kind, within the community concerned' (2005: 43).

2. See Milovanovic (2003), Hunt (1978), etc.

3. This chapter will draw mainly on a text that assembles much of this work on law in an edited volume (see Weber 1954).

4. For secondary sources on Weber generally, see classics like Runciman (1972), Giddens (1971), Wrong (1970), and Freund (1968); on law, see Milovanovic (2003), Kronman (1983), and Hunt (1978).

5. Misleadingly, this has led some to view Weber as a legal positivist. Weber may endorse empiricism and the prospect of objective science, but as Hunt (1978: 104) and Kronman (1983: 8, 16ff.) caution, he is no legal positivist; if anything, he studies values positivistically. Moreover, for Weber, the legal positivist idea that law is humanly posited, independently of value, is one instance of a broader 'rationalization' of society (2005: 79).

6. Interestingly, perhaps with reference to Durkheim, Weber (1994: 16) distinguishes two types of 'solidarity social relationships' as being either 'communal' (i.e., 'based on a subjective feeling of the parties . . . that they belong together') or 'associative' (where a rationally motivated, often mutually agreed, collective emerges).

7. Weber's discussions of bureaucracy and its development are detailed, describing the rise of its authority, in various contexts (see 2005: 341–58 and 2004: 59–107).

8. In passing, and probably referring critically to Marx, Weber argues that, '*The Bureaucratic Structure Goes Hand in Hand with the Concentration of the Material Means of Administration in the Hands of the Ruler*' (1994: 85).

9. Section 24 (2) reads; 'Where, in proceedings under subsection (1), a court concludes that evidence was obtained in a manner that infringed or denied any rights or freedoms guaranteed by this Charter, the evidence shall be excluded if it is established that,

having regard to all the circumstances, the admission of it in the proceedings would bring the administration of justice into disrepute.'

10. This is clearly laid out in *R. v. Rutten*, [2006] SJ No. 65.

11. Some might detect here an affinity with Austin's definition of law as a 'sovereign command', but Weber emphasizes neither the 'command' nor the 'sovereign'.

12. Thus, Rheinstein describes Weber's formulation of 'a set of normative ideas which are held in the minds of the members of a given community, which thus influence their conduct, and the effectiveness of which is increased by the existence of a staff of specialists . . . ' (in Weber 1954: lxvii). Such specialists coerce compliance with rules of law.

13. Much of this section is framed out of Weber (1954: chaps. 7, 8, 9, and intro.) and aided by interpretations in Milovanovic (2003), Kronman (1983), Hunt (1978), and Freund (1968).

14. Despite lapses, Weber's value-free sociology claims not to view 'irrationality' in pejorative terms.

15. On this type, he describes a shift from formal irrational to substantively rational law in this way: 'In criminal law, legal rationalisation has replaced the purely mechanistic remedy of vengeance by rational "ends of punishment" of an either ethical or utilitarian character, and has thereby introduced increasingly non-formal elements into legal practice' (1994: 216).

16. See Weber (1954: 73–97, 204, 301ff.).

Chapter 8

1. See Bauman (2002, 1996), Kairys (1990), Hutchinson (1989), Douzinas et al. (1994), Unger (1986), Fitzpatrick and Hunt (1987b), and so on.

2. The vibrant Conference of Critical Legal Studies in Britain provides a good example—see Fitzpatrick and Hunt (1987b).

3. For example, *Stanford Law Review* (1984) and *Cardoza Law Review* (1985, 6: 693–1031), with a more international perspective canvassed in the *Journal of Law and Society* (1987, 14: 1–197).

4. See Baer (1999), Rush et al. (1999), Barnett (1998), Lacey (1998), Smith (1993), Fineman and Thomadson (1991), and Naffine (1990).

5. Smart (1989: 77) argues that MacKinnon's theory is too overdetermined to allow her even to begin to frame the perspective of such a non-alienated 'woman', in all its diversity.

6. This consciousness-raising is perhaps better formulated in Irigaray's (1985) call for law to recognize not one but two sexes, and to enable women to define their own sexuality and eroticism.

Chapter 9

1. See Pavlich (2000) for an extended analysis of critique in Foucault's work.

2. See also Wickham (2002) and Hunt (1992).

3. As Foucault argues, '. . . so long as feudal-type societies survived, the problems dealt with by the theory of sovereignty, or to which it referred, were actually co-extensive with the general mechanics of power' (2004: 35).

Chapter 10

1. A further proclamation would have to be issued to declare 'that the insurrection no longer exists'. See http://faculty.marianopolis.edu/c.belanger/quebechistory/docs/october/wm-act.htm, accessed 27 April 2009.

2. See also Cover et al. (1992).

3. Cover insists, 'The meaning judges thus give to the law . . . is not privileged, not necessarily worth any more than that of the resister they put in jail' (1983: 60).

4. Note echoes of both Kelsen and Weber in the position that Cover critiques.

5. See, for example, Dolin (2007), Sanders (2007), Lockey (2006), Williams (2002), and Goodrich (1996).

6. One might note that in this, it reflects the logical law of the 'excluded middle' evident in such propositions as 'all propositions are either true or false'—to function effectively, so it seems, this proposition must exclude itself from its own decrees (see Rasch 2004: 89–90).

7. He refers directly to Nancy (1993) to make this point.

8. As Mills (2008) and several contributors to Norris (2005) note, this conclusion may be overblown, as it does entail quite a leap.

Chapter 11

1. See Davies (2008) and Milovanovic (2003) for discussions of how this scheme derives from, and relates to, semiotics and structuralism.

2. He means here the structures and institutions—'a system of regulated and coded prescriptions' (Derrida 2002: 250).

3. That is, the pre-legal, illimitable, infinite, incalculable, and not rule-driven, horizons that summon law.

4. This enables us, as Fitzpatrick notes, to engage Derrida on these terms: 'Derrida's "deconstruction" is notoriously tied to the dissolution of "presence" or fixed entities, but that seeming dissolution always "takes place" in a constituent relation between the entity and what is ever beyond it, and deconstruction would thence account for the iteratively enduring presence of the entity' (2005: 6).

5. Indeed, as Derrida cautions, 'If by community one implies, as is often the case, a harmonious group, consensus, and fundamental agreement beneath phenomena of discord or war, then I don't believe in it very much and I sense in it as much threat as promise' (Derrida 1995: 355). I have elsewhere referred to this as the 'force of community' (Pavlich 2001a).

6. As he puts it, 'What comes to light, then, is not a "social" or "communitarian dimension" added onto a primitive individual given . . . ' (2000: 44).

Conclusion

1. Franz Kafka, 'Before the Law', translated by Ian Johnston. http://records.viu.ca/~Johnstoi/Kafka/beforethelaw.htm..

2. Indeed, as Raz (2005: 324) argues, legal theory is predicated on the 'relation between the concept of a thing and its nature'. He takes for granted that a thing like 'law' exists, and sees the role of legal theory to provide an 'account of the nature of law'.

3. Even though referring specifically to Marx, Hunt reflects a more generally applicable idea: 'The law is a specific form of social relation. It is certainly not a "thing", nor is it reducible to a set of institutions. Law as a social relation provides the starting point most in keeping with Marxism because the focus on "people in relations" is what makes Marxism so strongly and distinctively social—more rigorously social than most sociology' (1993: 251).

4. Davies adds a further caution: 'Law—broadly understood—orders the way we view the world: it shapes our perception, and therefore cannot be identified merely as an "object" of our perception. It enters into the process of cognition' (2008: 7).

Bibliography ··

List of Cases

Buck v. Bell, 47 S.Ct. 584, 274 U.S. 200 (1927).

Martin v. Law Society of British Columbia, [1950] 3 DLR 173.

Regina v. Whalen, [1974] OJ 2293.

R. v. Smalbrugge, [1984] BCJ No. 133.

E. (Mrs.) v. Eve, [1986] SCJ No. 60.

R. v. Collins, [1987] SCJ No. 15.

Muir v. Alberta, [1996] AJ No. 37.

R. v. Brown, [1999] OJ 486.

R. v. Gladue, [1999] 1 SCR 688.

R. v. Rutten, [2006] SJ No. 65.

R. v. Kahpeaysewat, [2006] SJ No. 587.

Abel, R.L. (1995). *Politics by Other Means: Law in Struggle against Apartheid, 1980–1994*. London: Routledge.

Agamben, G. (1993). *The Coming Community*. Minneapolis: University of Minnesota Press.

———. (1998). *Homo Sacer: Sovereign Power and Bare Life*. Stanford: Stanford University Press.

———. (1999). *Remnants of Auschwitz: The Witness and the Archive*. New York: Zone Books.

———. (2004). *The Open: Man and Animal*. Stanford: Stanford University Press.

———. (2005). *State of Exception*. Chicago: University of Chicago Press.

———. (2007). *Profanations*. New York: Zone Books.

Albrow, M. (1981). 'Review: Law, Ideology . . . Sociology . . .?'. *British Journal of Sociology* 32(1), 127–36.

Alexander, J.C., & Smith, P. (2005). *The Cambridge Companion to Durkheim*. Cambridge: Cambridge University Press.

Althusser, L. (2005). *For Marx*. London: Verso.

Andersen, C. (2005). 'Residual Tensions of Empire: Contemporary Métis Communities and the Canadian Juridical Imagination', in M. Murphy (ed.), *Canada: The State of the Federation. Reconfiguring Aboriginal-State Relations*. Montreal: McGill-Queen's University Press, 295–332.

Angus, I. (1981). *Canadian Bolsheviks: An Early History of the Communist Party of Canada*. Montreal: Vanguard.

Aquinas, T. (1952). *The Summa Theologica of Thomas Aquinas*. Chicago: William Benton.

Aristotle. (2004). *Selections from Nichomachean Ethics, Politics*. London: CRW Publishing.

Arthurs, H.W. (1985). *'Without the Law': Administrative Justice and Legal Pluralism in Nineteenth-Century England*. Toronto: University of Toronto Press.

Atwood, W., Johnson, S., Coke, E., Petyt, W., & Cooke, E. (1682). *Argumentum Anti-Normannicum*. London: Sprint.

Auerbach, J.S. (1983). *Justice Without Law?* New York: Oxford University Press.

Augustine. (1950). *The City of God*. New York: Random House.

Austin, J. (1995). *The Province of Jurisprudence Determined*. Cambridge: Cambridge University Press.

Avakumovic, I. (1978). *Socialism in Canada: A Study of the CCF-NDP in Federal and Provincial Politics*. Toronto: McClelland & Stewart.

Aylward, C.A. (1999). *Canadian Critical Race Theory: Racism and the Law*. Halifax: Fernwood.

Azoulay, A. (2005). 'The Loss of Critique and the Critique of Violence'. *Cardozo Law Review* 26(3), 1005–39.

Badiou, A. (2009). *Logics of Worlds: Being and Event II*. London: Continuum.

Baer, J.A. (1999). *Our Lives Before the Law: Constructing a Feminist Jurisprudence*. Princeton: Princeton University Press.

Banakar, R., & Travers, M. (eds.) (2002). *An Introduction to Law and Social Theory*. Oxford: Hart.

———. (2005). *Theory and Method in Socio-Legal Research*. Oxford: Hart.

Barbour, C., & Pavlich, G. (eds.). (2010). *After Sovereignty: On the Question of Political Beginnings*. New York: Routledge-Cavendish.

Barnes, A.J., Dworkin, T.M., & Richards, E.L. (2006). *Law for Business*. New York: McGraw-Hill.

Barnett, H. (1998). *Introduction to Feminist*

Jurisprudence. London: Cavendish.

Baudrillard, J. (1983). *In the Shadow of the Silent Majorities: Or, the End of the Social and Other Essays*. New York: Semiotext(e).

Bauman, R.W. (1996). *Critical Legal Studies: A Guide to the Literature*. Boulder: Westview Press.

———. (2002). *Ideology and Community in the First Wave of Critical Legal Studies*. Toronto: University of Toronto Press.

Bauman, Z. (1992). *Intimations of Postmodernity*. New York: Routledge.

———. (1997). *Postmodernity and its Discontents*. New York: New York University Press.

———. (2002). *Society Under Siege*. Cambridge: Blackwell.

Baxter, H. (1996). 'Review Essay: Bringing Foucault into Law and Law into Foucault'. *Stanford Law Review* 48, 449–80.

Beardsworth, R. (1996). *Derrida & the Political: Thinking the Political*. New York: Routledge.

Beauvoir, S. de. (1983). *The Second Sex*. New York: Vintage Books.

Beck, A. (1996). 'Foucault and Law: the Collapse of Law's Empire'. *Oxford Journal of Legal Studies* 16, 489–502.

Beirne, P., & Quinney, R. (1982). *Marxism and Law*. New York: Wiley.

Bell, C.E., & Napoleon, V. (2008). *First Nations Cultural Heritage and Law: Case Studies, Voices, and Perspectives*. Vancouver: University of British Columbia Press.

Bell, D.A. (2000). *Race, Racism, and American Law*. Gaithersburg: Aspen Law & Business.

———. (2004). *Silent Covenants: Brown v. Board of Education and the Unfulfilled Hopes for Racial Reform*. New York: Oxford University Press.

Benjamin, W. (1996). 'Critique of Violence', in M. Bullock & M. Jennings (eds.), *Selected Writings v. 1*. Massachusetts: Harvard University Press, 236–52.

———. (1970). *The Limits of Jurisprudence Defined: Being Part Two of An Introduction to the Principles of Morals and Legislation*. Westport: Greenwood Press.

Bentham, J. (1988). *A Fragment on Government*. Cambridge: Cambridge University Press.

Benton, L.A. (2002). *Law and Colonial Cultures: Legal Regimes in World History, 1400–1900*. Cambridge: Cambridge University Press.

Bhabha, H.K. (2004). *The Location of Culture*. London: Routledge.

Bickenbach, J.E. (1989). 'Law and Morality'. *Law and Philosophy* 8(3), 291–301.

Bix, B. (2006). *Jurisprudence: Theory and Context*. London: Sweet & Maxwell.

Black, D.J. (1984). *Toward a General Theory of Social Control*. New York: Academic Press.

———. (1989). *Sociological Justice*. New York: Oxford University Press.

Blackstone, W. (2001). *Blackstone's Commentaries on the Laws of England in Four Volumes*. London: Cavendish.

Bonger, W.A. (1967). *Criminality and Economic Conditions*. New York: Agathon Press.

Boyle, J. (1992). *Critical Legal Studies*. New York: New York University Press.

Brickey, S.L., & Comack, E. (1997). *The Social Basis of Law Critical Readings in the Sociology of Law*. Halifax: Fernwood.

Brown, W., & Halley, J.E. (eds.). (2002). *Left Legalism/Left Critique*. Durham: Duke University Press.

Burgdorf, R.L.J., & Burgdorf, M.P. (1977). 'The Wicked Witch is Almost Dead: Buck v. Bell and the Sterilization of Handicapped Persons'. *Temple Law Quarterly* 50, 995–1034.

Burns, W.H. (1990). 'Law and Race in Early America', in D. Kairys (ed.), *The Politics of Law: A Progressive Critique*. New York: Pantheon Books, 115–20.

Butler, J. (1997a). *Excitable Speech: A Politics of the Performance*. New York: Routledge.

———. (1997b). *The Psychic Life of Power: Theories in Subjection*. Stanford: Stanford University Press.

———. (1999). *Gender Trouble Feminism and the Subversion of Identity*. New York: Routledge.

———. (2000). *Antigone's Claim: Kinship between Life & Death*. New York: Columbia University Press.

———. (2004). *Precarious Life: The Powers of Mourning and Violence*. New York: Verso.

Butler, W.E., & Kudriavtsev, V.N. (1985). *Comparative Law and Legal System: His-*

torical and Socio-Legal Perspectives. New York: Oceana.

Byrne, P.J. (1993). Criminal Law and Colonial Subject: New South Wales, 1810–1830. New York: Cambridge University Press.

Cavafy, C.P. (1992). 'Waiting For The Barbarians' in Collected Poems. Trans. E. Keeley & P. Sherrard. George Savidis (ed.), Princeton, NJ: Princeton University Press.

Cain, M. (1974). 'The Main Themes of Marx' and Engel's Sociology of Law'. British Journal of Law and Society 1(2), 136–48.

Cain, M.E., & Hunt, A. (1979). Marx and Engels on Law. London: Academic Press.

Campbell, C.M., & Wiles, P. (eds.). (1979). Law and Society. Oxford: M. Robertson.

Cardozo, B.N. (1960). The Nature of the Judicial Process. New Haven: Yale University Press.

Carson, W.G. (1982). The Other Price of Britain's Oil: Safety and Control in the North Sea. Oxford: M. Robertson.

Chanock, M. (1985). Law, Custom, and Social Order: The Colonial Experience in Malawi and Zambia. Cambridge: Cambridge University Press.

———. (2001). The Making of South African Legal Culture, 1902–1936: Fear, Favour, and Prejudice. Cambridge: Cambridge University Press.

Chomsky, N., & Foucault, M. (2006). The Chomsky-Foucault Debate: On Human Nature. New York: New Press.

Cicero (1971). Cicero: Selected Works. Harmondsworth: Penguin.

———. (1998). The Republic; and The Laws. New York: Oxford University Press.

Citron, R. (2006). 'The Nuremberg Trial and American Jurisprudence: The Decline of Legal Realism, the Revival of Natural Law, and the Development of Legal Process Theory'. Michigan State Law Review 2006(2), 385–410.

Collins, H. (1982). Marxism and Law. New York: Clarendon Press.

Comack, E. (1999). Locating Law: Race/Class/Gender Connections. Halifax: Fernwood.

Comack, E., & Brickey, S.L. (1991). The Social Basis of Law: Critical Readings in the Sociology of Law. Halifax: Garamond Press.

Comaroff, J. (1990). 'Re-Marx on Repression and the Rule of Law'. Law & Social Inquiry 15(4), 671–8.

Comaroff, J., & Comaroff, J. (2004a). 'Policing Culture, Cultural Policing: Law and Social Order in Postcolonial South Africa'. Law and Social Inquiry 29, 513–45.

———. (2004b). 'Criminal Justice, Cultural Justice: The Limits of Liberalism and the Pragmatics of Difference in the New South Africa'. American Ethnologist 31(2), 188–204.

Comaroff, J., & Comaroff, J.L. (eds.) (2006). Law and Disorder in the Postcolony. Chicago: University of Chicago Press.

Comte, A. (1975). Auguste Comte and Positivism: The Essential Writings. Ed. G. Lenzer. New York: Harper.

Constable, M. (2005). Just Silences: The Limits and Possibilities of Modern Law. Princeton: Princeton University Press.

Cornell, D. (1988). 'Post-Structuralism, The Ethical Relation, and the Law'. Cardozo Law Review 9, 1587–628.

Cotterrell, R. (2001). Sociological Perspectives on Law. Aldershot: Dartmouth.

———. (2003). The Politics of Jurisprudence: A Critical Introduction to Legal Philosophy. London: Butterworth.

———. (2004). 'Law in Social Theory and Social Theory in the Study of Law', in A. Sarat (ed.), The Blackwell Companion to Law and Society. Malden: Blackwell, 15–29.

———. (2008). Living Law: Studies in Legal and Social Theory. Aldershot: Dartmouth.

Couton, P. (2007). 'What is Sovereignty in Quebec?', in G.C. Pavlich & M.J. Hird (eds.), Questioning Sociology: A Canadian Perspective. Don Mills: Oxford University Press, 266–75.

Cover, R.M. (1983). 'The Supreme Court 1982 Term—Foreword: Nomos and Narrative'. Harvard Law Review 97, 4–68.

———. (1986). 'Violence and Word'. Yale Law Journal 95, 1601–30.

Cover, R.M., Minow, M., Ryan, M., & Sarat, A. (1992). Narrative, Violence, and the Law: The Essays of Robert Cover. Ann Arbor: University of Michigan Press.

Crenshaw, K. (1990). 'A Black Feminist Critique of Antidiscrimination Law and Politics', in D. Kairys (ed.), The Politics of Law: A Progressive Critique. New York: Pantheon Books, 195–218.

Daniels, D. (1973). Québec, Canada and the October Crisis. Montréal: Black Rose Books.

Danielsen, D., & Engle, K. (1995). After Identity: A Reader in Law and Culture. New York: Routledge.

Darian-Smith, E., & Fitzpatrick, P. (1999). Laws of the Postcolonial. Ann Arbor: University of Michigan Press.

Davies, M. (2008). Asking the Law Question. Sydney: Thompson Law Book Company.

Deflem, M. (2008). Sociology of Law: Visions of a Scholarly Tradition. Cambridge: Cambridge University Press.

Delgado, R. (1995). Critical Race Theory: The Cutting Edge. Philadelphia: Temple University Press.

Delgado, R., & Stefancic, J. (1993). 'Critical Race Theory: An Annotated Bibliography'. Virginia Law Review 79, 461–516.

———. (2001). Critical Race Theory: An Introduction. New York: New York University Press.

Derrida, J. (1976). Of Grammatology. Baltimore: Johns Hopkins University Press.

———. (1981). Positions. Chicago: University of Chicago Press.

———. (1994). Specters of Marx: The State of the Debt, The Work of Mourning, and the New International. New York: Routledge.

———. (1995). Points: Interviews, 1974–1994. Stanford: Stanford University Press.

———. (1997). Deconstruction in a Nutshell: A Conversation with Jacques Derrida. Edited with a commentary by John D. Caputo. New York: Fordham University Press.

———. (2002). 'Force of Law: The "Mystical Foundations of Authority"', in J. Derrida & G. Anidjar (eds.), Acts of Religion. New York: Routledge, 228–98.

———. (2009). The Beast and the Sovereign, vol. 1. Chicago: University of Chicago Press.

Derrida, J., & Tlili, M. (eds.) (1987). For Nelson Mandela. New York: Seaver Books.

Dolin, K. (2007). A Critical Introduction to Law and Literature. Cambridge: Cambridge University Press.

Douzinas, C., & Gearey, A. (2005). Critical Jurisprudence: The Political Philosophy of Justice. Oxford: Hart.

Douzinas, C., Goodrich, P., & Hachamovitch, Y. (1994). Politics, Postmodernity and Critical Legal Studies: The Legality of the Contingent. London: Routledge.

Douzinas, C., & Warrington, R. (1994). Justice Miscarried: Ethics and Aesthetics in Law. New York: Harvester Wheatsheaf.

Dugard, J. (1978). Human Rights and the South African Legal Order. Princeton: Princeton University Press.

———. (1988). 'Should Judges Resign?—Reply to Professor Wacks'. Bulletin of Australian Social and Legal Philosophy 12, 200–8.

———. (1990). 'A Bill of Rights for South Africa?'. Cornell International Law Journal 23, 441–66.

Durkheim, É. (1938). The Rules of Sociological Method. Chicago: The University of Chicago Press.

———. (1957). Professional Ethics and Civil Morals. London: Routledge & Kegan Paul.

———. (1964). Essays on Sociology and Philosophy. New York: Harper & Row.

———. (1973). On Morality and Society: Selected Writings. Chicago: University of Chicago Press.

———. (1983). Durkheim and the Law. New York: St. Martin's Press.

———. (1984). The Division of Labour in Society. London: Macmillan.

———. (1986). 'The Positive Science of Morality in Germany (1887)'. Economy & Society 15(3), 346.

Dworkin, R.M. (1978). Taking Rights Seriously. Cambridge: Harvard University Press.

———. (1986). Law's Empire. Cambridge: Belknap Press.

Dyzenhaus, D. 1998. Judging the Judges, Judging Ourselves: Truth, Reconciliation and the Apartheid Legal Order. Oxford: Hart.

Ehrlich, E. (2002). Fundamental Principles

of the Sociology of Law. New Brunswick: Transaction Publishers.

Ewald, F. (1986). 'A Concept of Social Law', in G. Teubner (ed.), Dilemmas of Law in the Welfare State. Berlin: Walter de Gruyter, 40–75.

———. (1988). 'The Law of Law', in G. Teubner (ed.), Autopoietic Law: A New Approach to Law and Society. Berlin: Walter de Gruyter, 36–50.

Fanon, F. (1965). The Wretched of the Earth. New York: Grove Press.

———. (1967). Black Skin, White Masks. New York: Grove Press.

Fine, B. (1984). Democracy and the Rule of Law: Liberal Ideals and Marxist Critiques. London: Pluto.

Fineman, M., & Karpin, I. (1995). Mothers in Law (Gender and Culture). New York: Columbia University Press.

Fineman, M., & Thomadsen, N.S. (1991). At the Boundaries of Law: Feminism and Legal Theory. New York: Routledge.

Finnis, J. (1967). 'Blackstone's Theoretical Intentions'. Natural Law Forum 12, 163–83.

———. (1980). Natural Law and Natural Rights. New York: Clarendon Press.

———. (1984). 'The Authority of Law in the Predicament of Contemporary Social Theory'. Notre Dame Journal of Law, Ethics and Public Policy 1(1), 115–38.

———. (1986). 'The "Natural Law Tradition"'. Journal of Legal Education 36(4), 492–5.

———. (1990). 'Natural Law and Legal Reasoning'. Cleveland State Law Review 38(1), 1–14.

———. (1998). Aquinas: Moral, Political, and Legal Theory. Oxford: Oxford University Press.

———. (2007). 'On Hart's Ways: Law as Reason and Law as Fact'. American Journal of Jurisprudence 52(1), 25–54.

Firestone, S. (1971). The Dialectic of Sex: The Case for Feminist Revolution. New York: Bantam Books.

Fitzpatrick, P. (1984). 'Law and Societies'. Osgoode Hall Law Journal 22(1), 115–38.

———. (1992). The Mythology of Modern Law: Sociology of Law and Crime. London: Routledge.

———. (1995). 'Being Social in Socio-Legal Studies'. Journal of Law and Society 22(1), 105–12.

———. (2001). Modernism and the Grounds of Law. Cambridge: Cambridge University Press.

———. (2003). 'Breaking the Unity of the World: Savage Sources and Feminine Law'. Australian Feminist Law Journal 19, 47–60.

———. (2005). 'Access as Justice'. Windsor Yearbook of Access to Justice 23, 3–16.

———. (2007). '"What are the Gods to Us Now?": Secular Theology and the Modernity of Law'. Theoretical Inquiry 8, 161–90.

Fitzpatrick, P., & Hunt, A. (1987a). 'Critical Legal Studies: Introduction'. Journal of Law and Society 14(1), 1–4.

———. (1987b). Critical Legal Studies. New York: Blackwell.

Fitzpatrick, P., & Tuitt, P. (2004). Critical Beings: Law, Nation, and the Global Subject. Aldershot: Ashgate.

Foucault, M. (1977). Language, Counter-Memory, Practice: Selected Essays and Interviews. Ithaca: Cornell University Press.

———. (1978). The History of Sexuality, vol.1. New York: Pantheon Books.

———. (1980). Power/Knowledge: Selected Interviews and Other Writings, 1972–1977. New York: Pantheon Books.

———. (1988). Politics, Philosophy, Culture: Interviews and other Writings, 1977–1984. New York: Routledge.

———. (1989). Foucault Live: Interviews, 1961–1984. New York: Semiotext(e).

———. (1993). The Archaeology of Knowledge and the Discourse on Language. New York: Barnes & Noble.

———. (1995). Discipline and Punish: The Birth of the Prison. New York: Vintage Books.

———. (1997). Ethics: Subjectivity and Truth. New York: New Press.

———. (2000). Power. New York: New Press.

———. (2004). Society Must be Defended: Lectures at the Collège de France, 1975–76. New York: Picador.

———. (2005). The Hermeneutics of the Subject: Lectures at the Collège de France, 1981–82. New York: Palgrave Macmillan.

———. (2006). Psychiatric Power: Lectures at the Collège de France, 1973–74. New York: Palgrave Macmillan.

———. (2007a). The Politics of Truth. Los

Angeles, CA: Semiotext(e).

———. (2007b). *Security, Territory, Population: Lectures at the Collège de France, 1977–78.* New York: Palgrave Macmillan.

———. (2009). *The Birth of Biopolitics: Lectures at the Collège de France, 1978–79.* New York: Palgrave Macmillan.

Frank, J. (1931). 'Are Judges Human? Part One: The Effect on Legal Thinking of the Assumption that Judges Behave Like Human Beings'. *University of Pennsylvania Law Review* 80(1), 17–53.

———. (1933a). 'What Constitutes a Good Legal Education?'. *American Bar Association Journal* 19, 723–8.

———. (1933b). 'Why Not a Clinical Law School?'. *University of Pennsylvania Law Review* 81(8), 907–23.

———. (1949). *Law and the Modern Mind.* New York: Coward-McCann.

———. (1953). 'Judicial Fact Finding and Psychology'. *Ohio State Law Journal* 14(2), 183–9.

———. (1955). 'A Conflict With Oblivion: Some Comments on the Founders of Legal Positivism'. *Rutgers Law Review* 9(2), 425–63.

———. (1970). *Courts on Trial: Myth and Reality in American Justice.* New York: Atheneum.

Fraser, A. (2001). 'A Marx for Managerial Revolution: Habermas on Law and Democracy'. *Journal of Law and Society* 28(3), 361–3.

Fraser, R.L. (1992). *Provincial Justice: Upper Canadian Legal Portraits from the Dictionary of Canadian Biography.* Toronto: University of Toronto Press.

Freund, J. (1968). *The Sociology of Max Weber.* New York: Pantheon Books.

Fuller, L. (1949). 'Pashukanis and Vyshinsky: A Study in the Development of Marxian Legal Theory'. *Michigan State Law Review* 47(8), 1157–66.

———. (1957). 'Positivism and Fidelity to Law: A Reply to Professor Hart'. *Harvard Law Review* 71(4), 672.

———. (1958). 'Natural Purpose and Natural Law'. *Natural Law Forum* 3, 68–76.

———. (1965). 'A Reply to Professors Cohen and Dworkin'. *Villanova Law Review* 10(4), 655–66.

———. (1969). *The Morality of Law* (revised edition). New Haven: Yale University Press.

———. (1970). 'Mediation: Its Forms and Functions'. *Southern California Law Review* 44(2), 305–39.

———. (1975). 'Law as an Instrument of Social Control and Law as a Facilitation of Human Interaction'. *Brigham Young Law Review* 1, 89–98.

———. (1979). 'The Forms and Limits of Adjudication'. *Harvard Law Review* 92(2), 353–409.

———. (1981). *The Principles of Social Order: Selected Essays of Lon L. Fuller.* Durham: Duke University Press.

Gabel, P., & Harris, P. (1983). 'Building Power and Breaking Images: Critical Legal Theory and the Practice of Law'. *New York University Review of Law and Social Change* 11, 369–412.

Gabel, P., & Kennedy, D. (1984). 'Roll Over Beethoven'. *Stanford Law Review* 36, 1–55.

Garland, D., & Sparks, R. (2000). *Criminology and Social Theory.* New York: Oxford University Press.

Geschiere, P. (2006). 'Witchcraft and the Limits of Law: Cameroon and South Africa', in J. Comaroff & J.L. Comaroff (eds.), *Law and Disorder in the Postcolony.* Chicago: University of Chicago Press, 219–46.

Giddens, A. (1971). *Capitalism and Modern Social Theory: An Analysis of the Writings of Marx, Durkheim and Max Weber.* Cambridge: Cambridge University Press.

Golder, B., & Fitzpatrick, P. (2009). *Foucault's Law.* London: Routledge.

Goodrich, P. (1996). *Law in the Courts of Love, Literature and Other Minor Jurisprudences.* London: Routledge.

Goodrich, P., et al. (eds.) (2008). *Derrida and Legal Philosophy.* Basingstoke: Palgrave Macmillan.

Gordon, R. (1984). 'Critical Legal Histories'. *Stanford Law Review* 36, 57–126.

———. (1990). 'New Developments in Legal Theory', in D. Kairys (ed.), *The Politics of Law: A Progressive Critique.* New York: Pantheon Books, 413–25.

Gouglas, S., & Weaver, J.C. (2003). 'A Postcolonial Understanding of Law and Society: Exploring Criminal Trials in Colonial Queensland'. *Australian Journal of Legal History* 7, 231–53.

Gramsci, A. (2001). *Selections from the Prison Notebooks of Antonio Gramsci.* Trans. Q. Hoare & G. Nowell-Smith. London: Electric Book Co.

Green, J. (2006). 'From *Stonechild* to Social Cohesion: Anti-Racist Challenges for Saskatchewan'. *Canadian Journal of Political Science* 39(3), 507–27.

Grotius, H. (1964). *De Jure Belli ac Pacis Libri Tres.* New York: Oceana Publications.

Gurvitch, G. (2001). *Sociology of Law.* New Brunswick: Transaction Publishers.

Hale, M. (1971). *The History of the Common Law.* Chicago: University of Chicago Press.

Harris, A.P. (1990). 'Race and Essentialism in Feminist Legal Theory'. *Stanford Law Review* 42, 581–616.

Hart, H.L.A. (1957). 'Positivism and the Separation of Law and Morals'. *Harvard Law Review* 71(4), 593–629.

———. (1963). 'Kelsen Visited'. UCLA *Law Review* 10(4), 709–28.

———. (1967). 'Social Solidarity and the Enforcement of Morality'. University of Chicago Law Review 35(1–13),13.

———. (1977). 'American Jurisprudence Through English Eyes: The Nightmare and the Noble Dream'. *Georgia Law Review* 11(5), 969–90.

———. (1994). *The Concept of Law.* New York: Oxford University Press.

Hay, D. (1975). *Albion's Fatal Tree: Crime and Society in Eighteenth-Century England.* London: A. Lane.

Hazlehurst, K.M. (1995). *Legal Pluralism and the Colonial Legacy: Indigenous Experiences of Justice in Canada, Australia, and New Zealand.* Aldershot: Avebury.

Hennessy, P.H. (1999). *Canada's Big House: The Dark History of the Kingston Penitentiary.* Toronto: Dundurn Press.

Hindess, B., & Hirst, P.Q. (1975). *Pre-Capitalist Modes of Production.* London: Routledge & Kegan Paul.

———. (1977). *Mode of Production and Social Formation: An Auto-Critique of Pre-capitalist Modes of Production.* London: Macmillan.

Hirst, P.Q. (1972). 'Marx and Engels on Law, Crime and Morality'. *Economy & Society* 1(1), 28–56.

———. (1979). *On Law and Ideology.* London: Macmillan.

Hobbes, T. (1651). *De Cive.* <http://www.constitution.org/th/decive06.htm>.

———. (1985). *Leviathan.* Harmondsworth: Penguin Books.

Hogeveen, Bryan. (2010). 'After Sovereignty: Spectres of Colonialism', in C. Barbour and G. Pavlich (eds.), *After Sovereignty: On the Question of Political Beginnings.* London: Routledge-Cavendish, 115–29.

Holmes, O.W. (1879). *Common Carriers and Common Law.* Boston: American Law Review.

———. (1897). 'The Path of the Law'. *Harvard Law Review* 110(5), 991–1009.

———. (1899). 'Law in Science and Science in Law'. *Harvard Law Review* 7(7), 21.

———. (1918). 'Natural Law'. *Harvard Law Review* 32(1), 5.

———. (1982). *The Common Law & Other Writings: Including the Common Law, Collected Legal Papers, Speeches.* Birmingham: Legal Classics Library.

Horner, J. (2007). *Canadian Law and the Canadian Legal System.* Toronto: Pearson.

Hull, N.E.H. (1989). 'Restructuring the Origins of Realistic Jurisprudence: A Prequel to the Llewellyn-Pound Exchange over Legal Realism'. *Duke Law Journal* 5, 1302–34.

Hunt, A. (1978). *The Sociological Movement in Law.* London: Macmillan.

———. (1986). 'The Theory of Critical Legal Studies'. *Oxford Journal of Legal Studies* 6(1), 1–45.

———. (1987). 'The "Critique" of Law: What is Critical about Critical Legal Theory?'. *Journal of Law and Society* 14(1), 5–19.

———. (1992). 'Foucault's Expulsion of Law: Toward a Retrieval'. *Law and Social Inquiry* 17(1), 1–38.

———. (1993). *Explorations in Law and Society: Toward a Constitutive Theory of Law.* London: Routledge.

Hunt, A., & Wickham, G. (1994). *Foucault and Law: Towards a Sociology of Law as Governance.* London: Pluto Press.

Hutchinson, A.C. (ed.) (1989). *Critical Legal Studies.* Totowa: Rowman & Littlefield.

Hutchinson, A.C., & Monahan, P.J.

(1984). 'Law, Politics, and the Critical Legal Scholars: The Unfolding Drama of American Legal Thought'. *Stanford Law Review* 36, 199–246.

Irigaray, L. (1985). *This Sex Which is Not One*. Ithaca: Cornell University Press.

Jaggar, A.M. (1983). *Feminist Politics and Human Nature*. Totowa: Rowman & Allanheld.

James, W. (2000). *Pragmatism and Other Writings*. New York: Penguin Books.

Joffe, J. (2009). *The State vs. Nelson Mandela: The Trial that Changed South Africa*. Oxford: Oneworld.

Johnson, D., Pete, S., & du Plessis, M. (2001). *Jurisprudence: A South African Perspective*. Durban: Butterworths.

Kainz, H. (2004). *Natural Law: An Introduction and Re-examination*. Chicago: Open Court.

Kairys, D. (ed.) (1990). *The Politics of Law: A Progressive Critique*. New York: Pantheon Books.

Kaplan, B., Atiyah, P.S., Vetter, J., Holmes, O.W., & Harvard Law School. (1983). *Holmes and the Common Law a Century Later, Three Lectures*. Cambridge: Harvard Law School.

Kelsen, H. (1934). 'The Pure Theory of Law: Its Method and Fundamental Concepts (Part 1)'. *Law Quarterly Review* 200, 477–81.

———. (1941). 'The Pure Theory of Law and Analytical Jurisprudence'. *Harvard Law Review* 55(1), 44–70.

———. (1946). *Society and Nature: A Sociological Inquiry*. London: Kegan Paul.

———. (1948). 'Law, State and Justice in the Pure Theory of Law'. *Yale Law Review* 57(3), 377–90.

———. (1959). 'On the Basic Norm'. *California Law Review* 47(1), 107–10.

———. (1960). 'Plato and the Doctrine of Natural Law'. *Vanderbilt Law Review* 14(1), 23–64.

———. (1961). *General Theory of Law and State*. New York: Russell & Russell.

———. (1966). 'Norm and Value'. *California Law Review* 54(4), 1624–9.

———. (1967). *Pure Theory of Law*. Berkeley: University of California Press.

———. (1981). 'On the Basis of Legal Validity'. *American Journal of Jurisprudence* 26(1), 178–89.

———. (1991). *General Theory of Norms*. Oxford: Clarendon Press.

Kennedy, D. (1971). 'How the Law School Fails: A Polemic'. *Yale Review of Law and Social Action* 1, 71–90.

———. (1973). 'Legal Formality'. *Journal of Legal Studies* 2, 351–98.

———. (1976). 'Form and Substance in Private Law Adjudication'. *Harvard Law Review* 89, 1685–9.

———. (1979). 'The Structure of Blackstone's Commentaries'. *Buffalo Law Review* 28, 205–382.

———. (1982). 'Legal Education and the Reproduction of Hierarchy'. *Journal of Legal Education* 32, 591–615.

———. (1983). 'The Political Significance of the Structure of the Law School Curriculum'. *Seton Hall Law Review* 14, 1–16.

———. (1985). 'The Role of Law in Economic Thought: Essays on the Fetishism of Commodities'. *American University Law Review* 34, 939–1002.

———. (1986). 'Liberal Values in Legal Education'. *Nova Law Journal* 10, 603–18.

———. (1987). 'Are Lawyers Really Necessary? Barrister Interview with Duncan Kennedy'. *The Barrister* 14, 12–37.

———. (1990). 'Legal Education as Training for Hierarchy', in D. Kairys (ed.), *The Politics of Law: A Progressive Critique*. New York: Pantheon Books, 38–58.

———. (1991). 'The Stakes of Law, or Hale and Foucault!'. *Legal Studies Forum* 15(4), 327–66.

———. (1992). 'Sexual Abuse, Sexy Dressing and the Eroticization of Domination'. *New England Law Review* 26, 1309–94.

———. (1997). *A Critique of Adjudication: Fin de Siècle*. Cambridge: Harvard University Press.

———. (2002). 'The Critique of Rights in Critical Legal Studies', in W. Brown & J.E. Halley (eds.), *Left Legalism/Left Critique*. Durham: Duke University Press, 178–228.

———. (2004). 'The Disenchantment of Logically Formal Legal Rationality, or Max Weber's Sociology in the Genealogy of the Contemporary Mode of Western Legal Thought'. *Hastings Law Journal* 55, 1031–76.

———. (2005). 'Introduction'. UMKC *Law*

Review 73, 231–6.

Kennedy, D., & Carrington, P. (2004). *Legal Education and the Reproduction of Hierarchy: A Polemic against the System.* New York: New York University Press.

Kronman, A.T. (1983). *Max Weber.* London: E. Arnold.

Lacey, N. (1998). *Unspeakable Subjects: Feminist Essays in Legal and Social Theory.* Oxford: Hart.

Latour, B. (2005). *Reassembling the Social: An Introduction to Actor-Network-Theory.* Oxford: Oxford University Press.

Lattimore, O. (1971). *Ordeal by Slander.* Westport: Greenwood Press.

Laxer, G. (1989). *Open for Business: The Roots of Foreign Ownership in Canada.* Don Mills: Oxford University Press.

Lewis, R. (1986). *Apartheid: Capitalism or Socialism? The Political Economy of the Causes, Consequences and Cure of the Colour Bar in South Africa.* London: Institute of Economic Affairs.

Lipson, L., & Wheeler, S. (1986). *Law and the Social Sciences.* New York: Russell Sage Foundation.

Litowitz, D.E. (1997). *Postmodern Philosophy and Law.* Lawrence: University Press of Kansas.

Littleton, C.A. (1987). 'In Search of a Feminist Jurisprudence'. *Harvard Women's Law Journal* 10, 1–8.

Llewellyn, K.N. (1930). *The Bramble Bush, Some Lectures on Law and its Study.* New York: K.N. Llewellyn.

———. (1931). 'Some Realism about Realism: Responding to Dean Pound'. *Harvard Law Review* 44(8), 1222–64.

———. (1935). 'Holmes'. *Columbia Law Review* 35(4), 485–92.

———. (1940). 'The Normative, the Legal, and the Law-jobs: The Problem of Jurisitic Method'. *Yale Law Journal* 49(8), 1355–400.

———. (1942). 'On The Good, The True, The Beautiful, In Law'. *University of Chicago Law Review* 9, 224–65.

———. (1949). 'Law and the Social Sciences—Especially Sociology'. *Harvard Law Review* 62(8), 1286–305.

———. (1960). *The Common Law Tradition: Deciding Appeals.* Boston: Little, Brown & Co.

Llewellyn, K.N., & Gewirtz, P. (1989). *The Case Law System in America.* Chicago: University of Chicago Press.

Llewellyn, K.N., & Hoebel, E.A. (1941). *The Cheyenne Way: Conflict and Case Law in Primitive Jurisprudence.* Norman: University of Oklahoma Press.

Lockey, B. (2006). *Law and Empire in English Renaissance Literature.* Cambridge: Cambridge University Press.

Lucey, F.E. (1942). 'Natural Law and American Legal Realism: Their Respective Contributions to a Theory of Law in a Democratic Society'. *Georgetown Law Journal* 30(6), 493–533.

Lyotard, J.F. (1984). *The Postmodern Condition: A Report on Knowledge.* Manchester: Manchester University Press.

Maaka, R., & Andersen, C. (2006). *The Indigenous Experience: Global Perspectives.* Toronto: Canadian Scholars' Press.

Macaulay, S., Friedman, L.M., & Mertz, E. (2007). *Law in Action: A Socio-legal Reader.* New York: Thomson/West.

MacKinnon, C.A. (1983). 'Feminism, Marxism, Method and the State: Towards Feminist Jurisprudence'. *Signs* 8(4), 635–58.

———. (1987). *Feminism Unmodified: Discourses on Life and Law.* Cambridge: Harvard University Press.

———. (1989). *Toward a Feminist Theory of the State.* Cambridge: Harvard University Press.

———. (1991a). 'From Practice to Theory, or What is a White Woman Anyway?'. *Yale Journal of Law and Feminism* 4, 13–22.

———. (1991b). 'Reflections on Sex Equality Under Law'. *Yale Law Journal* 100, 1281–328.

———. (2000). 'Points against Postmodernism'. *Kent Law Review* 75, 687–712.

———. (2007). *Sex Equality.* New York: Foundation Press.

Maine, H.S. (1979). 'Law in Progressive Societies', in C.M. Campbell & P. Wiles (eds.), *Law and Society.* Oxford: M. Robertson, 18–23.

———. (2002). *Ancient Law.* New Brunswick: Transaction Publishers.

Martel, J.R. (2007). *Subverting the Leviathan: Reading Thomas Hobbes as a Radical Democrat.* New York: Columbia University Press.

Marx, K. (1844). Economic and Philosophical Manuscripts. <http://www.

marxists.org/archive/marx/works/1844/epm/3rd.htm>.

———. (1959). *Excerpts from Capital: A Critique of Political Economy*. New York: Anchor Publishing Company.

———. (1964). *Early Writings, Karl Marx*. New York: McGraw-Hill.

———. (1970). *A Contribution to the Critique of Political Economy*. Moscow: Progress Publishers.

———. (1976). *Capital: A Critique of Political Economy*. Harmondsworth: Penguin.

Marx, K., & Engels, F. (1965). *The German Ideology (Selections)*. London: International.

———. (2001). *Critique of the Gotha Programme*. London: Electric Book Co.

———. (2004). *The Communist Manifesto*. Peterborough: Broadview Press.

Matsuda, M.J. (1986). 'Liberal Jurisprudence and the Abstracted Visions of Human Nature: A Feminist Critique of Rawls' Theory of Justice'. *New Mexico Law Review* 16, 613–30.

———. (1989). 'Public Response to Racist Speech: Considering the Victim's Story'. *Michigan State Law Review* 87, 2320–81.

———. (2008). 'Are We Dead Yet? The Lies We Tell to Keep Moving Forward Without Feeling'. *Connecticut Law Review* 40(4), 1035–43.

Matsuda, M.J., Fiss, O., Finley, L., Guido, C., & Williams, P.J. (1989). 'Untitled Text on Law and Liberation'. *Yale Journal of Law and Liberation* 1, 1–4.

Matsuda, M.J., Lawrence, C., Delgado, R., & Crenshaw, K. (1993). *Words that Wound: Critical Race Theory, Assaultive Speech, and the First Amendment*. Boulder: Westview Press.

Mawani, R. (2002). 'In Between and Out of Place', in S. Razack (ed.), *Race, Space, and the Law: Unmapping a White Settler Society*. Toronto: Between the Lines, 47–70.

Mbembe, A. (1992). 'Provisional Notes on the Postcolony'. *Africa: Journal of the International African Institute* 62(1), 3–37.

———. (2001). *On the Postcolony*. Berkeley: University of California Press.

———. (2003). 'Necropolitics'. *Public Culture* 15(1), 11–40.

McLaren, A. (1990). *Our Own Master Race: Eugenics in Canada, 1885–1945*.

Toronto: McClelland & Stewart.

McLeod, J. (2007). *The Routledge Companion to Postcolonial Studies*. London: Routledge.

Mensch, E. (1990). 'The History of Mainstream Legal Thought', in D. Kairys (ed.), *The Politics of Law: A Progressive Critique*. New York: Pantheon Books, 13–37.

Merry, S.E. (1988). 'Legal Pluralism'. *Law and Society Review* 22(5), 869–901.

———. (2000). *Colonizing Hawai'i: The Cultural Power of Law*. Princeton: Princeton University Press.

———. (2004). 'Colonial and Postcolonial', in A. Sarat (ed.), *The Blackwell Companion to Law and Society*. Malden: Blackwell, 569–88.

———. (2006). *Human Rights and Gender Violence: Translating International Law into Local Justice*. Chicago: University of Chicago Press.

Miliband, R. (1973). *The State in Capitalist Society*. London: Quartet Books.

Mills, C. (2006). 'Biopolitics, Law and Futurity in Coetzee's *Life and Times of Michael K*'. *Griffith Law Review* 15(1), 177–95.

———. (2008). *The Philosophy of Agamben*. Kingston: McGill-Queen's University Press.

Milovanovic, D. (1988). *A Primer in the Sociology of Law*. New York: Harrow and Heston.

———. (2003). *An Introduction to the Sociology of Law*. Monsey: Criminal Justice Press.

Monture, P. (2007). 'What is Sovereignty for Indigenous People?', in G. Pavlich & M.J. Hird (eds.), *Questioning Sociology: A Canadian Perspective*. Don Mills: Oxford University Press, 253–65.

Moodie, T.D. (1975). *The Rise of Afrikanerdom: Power, Apartheid, and the Afrikaner Civil Religion*. Berkeley: University of California Press.

Moore, S.F. (1978). *Law as Process: An Anthropological Approach*. London: Routledge & Kegan Paul.

———. (1986). *Social Facts and Fabrications: 'Customary' Law on Kilimanjaro, 1880–1980*. Cambridge: Cambridge University Press.

———. (2005). *Law and Anthropology: A Reader*. Malden: Blackwell.

Moreton-Robinson, A. (2000). *Talkin' Ip to the White Woman: Aboriginal Women and Feminism.* St. Lucia, Australia: University of Queensland Press.

Mulcahy, L. (2003). *Disputing Doctors: The Socio-Legal Dynamics of Complaints about Medical Care.* Maidenhead: Open University Press.

Munger, F. (1998). 'Mapping Law and Society', in A. Sarat (ed.), *Crossing Boundaries: Traditions and Transformations in Law and Society Research.* Evanston: Northwestern University Press, 21–80.

Murphy, M.C. (1996). 'Natural Law and the Moral Absolute against Lying'. *American Journal of Jurisprudence* 41, 81–102.

———. (2006). *Natural Law in Jurisprudence and Politics.* New York: Cambridge University Press.

Naffine, N. (1990). *Law and the Sexes: Explorations in Feminist Jurisprudence.* Sydney: Allen & Unwin.

Naffine, N., & Owens, R.J. (1997). *Sexing the Subject of Law.* North Ryde: Sweet and Maxwell.

Nancy, J.L. (1993). *The Experience of Freedom.* Stanford: Stanford University Press.

———. (2000). *Being Singular Plural.* Stanford: Stanford University Press.

Napoleon, V., & Overstall, R. (2007). 'Indigenous Laws: Some Issues, Considerations and Experiences'. Winnipeg: Centre for Indigenous Environmental Resources.

Nietzsche, F.W. (1967). *The Will to Power.* New York: Random House.

———. (2001). *The Gay Science: With a Prelude in German Rhymes and an Appendix of Songs.* New York: Cambridge University Press.

Nonet, P., & Selznick, P. (2007). *Law & Society in Transition: Toward Responsive Law.* New Brunswick: Transaction Publishers.

Norris, A. (2005). *Politics, Metaphysics, and Death: Essays on Giorgio Agamben's Homo Sacer.* Durham: Duke University Press.

O'Malley, P. (1996). 'Post-social Criminologies: Some Implications of Current Political Trends for Criminology Theory and Practice'. *Current Issues in Criminal Justice* 8, 26–38.

Parsons, T. (1965). 'Max Weber 1864–1964'. *American Sociological Review* 30(2), 171–5.

Pashukanis, E. (2002). *The General Theory of Law & Marxism.* Ed. D. Milovanovic. New Brunswick: Transaction Publishers.

Pavlich, G.C. (1996). *Justice Fragmented: Mediating Community Disputes Under Postmodern Conditions.* New York: Routledge.

———. (1998). 'Political Logic, Colonial Law and the "Land of the Long White Cloud"'. *Law and Critique* 9(2), 175–206.

———. (2000). *Critique and Radical Discourses on Crime.* Aldershot: Ashgate.

———. (2001a). 'Transforming Images: Society, Law and Critique', in G. Wickham & G. Pavlich (eds.), *Rethinking Law, Society and Governance: Foucault's Bequest.* Oxford: Hart, 1–9.

———. (2001b). 'The Force of Community', in H. Strang & J. Braithwaite (eds.), *Restorative Justice and Civil Society.* Cambridge: Cambridge University Press, 56–69.

———. (2002). 'Deconstructing Restoration: The Promise of Restorative Justice', in E. Wietekamp & H.J. Kerner (eds.), *Restorative Justice: Theoretical Foundations.* Portland: Willan Publishing, 322–38.

———. (2004). 'What are the Dangers as Well as the Promises of Community Involvement', in B. Toews & H. Zehr (eds.), *Critical Issues in Restorative Justice.* New York: Criminal Justice Press, 173–84.

———. (2005). *Governing Paradoxes of Restorative Justice.* London: Glass House Press.

———. (2007a). 'Deconstruction', in George Ritzer (ed.), *The Blackwell Encyclopedia of Sociology.* Oxford: Blackwell Publishing, 986–9.

———. (2007b) 'The Lore of Criminal Accusation'. *Criminal Law and Philosophy* 1(1), 79–97.

———. (2009a). 'Being Accused, Becoming Criminal', in D. Crewe & R. Lippen (eds.), *Being, Justice, and Crime: Essays in Existentialist Criminology.* London: Routledge-Cavendish, 171–90.

———. (2009b). 'The Subject of Criminal

Identification'. *Punishment and Society* 11(2), 171–90.

———. (2010). 'On Subjects and Sovereigns', in C. Barbour & G. Pavlich (eds.), *After Sovereignty: On the Question of Political Beginnings*. Routledge-Cavendish, 22–36.

Pavlich, G.C., & Hird, M.J. (2007). *Questioning Sociology: A Canadian Perspective*. Don Mills: Oxford University Press.

Phillips, P. (1980). *Marx and Engels on Law and Laws*. Totowa: Barnes & Noble.

Pick, D. (1989). *Faces of Degeneration: A European Disorder, c.1848–c.1918*. New York: Cambridge University Press.

Plato. (1964). *The Dialogues of Plato*. Oxford: Clarendon Press.

———. (1971). *The Republic*. Harmondsworth: Penguin.

———. (2004). *The Laws*. Whitefish: Kessinger Publishing.

Poulantzas, N.A. (1978). *State, Power, Socialism*. London: NLB.

———. (2000). *State, Power, Socialism*. London: Verso.

Pound, R. (1907). 'The Need of a Sociological Jurisprudence'. *Green Bag* 19, 607–15.

———. (1910). 'Law in Books and Law in Action'. *American Law Review* 44(1), 12–36.

———. (1911). 'The Purpose and Scope of Sociological Jurisprudence'. *Harvard Law Review* 24(8), 591–619.

———. (1922). 'An Appreciation of Eugen Ehrlich'. *Harvard Law Review* 36(2), 129–45.

———. (1931). 'The Call for a Realist Jurisprudence'. *Harvard Law Review* 44(5), 697–711.

———. (1954). *An Introduction to the Philosophy of Law*. New Haven: Yale University Press.

———. (1959). *Jurisprudence*. St. Paul, Minnesota: West Publishing.

———. (1968). *Social Control Through Law*. Hamden: Archon Books.

Pruitt, L.R. (1994). 'A Survey of Feminist Jurisprudence'. *UALR Law Journal* 16, 183–210.

Pue, W.W. (1985). *Socio-legal Scholarship in Canada: The Jurisprudence Centre Working Papers*. Ottawa: Faculty of Social Sciences, Carleton University.

Quinney, R. (1980). *Class, State, & Crime.* New York: Longman.

Rafter, N.H. (1997). *Creating Born Criminals*. Urbana: University of Illinois Press.

Rasch, W. (2004). *Sovereignty and its Discontents: On the Primacy of Conflict and the Structure of the Political*. London: Birkbeck Law.

Raz, J. (1979). *The Authority of Law: Essays on Law and Morality*. Oxford: Clarendon Press.

———. (2005). 'Can There Be a Theory of Law?', in M. Golding & W. Edmundson (eds.), *The Blackwell Guide to Philosophy and Legal Theory*. Oxford: Blackwell, 324–42.

Razack, S. (1991). 'Speaking For Ourselves: Feminist Jurisprudence and Minority Women'. *Canadian Journal of Women and Law* 4, 440–58.

———. (2000). 'Gendered Racial Violence and Spatialized Justice: The Murder of Pamela George'. *Canadian Journal of Law and Society* 15(2), 91–130.

———. (ed.) (2002). *Race, Space, and the Law: Unmapping a White Settler Society*. Toronto: Between the Lines.

Reiman, J.H. (2004). *The Rich Get Richer and the Poor Get Prison: Ideology, Class, and Criminal Justice*. Boston: Pearson.

Ricouer, P. (2000). *The Just*. Chicago: University of Chicago Press.

Robertson, R., & Taylor, L. (1973). *Deviance, Crime and Socio-legal Control: Comparative Perspectives*. London: M. Robertson.

Rose, G. (2009). 'Who Cares For Which Dead and How? British Newspaper Reporting of the Bombings in London, July 2005'. *Geoforum* 40(1), 46–54.

Rose, N., & Valverde, M. (1998). 'Governed by Law?'. *Social and Legal Studies* 7(4), 551–2.

Rose, N.S. (1999). *Powers of Freedom: Reframing Political Thought*. Cambridge: Cambridge University Press.

Ross, E.A. (1905). *Foundations of Sociology*. New York: The Macmillan Company.

———. (1969). *Social Control: A Survey of the Foundations of Order*. Cleveland: Case Western Reserve University.

Roth, G. (1975). 'Untitled'. *Contemporary Sociology* 4(4), 366–73.

Rousseau, J.J. (1979). *Émile: Or, On Edu-*

cation. United States: Basic Books.

———. (1997). *The Social Contract and Other Later Political Writings*. New York: Cambridge University Press.

Runciman, W.G. (1972). *A Critique of Max Weber's Philosophy of Social Science*. Cambridge: Cambridge University Press.

Rush, S., Munro, R.J., & Taylor, B.W. (1999). *Feminist Jurisprudence, Women and the Law: Critical Essays, Research Agenda, and Bibliography*. Littleton: F.B. Rothman.

Said, E.W. (2003). *Orientalism*. London: Penguin.

Sanders, M. (2007). *Ambiguities of Witnessing: Law and Literature in the Time of a Truth Commission*. Stanford: Stanford University Press.

Santos, B.D.S. (1987). 'Law: A Map of Misreading. Toward a Postmodern Conception of Law'. *Journal of Law and Society* 14(3), 279–302.

Sarat, A. (1999). *The Killing State: Capital Punishment in Law, Politics, and Culture*. New York: Oxford University Press.

———. (2001). *Law, Violence, and the Possibility of Justice*. Princeton: Princeton University Press.

———. (2004a). *The Blackwell Companion to Law and Society*. Malden: Blackwell.

———. ed. (2004b). *The Social Organisation of Law*. Los Angeles: Roxbury Publishing Company.

Sarat, A., Douglas, L., & Umphrey, M.M. (2007). *Law and the Sacred*. Stanford: Stanford University Press.

Sarat, A., & Kearns, T.R. (2001). *Human Rights: Concepts, Contests, Contingencies*. Ann Arbor: University of Michigan Press.

Sarat, A., Constable, M., Engel, D., Hans, V., & Lawrence, S. (1998). *Crossing Boundaries: Traditions and Transformations in Law and Society Research*. Evanston: Northwestern University Press and the American Bar Association..

Sarat, A., & Simon, J. (2003). *Cultural Analysis, Cultural Studies, and the Law: Moving Beyond Legal Realism*. Durham: Duke University Press.

Saywell, J. (1971). *Quebec 70: A Documentary Narrative*. Toronto: University of Toronto Press.

Scales, A.C. (1986). 'The Emergence of Feminist Jurisprudence: An Essay'. *Yale Law Journal* 95, 1373–404.

Scruton, R. (1988). 'Review Essay'. *British Journal of Sociology* 39(4), 625–8.

Selznick, P. (1961). 'Sociology and Natural Law'. *Natural Law Forum* 6, 84–108.

Smart, C. (1989). 'Feminism and the Power of Law'. *Sociology of Law and Crime*. London: Routledge.

———. (1995). *Law, Crime and Sexuality: Essays in Feminism*. London: Sage Publications.

Smith, G.P. (1993). *Bioethics and the Law: Medical, Socio-legal and Philosophical Directions for a Brave New World*. Lanham: University Press of America.

Smith, P. (1993). *Feminist Jurisprudence*. New York: Oxford University Press.

Sophocles. (2003). *Antigone*. Trans. Gibbons & Segal. New York: Oxford University Press.

Spitzer, S. (1975). 'Toward a Marxian Theory of Deviance'. *Social Problems* 22(4), 638–52.

Spivak, G.C. (1990). *The Post-Colonial Critic: Interviews, Strategies, Dialogues*. New York: Routledge.

Stone, J. (2007). *When She Was White: The True Story of a Family Divided by Race*. New York: Hyperion.

Stoner, J.R. (1992). *Common Law and Liberal Theory: Coke, Hobbes, and the Origins of American Constitutionalism*. Lawrence: University Press of Kansas.

Sumner, C. (1979). *Reading Ideologies: An Investigation into the Marxist Theory of Ideology and Law*. New York: Academic Press.

Sydie, R.A. (1994). *Natural Women, Cultured Men: A Feminist Perspective on Sociological Theory*. Vancouver: University of British Columbia Press.

Tadros, V. (1998). 'Between Governance and Discipline: The Law and Michel Foucault'. *Oxford Journal of Legal Studies* 18, 75–104.

Taiwo, O. (1996). *Legal Naturalism: A Marxist Theory of Law*. Ithaca: Cornell University Press.

Taub, N., & Schneider, E. (1990). 'Women's Subordination and the Role of Law', in D. Kairys (ed.), *The Politics of Law: A Progressive Critique*. New York: Pantheon Books, 151–76.

Taylor, I.R., Walton, P., & Young, J.

(1973). *The New Criminology: For a Social Theory of Deviance*. London: Routledge & Kegan Paul.

———. (1975). *Critical Criminology*. London: Routledge and Kegan Paul.

Tetley, W. (2007). *The October Crisis, 1970: An Insider's View*. Montréal: McGill-Queen's University Press.

Thompson, E.P., & Great Britain. (1975). *Whigs and Hunters: The Origin of the Black Act*. New York: Pantheon Books.

Thompson, L.M. (1990). *A History of South Africa*. New Haven: Yale University Press.

Tie, W. (1999). *Legal Pluralism: Toward a Multicultural Conception of Law*. Aldershot: Dartmouth.

Timasheff, N.S. (1937). 'What Is "Sociology of Law"?'. *American Journal of Sociology* 43(2), 225–35.

Travers, M., & Manzo, J.F. (1997). *Law in Action: Ethnomethodological and Conversation Analytic Approaches to Law*. Aldershot: Dartmouth.

Trubeck, D.M. (1984). 'Where the Action Is: Critical Legal Studies and Empiricism'. *Stanford Law Review* 36, 575–622.

———. (1985). 'Review: Reconstructing Max Weber's Sociology of Law'. *Stanford Law Review* 37(3), 919–36.

Tuitt, P. (2004). *Race, Law, Resistance*. London: GlassHouse.

Turk, A.T. (1980). 'Review: *Marx and Engels on Law*, by Cain, Maureen & Hunt, Alan 1980'. *Contemporary Sociology* 9(4), 556–7.

Turkel, G. (1990). 'Michel Foucault: Law, Power, Knowledge'. *Journal of Law and Society* 17, 170–93.

Tushnet, M. (1980). 'Review Essay'. *British Journal of Law and Society* 7(1), 122–6.

———. (1984). 'Critical Legal Studies and Constitutional Law: An Essay in Deconstruction'. *Stanford Law Review* 36, 623–48.

———. (1991). 'Critical Legal Studies: A Political History'. *Yale Law Journal* 100, 1515–44.

Twining, W.L. (1968). 'Two Works of Karl Llewellyn'. *Modern Law Review* 31(2), 165–82.

———. (1973). *Karl Llewellyn and the Realist Movement*. London: Weidenfeld and Nicolson.

Unger, R.M. (1986). *The Critical Legal Studies Movement*. Cambridge: Harvard University Press.

Valverde, M. (2003). *Law's Dream of a Common Knowledge*. Princeton: Princeton University Press.

———. (2006). *Law and Order: Images, Meanings, Myths*. New Brunswick: Rutgers University Press.

Van der Walt, J.C. (2005). *Law and Sacrifice: Towards a Post-Apartheid Theory of Law*. London: Birkbeck Law Press.

Van Marle, K. (2001). 'Reflections on Teaching Critical Race Theory at South African Universities/Law Faculties'. *Stellenbosch Law Review* 12, 86–100.

Veitch, S., Christodoulidis, E.A., & Farmer, L. (2007). *Jurisprudence: Themes and Concepts*. New York: Routledge-Cavendish.

Verund-Jones, S. (1974). 'The Jurisprudence of Karl Llewellyn'. *Dalhousie Law Journal* 1(3), 441–81.

Vincent, A. (1993). 'Marx and Law'. *Journal of Law and Society* 20(4), 371–97.

Wacks, R. (1984). 'Judges and Injustice'. *South African Law Journal* 101, 266–85.

———. (2005). *Understanding Jurisprudence: An Introduction to Legal Theory*. New York: Oxford University Press.

———. (2006). *Philosophy of Law: A Very Short Introduction*. Oxford: Oxford University Press.

Watson, I. (1998). 'Power of the Muldarbi, the Road to its Demise'. *Australian Feminist Law Journal* 11(28), 30–45.

Weber, M. (1954). *Max Weber on Law in Economy and Society*. New York: Simon and Schuster.

———. (1967). *Ancient Judaism*. New York: Free Press.

———. (1968). *Economy and Society: An Outline of Interpretive Sociology*. New York: Bedminster Press.

———. (1980). *Basic Concepts in Sociology*. New York: Citadel Press.

———. (1994). *Sociological Writings*. New York: Continuum.

———. (2003). *The Protestant Ethic and the Spirit of Capitalism*. London: Courier Dover.

———. (2005). *Max Weber: Selections in Translation*. Cambridge: Cambridge University Press.

Wickham, G. (2002). 'Foucault and Law',

in R. Banakar & M. Travers (eds.), *An Introduction to Law and Social Theory*. Oxford: Hart, 249–66.

Wickham, G., & Pavlich, G.C. (2001). *Rethinking Law, Society and Governance: Foucault's Bequest*. Oxford: Hart.

Williams, M. (2002). *Empty Justice: One Hundred Years of Law, Literature, and Philosophy*. London: Cavendish.

Williams, P.J. (1986). 'A Brief Comment, with Footnotes, on the Rights Chronicles'. *Harvard Blackletter Journal* 3, 79–82.

———. (1988). 'Spirit-Murder the Messenger: The Discourse of Fingerpointing as Law's Response to Racism'. *University of Miami Law Review* 42, 127–58.

———. (1989). 'The Obliging Shell: An Informal Essay on Formal Equal Opportunity'. *Michigan Law Review* 87, 2128–51.

———. (1991). *The Alchemy of Race and Rights*. Cambridge: Harvard University Press.

Williams, R.V. (2006). *Postcolonial Politics and Personal Laws: Colonial Legal Legacies and The Indian State*. New York: Oxford University Press.

Willrich, M. (1998). 'The Two Percent Solution: Eugenic Jurisprudence and the Socialization of American Law, 1900–1930'. *Law and History Review* 16(1), 63–111.

Woolford, A. (2009). *The Politics of Restorative Justice: A Critical Introduction*. Halifax: Fernwood.

Woolford, A., & Ratner, R.S. (2008). *Informal Reckonings: Conflict Resolutions in Mediation, Restorative Justice, and Reparations*. London: Routledge-Cavendish.

Worden, N. (2007). *The Making of Modern South Africa: Conquest, Apartheid, Democracy*. Malden: Blackwell.

Wrong, D. H. (1970). *Max Weber*. Englewood Cliffs: Prentice-Hall.

Young, J., & Matthews, R. (1992). *Rethinking Criminology: The Realist Debate*. London: Sage Publications.

Zeitlin, I.M. (1985). 'Max Weber's Sociology of Law'. *University of Toronto Law Journal* 35(2), 183–214.

Credits

Grateful acknowledgement is made for permission to reprint the following:

Page 15: ANTIGONE by Sophocles, translated by Gibbons and Segal (2003) Lines 495–501, 512–518 p.73. Reprinted by permission of Oxford University Press.

Pages 20-1: Excerpt from Book III , pp 68–69, total 220 words from "Republic; The Law" by Cicero MT (1998). By permission of Oxford University Press, Inc

Pages 50-1: Excerpts © 1959 by California Law Review, Inc. Reprinted from the California Law Review Vol. 47 , No. 1 by California Law Review, Inc.

Pages 74, 78, 79, 84, 85: Excerpts from Durkheim, E. (1984). The Division of Labour in Society. London: Macmillan.

Pages 79, 80, 81, 82, 83, 84: Excerpts from Durkheim, E. (1983). Durkheim and the Law,eds, Steven Lukes and Andrew Scull. New York: Martin Robinson Press.

Page 103, 105: Excerpts from Weber, M. (1994). Sociological Writings. New York: Continuum. Used by permission of Continuum.

Page 175-6: Excerpts from 'Waiting For The Barbarians' by C.P Cavafy. KEELEY, EDMUND; C.P. CAVAFY. © 1975 by Edmund Keeley and Phillip Sherrard. Reprinted by permission of Princeton University Press.

Page 174: Excerpt Derrida, J. (2002). 'Force of Law: The "Mystical Foundations of Authority"', in J. Derrida & G. Anidjar (eds.), Acts of religion. New York: Routledge, 228–298.

Page 183: Franz Kafka, 'Before the Law', translated by Ian Johnston.

Index